SUBSTANCE ABUSE
AND THE NEW ROAD
TO RECOVERY

SUBSTANCE ABUSE AND THE NEW ROAD TO RECOVERY
A Practitioner's Guide

Glenn D. Walters
Federal Correctional Institution
Schyulkill, Pennsylvania

Taylor & Francis
Publishers since 1798

USA	Publishing Office:	Taylor & Francis 1101 Vermont Ave., N.W., Suite 200 Washington, DC 20005 Tel: (202) 289-2174 Fax: (202) 289-3665
	Distribution Center:	Taylor & Francis 1900 Frost Road, Suite 101 Bristol, PA 19007-1598 Tel: (215) 785-5800 Fax: (215) 785-5515
UK		Taylor & Francis, Ltd. 1 Gunpowder Square London EC4A 3DE Tel: 071 538 0490 Fax: 071 538 0581

SUBSTANCE ABUSE AND THE NEW ROAD TO RECOVERY: A Practitioner's Guide

1 2 3 4 5 6 7 8 9 0 BRBR 9 8 7 6 5

This book was set in Times Roman by Princeton Editorial Associates. The editors were Holly Seltzer and Christine Winter. Cover design by Michelle Fleitz. Prepress supervisor was Miriam Gonzalez. Printing and binding by Braun-Brumfield, Inc.

A CIP catalog record for this book is available from the British Library.
∞ The paper in this publication meets the requirements of the ANSI Standard Z39.48-1984 (Permanence of Paper)

Library of Congress Cataloging-in-Publication Data
Walters, Glenn D.
    Substance abuse and the new road to recovery: a practitioner's guide/Glenn D. Walters
      p. cm.
    Includes bibliographical references.

    1. Drug abuse—United States—Psychological aspects. 2. Substance abuse—United States—Psychological aspects. 3. Life style—United States—Psychological aspects. 4. Narcotic addicts—Rehabilitation—United States. 5. Narcotic addicts—Counseling of—United States.
I. Title.
HV5825.W381275 1996
616.86′03—dc20

95-40600
CIP

ISBN 1-56032-427-9 (case)
ISBN 1-56032-428-7 (paper)

Contents

Preface

The drug lifestyle leads nowhere, as many who have entered its labyrinthine hallways can attest. Nonetheless, it is a path that is well worn by the footsteps of persons attempting to find a solution to the problems and responsibilities of everyday living by misusing substances and engaging in drug-related activities. This is because a drug lifestyle, like any other lifestyle, supplies people with a script or blueprint of the rules, roles, and rituals to be followed in interacting with their environment. Although this may appeal to the part of ourselves that cringes with fear and trepidation at the prospect of change and personal responsibility, the patterned behavior that evolves from a growing preoccupation with drugs stifles personal development, affronts individuality, and destroys the possibility of meaningful social relationships. In the sense that no two people share the same exact thoughts, feelings, and experiences, the notion of a script or blueprint for living is pure fantasy. Unfortunately, it is a fantasy that many people try to live out in the form of a drug or other lifestyle. This is why the drug lifestyle is considered a journey to nowhere.

The assertions and opinions contained herein are the private views of the author and should not be construed as official or as reflecting the views of the Federal Bureau of Prisons or the U.S. Department of Justice.

Escaping the Journey to Nowhere: The Psychology of Alcohol and Other Drug Abuse (Walters, 1994c) offered a model of substance misuse that deviates noticeably from traditional views on the etiology and treatment of alcohol and other drug abuse. Instead of conceptualizing drug-seeking behavior as an addiction or disease, the lifestyle model envisions the misuse of substances as a lifestyle, around which many of the person's activities are organized. With this in mind, the present book introduces the reader to an intervention model founded on three influences. The first influence is that of the theory itself. Lifestyle theory not only provides an organizing framework for the change model described in this book, but also raises certain issues, such as existential fear, commonly ignored by more traditional therapies. A second contributing influence to the lifestyle model of change is cognitive-behavioral intervention as represented by specific skill-based techniques (e.g., cognitive restructuring) and concepts (e.g., self-efficacy). A third influence contributing to a lifestyle model of change is research on natural recovery. Studies show that a majority of persons who terminate their involvement with drugs do so on their own (Biernacki, 1990; Tuchfeld, 1981). Several of the procedures utilized by persons who have abandoned the drug lifestyle without treatment (e.g., identity transformation) have therefore been incorporated into the intervention model described in this book.

The overarching objective of intervention, as described in this book, is to help clients escape the journey to nowhere. If change is to take root and endure, however, intervention must extend beyond the initial avoidance of drug usage. Helping clients find a new way of life that is incompatible with future misuse of substances also entails a journey. But this journey leads somewhere, because it takes into account the unique attributes, beliefs, and experiences of the individual traveler. In lifestyle theory terms, this is known as the new road to recovery. Although the client may meet others over the course of his or her travels, the road he or she takes will be unique and not nearly as well worn as that which guides a drug lifestyle. This book is designed to provide mental health professionals with strategies and information to help clients find this road. However, the new road is not a blueprint, but merely a series of guidelines and suggestions that will be differentially effective, depending on the traveler. Determining the proper combination of interventions and strategies is the responsibility of the mental health professional. However, the professional must avoid getting so preoccupied with effecting a client's escape from the journey to nowhere, that he or she loses sight of the fact that the client must be prepared for another journey, a journey into meaning (Frankl, 1984). That these two objectives are mutually dependent and vital to the success of a change program appears self-evident; that they can be effectively integrated to form a practical and comprehensive program of intervention is a question that has, in large part, been a motivating force in the writing of this book.

Glenn D. Walters

Chapter 1

Introduction: In Search of the Path Less Traveled

Before entertaining the applications for which this book was intended, it may be helpful to consider the applications for which it was not intended, in the knowledge that negative examples can sometimes be just as valuable as positive depictions in clarifying a subject. The absent or negative example is, in actuality, fundamental to human learning, development, and growth, whether reference is being made to a young child who forms an incipient sense of self by learning to differentiate him or herself from the surrounding environment, or an adult who settles on a career in marketing after discovering that accounting and finance do not coincide with his or her temperament and interests. Learning from the negative instance may be particularly helpful in defining the purpose of a published work, a task that may seem unnecessary and tedious to some, but which is actually vital to the success of any such work. Numerous books and manuals have been published on the topic of substance abuse treatment; some have failed because they have tried to be all things to all people. This could perhaps have been avoided had the authors taken the time to discuss their reasons for writing the book. With this in mind, I will attempt to elucidate my rationale for drafting the current text by contrasting the purposes for which this book was intended with those for which it was not intended, beginning with the former.

First and foremost, the reader should understand that this book was not meant to serve as a self-help manual. Lifestyle theory respects the fact that many people desist from problematic drug use without formal treatment. Accordingly, many of the incentives mentioned by people who have exited a drug lifestyle on their own (Biernacki, 1990; Ludwig, 1985; Tuchfeld, 1981; Vaillant & Milofsky, 1982; Walters, 1995b) have been integrated into the present program. However, the concepts, procedures, suggestions, and exercises outlined herein are subject to misinterpretation and misapplication in situations where the user lacks sufficient training or experience to appreciate the limits of the knowledge acquisition process. The fact that competent self-help programming is critical to continued desistance from drug use in no way relieves the clinician of the responsibility for supervising the therapeutic activities of his or her clients. Although lifestyle theory readily acknowledges that self-directed intervention is vital to program effectiveness, it insists that such interventions be overseen by trained professionals who appreciate the limitations inherent in any organized program of assessment and intervention. The respect lifestyle theory affords self-help programming is exemplified, in part, by Appendix 1: Participant Handbook.

A limitation that may be apparent only to trained professionals is the minimal reliability and validity data that is currently available for the assessment procedures reproduced in the appendixes, with the exception of the Drug Lifestyle Screening Interview (DLSI) and the Psychological Inventory of Drug-Based Thinking Styles (PIDTS). Although many of the assessment procedures do not conform to strict scientific standards, this is probably not a fatal flaw unless the supervising clinician fails to identify and discuss these limitations with his or her clients. These assessments are designed to serve only as general clinical aids, rather than as standardized psychometric instruments. Unfortunately, people unfamiliar with measurement theory tend to confuse publication, whether in a newspaper, magazine, or book, with validity. This is a dangerous assumption and one that violates the basic principles of lifestyle theory. It would therefore be hypocritical of me to profess greater confidence in these measures than is scientifically or methodologically warranted. These procedures should therefore be treated as working tools, potentially capable of defining certain change goals and issues, but limited by their simplicity and general absence of reliability and validity data. As such, they should be used only under the continuing supervision of a trained professional so as to avoid misinterpretation and misapplication.

This manual is not a cookbook. Helping someone with a substance abuse problem is not like changing a tire. Substituting one lifestyle for another is not the goal of lifestyle intervention. Rather, the purpose is to provide the client with information, skills, and support as a way of stimulating a change in attitude and behavior. Unlike a drug lifestyle, change does not follow a script or blueprint, but is a path unique to itself. The Minnesota Multiphasic Personality Inventory

(MMPI; Hathaway & McKinley, 1940) is an instrument for which various cookbooks have been constructed and successfully applied. In devising an MMPI cookbook, the researcher examines the behavioral correlates of a defined set of varying MMPI scale patterns, called high-point codes, and generates interpretative statements from these correlates. Some of the more popular MMPI cookbooks include those by Gilberstadt and Duker (1965) and Marks, Seeman, and Haller (1974). Whereas such an approach may be helpful in interpreting the results of a standardized personality inventory, there are at least two reasons why a cookbook will likely never be successfully assembled for intervention. First, the unique thoughts, feelings, and experiences of the individual client cannot be properly covered by a cookbook. Change is not typically realized in a blueprint or well-worn path, but in a path less traveled. One way to conceive of lifestyle intervention, then, is as an attempt by clinicians to assist clients in their search for a life path that takes their unique life circumstances and abilities into account, rather than forcing them onto the well-worn path of a drug or other lifestyle. Second, the working relationship that forms between a therapist and client defies simplistic cookbook reductionism. Procedures, suggestions, and guidelines are possible; but they must be flexibly applied in order to facilitate, rather than inhibit, the therapist–client relationship.

Lifestyle theory also rejects the mechanistic theorems of the medical, disease, and conditioning models in favor of a more existential, teleological conceptualization of human deportment. The medical model assumes that drug use symptomatology is an expression of some underlying, often emotion-based, problem. Like a mechanic who checks the carburetor when the engine won't start, practitioners of the medical model search for childhood traumas and emotional disturbances to explain the current drug use difficulties of their clients. This approach has spawned the self-medication hypothesis, but not all, or even most, of the drug-seeking behavior of substance abusers is driven by self-medicating motives, particularly during the early stages of drug involvement (see Walters, 1994c). The disease model assumes that substance abusers suffer from a progressive and potentially fatal disease that can be arrested only by providing the client with a counter-dependency. In many cases the prescribed treatment for the "disease" of alcoholism or drug abuse is regular attendance at 12-step meetings (e.g., Alcoholics Anonymous, Narcotics Anonymous). The conditioning model rejects the disease concept of addiction, but holds that environmental conditions are fully responsible for substance abuse difficulties. As such, supporters of the conditioning approach consider modification of external conditions to be the primary vehicle by which a person terminates his or her relationship with drugs. Lifestyle theory repudiates the passivity and pessimism of all three models by holding the individual accountable for his or her actions, discouraging dependency on outside influences and standards, and encouraging increased commitment to personal goals, values, and expectancies.

The reader also needs to understand that this manual is not a panacea or cure-all, but rather, an alternative to traditional views on drug-seeking behavior. It is well recognized that the lifestyle model does not apply to all drug-involved clients any more than Alcoholics Anonymous benefits all persons who have ever abused ethyl alcohol. If the reader harbors any skepticism about the need for alternative methods of intervention, research documenting the efficacy of client–treatment matching (Hester & Miller, 1988) should fairly well convince him or her that when it comes to substance abuse programming, one size clearly does not fit all. Further advances in the substance abuse field will depend on the field's ability to entertain many more perspectives than currently exist. Although some clients may profit from the traditional disease concept of addiction, there will be others who resist the model, not because they are denying their problem, but because the approach is irrelevant to their current life situation. The lifestyle model is viewed by its proponents as one alternative to the traditional disease, medical, and social work models that have dominated the substance abuse field for decades, mindful of the fact that not everyone will respond favorably to any one approach. Consequently, a change in mindset needs to occur wherein the question, "Which approach works best with substance abusers?" is replaced by the query, "Which approach works best with which type of clients under which specific sets of circumstances?"

With the purposes for which this book is not intended clearly delineated, it is now time to turn our attention to the purposes for which this book was originally designed. Throughout this introductory chapter, I have asserted that the lifestyle model is an alternative to traditional conceptualizations of substance abuse and substance abuse treatment. The overriding purpose of this book, then, is to introduce the reader to a perspective on substance abuse and substance abuse intervention that is novel, user friendly, and sufficiently inclusive to serve as the basis for a comprehensive program of assisted change. This purpose is supported by three subpurposes: (a) to demonstrate the feasibility of a skill-based approach to intervention, (b) to illustrate precisely how affirming respect for human dignity and choice can facilitate change in drug-involved individuals, and (c) to describe the manner in which adaptability promotes change and prevents relapse.

Skill development and education are both features and goals of lifestyle intervention. In fact, lifestyle theory conceives of the drug lifestyle as a form of acquired developmental disability characterized by arrested emotional development and reduced opportunities for adaptive learning. In addressing these issues, lifestyle therapists search for solutions, rather than becoming preoccupied with problems. It is important to understand that although problems are not ignored by lifestyle therapists, they are clearly deemphasized in favor of potential solutions and the component skills of each solution. For this reason, the model begins by identifying relevant core and ancillary skills, follows up with an evaluation of each skill, and concludes with an organized plan of action. This three-step procedure is summarized by the acronym SAP (Skill-Assessment-Plan). Although an awareness of problems may activate the treatment process by highlighting the need for change, the identification of skills is the point at which intervention formally begins. Within this framework, lifestyle therapists attempt to define the spectrum of relevant skills, gradually breaking them down into their component subskills so that treatment can be optimally effective for clients, each of whom displays a unique pattern of skill strengths and weaknesses. In brief, a comprehensive evaluation of skills is implemented, rather than an assessment based simply on the presenting problem.

Skills come in a multitude of shapes, sizes, and forms. Some of the major categories of skill addressed by lifestyle therapists include educational skills, occupational skills, intellectual/learning skills, social skills, coping skills, communication skills, and thinking skills. The identification of skills and their component subskills is the initial step in the change process; the next step is to assess these skills. The assessment procedures outlined in the appendixes of this book are designed to assist clinicians with the assessment process. However, assessment procedures for all skills and subskills potentially relevant to clinical work with substance abusing clients would require a book many times the size of the present one. For this reason, the majority of assessment devices found in this book provide only a general overview of a skill area that will need to be modified or delineated further when addressing an individual client's unique issues. Clinicians, however, must take pains to avoid getting so "bogged down" in assessment that they have little time left for intervention. It is imperative, then, that the purpose for which assessment is intended be kept firmly in mind: Assessment is designed to identify strengths, weaknesses, and targets for future intervention and to document any changes that occur in these skills as a consequence of intervention. Assessments are enacted, not for their own sake, but for the sake of intervention or, in some cases, prediction. The degree to which the feedback loop from assessment to intervention assists with the planning and modification of specific therapeutic interactions is an estimate of the value of that assessment.

The development of a skill-based change plan follows from the identification and assessment of skills. The plan may involve remediation of a previously learned skill, acquisition of a previously unlearned skill, or transfer of a skill strength to cover an area of weakness. Stress management training may therefore be helpful to clients who no longer remember how to relax without drugs, and negotiation skills training may potentially benefit an individual who has never learned the fine art of interpersonal persuasion and compromise. In some cases, however, the client may already possess the skill being assessed. Although remediation or skill development is unnecessary under these circumstances, such skills may still work their way into a client's change plan. A person holding an advanced degree in accounting, for instance, can probably forgo the academic enrichment portion of a change program, whereas a client with strong imagery skills probably does not require additional training in imagery enhancement. Nevertheless, the well-developed academic and intellectual skills of the first individual could be employed as part of an intervention aimed at irrational thinking by assigning articles on rational restructuring for the client to read; the second individual's strong imagery skills might be used to improve social isolation through implementation of an imagery-enhanced rehearsal technique designed to improve his or her communication skills. It is also essential that the change plan adapt as new information is brought to bear on a subject. Consequently, the second (assessment) and third (plan) stages of lifestyle intervention overlap extensively.

Traditional substance abuse treatment may encourage dependency on a treatment philosophy, program, or group. The lifestyle model rejects this approach, arguing that dependency is one of the building blocks of a drug lifestyle with the strength to reactivate drug-related thinking and behavioral patterns in currently abstaining individuals. Shifting the dependency from one source to another may assist some clients, but will leave many others vulnerable to relapse. Perhaps this explains, in part, the disappointing outcomes attained by persons graduating from traditional inpatient substance abuse programs (Hunt, Barnett, & Branch, 1971). In contrast to dependency-fostering models such as Alcoholics Anonymous, the lifestyle approach strives to promote independence by focusing on issues such as responsibility, choice, and the ongoing evaluation of consequences. Instead of imposing preconceived notions and ideas on clients, the lifestyle approach teaches its consumers to think for themselves in the belief that a lack of self-confidence and an overreliance on externalized standards of success and happiness may have been what encouraged development of a drug lifestyle in the first place. Accordingly, the lifestyle model honors the dignity of the individual client by encouraging independence and the formation of personal skills designed to enhance the client's decision-making competence. The focus of lifestyle intervention, then, is on teaching clients how to more effectively manage their lives through choice, responsibility, and autonomy. Demonstrating exactly how this might be accomplished is the second subpurpose of this book.

Lifestyle intervention is guided not only by skill-based training and respect for client autonomy, but also by a pursuit of adaptive goals. In actuality, the manner in which autonomy and skill development are attained centers on fortification of a person's adaptive resources. Whereas a lifestyle furnishes people with the rules, roles, rituals, and relationships that allow them to function within the rigid boundaries of an established lifestyle, adaptation supplies people with skills they can use to modify their behavior and learn from their environment. Survival, in fact, depends on our ability to adapt to certain physical and psychological demands. Unfortunately, as people grow accustomed to depending on lifestyles to cope with the pressures, disappointments, and hassles of everyday living, they experience a corresponding atrophy in their ability to think for themselves. Lifestyle therapists attempt to remedy this situation by assisting clients in identifying, rediscovering, and developing their adaptive resources by teaching and reinforcing basic skills. As a client begins to clarify and expand his or her repertoire of adaptive responses he or she becomes less dependent on the drug lifestyle to meet life's challenges and moves further down the path less traveled. This illustrates the interactive nature of the relationship that forms among the three subpurposes of this book (skill development, facilitation of independence, and increased adaptability) in the evolution of an alternative program of substance abuse intervention. The tools designed to assist with the implementation of a lifestyle-based program of change will be explored in Chapters 3 through 8, but first Chapter 2 will provide a review of the underlying tenets of the lifestyle model.

An Overview of Lifestyle Theory

The differences and interrelationships between the structural and functional divisions of lifestyle theory can perhaps be best explained using the analogy of an automobile engine. A car's engine is made up of rods and pistons, plugs and points, belts and hoses, a battery, a carburetor, and a wide assortment of gears and wires. In this analogy, these automobile parts represent the structural division of lifestyle theory. The functional division, on the other hand, is represented by processes that place the battery in interaction with the points and plugs in order to create chemical and mechanical reactions that then start the engine. This insinuates that the structural elements of a car engine or lifestyle must be clarified before the functional features can be understood. Conversely, examining the structural components of a car's engine or lifestyle, without simultaneously considering the dynamic interrelationships that exist between these individual components, is equally unwise. This overview of lifestyle theory is organized around these two major divisions—structural and functional—with the first part of the chapter devoted to a review of the primary structural elements of a drug lifestyle and the second part exploring the functional features of this lifestyle.

STRUCTURAL COMPONENTS OF THE
DRUG LIFESTYLE

The structural division of lifestyle theory follows along the lines of the so-called three Cs: conditions, choice, and cognition.

Conditions

Conditions are internal (e.g., heredity, anger) or external (e.g., socioeconomic status, drug-related cues) variables that increase or decrease a person's propensity to engage in drug use. These conditions may be either historical–developmental or current–contextual in nature. Historical–developmental conditions are past events (e.g., family relationships) and innate characteristics of the individual (e.g., autonomic response) that increase or decrease the person's future probability of using and/or abusing drugs. Current–contextual conditions, on the other hand, are prevailing emotional states (e.g., depression) and situational events (e.g., access to drugs) that increase or decrease a person's chances of engaging in a concurrent drug use episode. Some variables exert both a historical–developmental and current–contextual effect. Receiving pressure from peers to use drugs may enhance a subject's chances of using drugs in a particular situation (current–contextual), but also may increase his or her odds of entering into drug lifestyle activities at some future point (historical–developmental). Because nothing can be done to effect change in past events and emotional reactions the emphasis of lifestyle intervention is on helping clients learn to manage current–contextual conditions. Historical–developmental conditions, on the other hand, can be useful in identifying major targets for primary and secondary prevention (see Walters, 1994c).

Lifestyle theory takes issue with the addictive personality and disease concepts of substance misuse on the grounds that these perspectives ignore important situational influences. Opportunities for drug use, as represented by a person's access to abusable substances and the availability of drug use paraphernalia (e.g., syringes, hashish pipes) and money, are situational conditions that explicitly impact on a person's current and future proclivity to use drugs. The interaction of various person and situation variables, however, is said to be even more critical in explaining substance use and abuse. Lifestyle theory, therefore, contends that the person × situation interaction is of prime etiological significance in explaining drug use patterns and predilections. The three primary domains of person × situation interaction believed to put a person at risk for future substance use difficulties are (a) idiosyncratic physiological reactions to internal and external stimuli that allow some people to experience initial drug use as more rewarding or less punishing than most first-time users, (b) a weak socialization to conventional (societal) definitions of drug use, and (c) a strong socialization to deviant definitions of drug use

(Walters, 1994c). These interacting influences contribute to the formation of the three early life tasks described later in this chapter.

Choice

Conditions do not cause behavior directly. Rather, they limit or expand a person's options in a specific situation. It is important to keep in mind, then, that lifestyle theory holds that a person makes a choice to engage in a specific activity based on his or her evaluation of the available options. Factors believed to influence the choices people make include development, motivation, reinforcement history, and the natural fallibility of the human decision-making process. Lifestyle theory contends that choice is not an all-or-nothing proposition, but one that unfolds in concert with the person's growing capacity for informed decision making, the consequence of increased brain development and exposure to an ever-widening sphere of environmental experience and information. Appreciating expectancies, articulating values, delaying gratification, and learning to anticipate and balance the long- and short-term consequences of one's actions are critical elements of the decision-making process that evolves and grows as one matures. Accordingly, these potential vehicles for change will be discussed at length in the chapter on choice-based intervention (Chapter 5). For the purposes of the present discussion, however, a person's capacity for choice and informed decision making expands as a direct result of developmental changes taking place within the individual.

Motivation is a second factor that must be considered if one is to form a complete understanding of the choice process that gives rise to the use and abuse of substances. Researchers have identified three primary incentives for drug use behavior: enhancement, coping, and socially oriented motives (Critchlow, 1986). The enhancement motive centers on the use of drugs as a means of achieving a positive affective state; the coping motive directs one to ingest substances in order to suppress or eliminate negative affect; the social motive entails the use of chemical substances for ceremonial and religious reasons, or for conviviality. Dividing two of the above motives (enhancement and coping) by their sources (personal versus social), I have developed a four-function motivational scheme for drug-seeking behavior: personal enhancement, social enhancement, personal coping, and social coping (Walters, 1994c). This is similar to Cox and Klinger's (1988) four-factor model of drinking motivation, which highlights internally generated positive reinforcement motives, externally generated positive reinforcement motives, internally generated negative reinforcement motives, and externally generated negative reinforcement motives. A recent confirmatory factor analysis of interview data collected on a group of 1,243 Black and White adolescents provides support for a four-factor model of drug use motivation (Cooper, 1994) as represented in my work (Walters, 1994c) and that of Cox and Klinger (1988).

People tend to engage in behaviors for which they have received reinforcement in the past. Hence, reinforcement history is a third factor that influences the human decision-making enterprise. If a person is reinforced for using drugs by peers he or she holds in high esteem, then he or she is likely to continue using drugs. In most situations, however, a complex system of reinforcers operates continuously. The pleasure associated with drug use must be tempered with the realization that habitual drug use comes with certain long-term negative consequences—the pain of drug dependency, the prospect of getting caught, and the fear of disappointing one's parents, among others. Because the positive effects of drug use tend to be more immediate than the negative effects, they normally weigh more heavily in the decisions of people committed to the drug lifestyle. One goal of intervention, therefore, is to arm clients with coping strategies designed to assist them with balancing the anticipated long- and short-term consequences of a particular behavior such as drug use. It is vital that clinicians understand that even though reinforcement history undoubtedly impacts on the decision-making process, it is still possible for people to violate the conditions of this history by making decisions that could never have been anticipated from a knowledge of their reinforcement history.

A fourth factor that contributes to the nonlinear character of choice behavior is the flawed nature of the choice process itself. Contrary to the predictions of rational choice theorists (Becker, 1968), most people, regardless of whether they misuse drugs, fail to consider all potential options before arriving at a decision. Rather, people tend to select the option that has worked for them in the past or that requires the least amount of effort. Research studies examining shortcut decision making (Corbin, 1980) and perseverative choice selection (Einhorn & Hogarth, 1978) insinuate that human decision making is often irrational and nonoptimizing. Furthermore, a substantial loss of information occurs when people attempt to organize, integrate, and merge data from different sources (Reitman, 1974). Several researchers have determined that the thought processes of drug abusers are often irrational and error-filled and that this would appear to play some role in these individuals' preoccupation with drugs (Denoff, 1988; Shorkey & Sutton-Smith, 1983). It is critical, then, that clinicians working with drug-involved clients appreciate the flawed nature of the human decision-making enterprise, particularly in light of the fact that the drug lifestyle encourages a high degree of irrationality, automaticity, and self-justification (Walters, 1994b).

Cognition

Lifestyle theory divides cognition, or thinking, into two basic functions: constructive and defensive. The constructive function of human thought assists with the derivation of a self- and world-view, whereas the defensive function is geared toward promoting and protecting a person's current self- and world-views. The constructive function is divided into four subcategories that run the gamut from primitive (mythical), to rational (empirical), to complex (teleological, epistemological). Mythical constructions are believed to be fertile soil for the development of the drug or other lifestyle, whereas empirical, teleological, and epistemological constructions open the door to novel and innovative interpretations of events and, as such, are often incompatible with development and maintenance of the drug lifestyle. The constructive function of human thought is discussed in greater detail in Chapter 6. The focus of the present discussion, however, will be on the defensive function, which is also divided into four subcategories: denial, distortion, diversion, and justification.

The four subcategories of defensive thinking can be viewed as mechanisms the client may employ to modify his or her thinking so as to protect his or her chosen lifestyle against forces, like alternative constructions of reality, that threaten the lifestyle. It is easier to deny certain facts when one's thinking is irrational, routinized, and inattentive to new information than when one's thinking is rational, organized, and open to different interpretations. Using Yochelson and Samenow's (1976) insights on the criminal personality as a starting point, I designed a system of eight thinking styles in an effort to capture the denial, distortion, diversion, and justification displayed by persons who follow the criminal lifestyle in managing the problem of existential fear (Walters, 1990). Subsequent work has demonstrated that a similar set of defensive operations may support the drug lifestyle (Walters, 1992, 1994c). According to lifestyle theory, the eight thinking styles that support the defensive function of human cognition are mollification, cutoff, entitlement, power orientation, sentimentality, superoptimism, cognitive indolence, and discontinuity.

Mollification   People who abuse drugs frequently seek to avoid responsibility for their actions by pointing out how little control they have over their use of chemical substances. They may consequently seek to blame someone or something for problems attributable to their own poor decision making. Mollification necessitates minimizing the seriousness of one's drug-related difficulties, or diverting attention and responsibility away from one's own actions onto factors external to oneself. This thinking style is often difficult to challenge, however, because patches of truth are sometimes woven into the fabric of one's distortions and rationalizations. By blaming their parents, peers, or society in general, drug-involved clients have ready-made excuses for their failures in life. In so doing, the drug-involved individual is shutting him or herself off from potential avenues of change and intervention, which in the end, only serves to protect the lifestyle and prevents him or her from recognizing other options and life goals.

Cutoff   All people, including drug abusers, respond to deterrents. Drug abusers are just better at eliminating these deterrents from consideration. Therefore, engagement in the drug lifestyle presupposes the ability to eradicate common deterrents to drug use in a moment's notice. This is referred to by lifestyle theory as implosion or cutoff. The most popular form of cutoff in drug-abusing populations is the two-word phrase "fuck it." However, it is also possible to use drugs as a cutoff for future or continued drug use. Hence, a person who initially plans to limit him or herself to two drinks, may wind up consuming an entire case of beer, along with a fifth of whisky, because of the power of the first two drinks to implode common deterrents—such as fear and good judgment—to additional drug use. The cutoff is generally very rapid; a more gradual wearing down of concerns or deterrents to drug use is more appropriately classified under cognitive indolence.

Entitlement   Before people can enact a behavior they must first grant themselves permission to engage in the behavior. This is particularly true of drug use, where the individual may be violating certain societal, legal, family, and moral codes. The drug user must find some way to free him or herself from the moral, ethical, or legal constraints that would normally interfere with the intent to use drugs. The cutoff is one way a person might choose to eliminate these constraints; entitlement is another. Entitlement involves granting oneself permission to use and abuse drugs based on a perception of being special, privileged, or uniquely deserving. Some people use a form of entitlement in which they frame their situation as a special occasion, but then any day can be a special occasion for someone with a drug problem; others may set up or arrange a conflict with their spouse or employer in order to justify using drugs. The misidentification of wants as needs ("I need to get high tonight because I'm addicted") is a further reflection of entitlement and one that is unwittingly reinforced by the disease and addiction models of substance abuse treatment.

Power Orientation   The thinking that supports the drug lifestyle is not only geared toward immediate gratification, but also emphasizes interpersonal power and control. One way to compensate for weak personal control is to exercise control over one's external environment. This might entail physically assaulting another person, verbally intimidating a weaker individual, or subtly manipulating someone into doing something they don't want to do. The power orientation is also present when one uses drugs to achieve a sense of control and predictability over one's mood. Because drugs have a fairly predictable influence on one's emotional state, a person can gain a temporary sense of predictability over one's seemingly unmanageable life by ingesting these substances and experiencing the anticipated effect, even if this effect is no longer enjoyable. Yochelson and Samenow (1976) assert that when criminal offenders and substance abusers see themselves as not being in control they experience a zero state. The individual frees him or herself from this zero state by taking control of the situation, which may materialize into an assault, intimidation, manipulation, or drug binge. This is labeled a power thrust by Yochelson and Samenow (1976).

Sentimentality   It is natural for people to want to feel justified in their actions. Commitment to the drug lifestyle, however, magnifies these tendencies. One way people justify their behavior is by projecting blame for their decisions onto others. This is referred to as mollification. Another way people justify their actions is by performing various good deeds for the purpose of creating an image of themselves as kind and generous. Lifestyle theory refers to this as sentimentality (Yochelson & Samenow, 1976). Examples include purchasing a bouquet of flowers for one's spouse following a drug binge, lending money to another drug user in an attempt to gain access to that person's circle of suppliers, and encouraging a younger sibling to stop using drugs. The problem with sentimentality is that it provides drug users with the opportunity to deny or minimize the harm they have done to themselves and others through their involvement in the drug lifestyle. What clients need to realize is that a few good deeds do not erase the harm that has been created by their misuse of substances.

Superoptimism   The human body can withstand a great deal before it begins to deteriorate under the strain of chronic drug use. People introduce all manner of foreign substances into their bodies, and the body characteristically responds by cleansing itself of these impurities. People can use drugs for months, years, even decades, before suffering the negative physical side effects of a drug lifestyle. Over time, this resiliency contributes to a growing belief on the part of the habitual drug user that he or she can continue misusing substances and avoid the adverse consequences he or she observes in others who ingest a comparable amount of chemical substance. Cavalier disregard for the negative long-term consequences of drug abuse and the associated attitude of invulnerability are labeled superoptimism by lifestyle theory, a term originally coined by Yochelson and Samenow (1976) to describe a similar attitude observed in criminal offenders. The fantasy, illusion, and irrationality of superoptimism must be addressed with clients if they are to have a shot at abandoning the drug lifestyle; for as long as superoptimism thrives, the individual will continue to deny the destructiveness of his or her drug lifestyle with statements such as, "It (drug-related difficulties) could never happen to me" and "I can stop anytime I want."

Cognitive Indolence   Drug abusers are as lazy in thought as they are in action. Like water running down hill, people committed to a drug lifestyle take the path of least resistance, although this path is replete with pitfalls, snares, and sundry other hazards at every turn. If a person is committed to the drug lifestyle, then he or she has grown accustomed to taking shortcuts, knowing full well that these shortcuts hold a strong possibility of creating serious problems in the future. However, people engaged in the drug lifestyle are more interested in pursuing short-term pleasure than worrying about the long-term difficulties associated with habitual drug use. The lazy thinking that is cognitive indolence also causes many drug abusers to take an uncritical view of their plans, ideas, and methods. The thinking pattern of cognitive indolence often combines with superoptimism to create numerous obstacles for clients and block future opportunities for success; unbridled fantasy and blatant laziness ultimately lead the individual into failure.

Discontinuity   Persons committed to the drug lifestyle often have trouble following through on commitments and initially good intentions. Because the drug lifestyle contributes to the users' increased susceptibility to distraction in their thinking patterns, one frequent complaint of drug-involved persons is that they have fallen short of accomplishing many of their goals in life. This thinking style is referred to as discontinuity and can cause the individual to jump from one topic to another in conversations so that other people have trouble following his or her train of thought. Low consistency of thought and behavior can frustrate a client's efforts at change and render formal treatment ineffective. Discontinuity may also give rise to a Jekyll and Hyde orientation, whereby the client assumes two separate personas, one when using drugs and the other when sober. The chameleon-like demeanor of the habitual drug user, which can also be traced back to discontinuity, protects the lifestyle because it helps the individual indefinitely avoid the consequences of his or her actions.

Condition–Choice–Cognition Interactions

Lifestyle theory asserts that interactions among drug-related conditions, choices, and cognitions give rise to specific behavioral styles and patterns. The four behavioral styles hypothesized to be diagnostic of the drug lifestyle include irresponsibility/pseudoresponsibility, stress-coping imbalance, interpersonal triviality, and social rule breaking/bending. The drug lifestyle is conceptualized by lifestyle theory as a caricature (exaggerated picture of reality) or fiction that people approach, but rarely achieve in its entirety. One's proximity to the caricature of the drug lifestyle can be assessed using these four behavioral markers. In fact, these behavioral styles are often a good starting point in the development of a change plan for drug-seeking clients. A review of these characteristics should therefore occur early in intervention with the aid of the Participant Handbook reproduced in Appendix 1.

Irresponsibility/Pseudoresponsibility   Irresponsibility refers to the individual's failure to meet his or her obligations to others (family, friends, employers) or lack of accountability, as demonstrated by missing appointments, being negligent in paying bills, or dismissing the potential consequences of his or her actions. Pseudoresponsibility, on the other hand, is a false sense of responsibility in which the person meets certain obligations (e.g., providing financial support for self and family, maintaining employment, staying out of serious legal trouble) but neglects obligations in other areas (e.g., missing important family functions because of a growing preoccupation with drugs).

Stress-Coping Imbalance   Drug use often begins as an attempt to feel good and indulge oneself. Over time, however, the motivation for drug use changes. The individual's motivation shifts from seeking pleasure to searching for ways to avoid pain. Self-indulgence, therefore, is gradually replaced by stress-coping imbalance in the evolution of a drug lifestyle. As the lifestyle progresses, so too does the stress that the drug abuser has learned to momentarily circumvent by ingesting drugs or engaging in other forms of escape. The meaning behind the term stress-coping imbalance is that the person's habitual style of managing stress (i.e., escaping from stress by using drugs) creates long-term stress problems that then contribute to an escalating pattern of drug use designed to alleviate the mounting level of stress brought on by the person's use of drugs—a vicious cycle. In addition, because drugs are effective in reducing short-term discomfort, the person has little motivation to learn more effective long-term coping strategies.

Interpersonal Triviality   As a person becomes increasingly committed to the drug lifestyle there is a corresponding increase in the amount of time spent with other drug users and a corollary decrease in the amount of time spent with family members and others who do not abuse drugs (assuming, of course, that family members do not abuse drugs). Deep, meaningful relationships are replaced by superficial, often exploitive associations because intimacy threatens the lifestyle by interfering with the untethered use of drugs. This pattern is referred to as interpersonal triviality. Interpersonal triviality is also displayed in a person's use of drugs as a substitute for meaningful human contact. For this reason, rituals (i.e., repeated patterns of behavior centering on the purchase, preparation, and use of drugs) become increasingly more common as people move into the more advanced stages of the drug lifestyle. These rituals can become so powerful that drug users frequently display agitation and anger at being interrupted in the performance of such routinized patterns of behavior.

Social Rule Breaking/Bending   People who engage in problematic drug use generally experience little compunction in breaking rules to finance a drug habit. However, if the user is caught, his or her access to drugs may be reduced. This is why people committed to the drug lifestyle generally prefer to bend the rules—lying, conning, deceiving—as opposed to breaking them. One is less likely to be apprehended for social rule–bending behavior than for social rule–breaking conduct, and even if caught in the act of bending the rules, the sanctions are ordinarily less severe than if one were caught stealing, robbing, or committing some other social rule–breaking act. It should come as no surprise that clients committed to the drug lifestyle will resort to breaking the rules if they believe their opportunities for social rule bending are limited; however, given the choice between social rule breaking and social rule bending, most substance abusers will select the social rule–bending option because it is much less likely to separate them from the source of their motivation (namely, drugs).

Drug Lifestyle Screening Interview

The Drug Lifestyle Screening Interview (DLSI) is a structured interview that can be used to assess each of the four behavioral characteristics of a drug lifestyle. The interview takes 15 to 30 minutes to administer, depending on the level of detail in the answers provided by the client and the degree to which the clinician is experienced in its use. This interview, which has received preliminary research support (Walters, 1994a, 1995a), is reproduced in Appendix 2: Drug Lifestyle Screening Interview. Research indicates that scores of 12 or higher signify strong identification with the drug lifestyle ideal; scores between 8 and 11 denote moderate identification with the drug lifestyle ideal; and scores below 8 reflect little or no identification with this ideal. The interrater reliability ranges between .57 and .75 for the four subscales and is .83 for the total DLSI score (Walters, 1994a). It is recommended that program participants be interviewed with the DLSI early in the program but that this be only one of several tools used to assess a client's level of commitment, preoccupation, and identification with the drug lifestyle. Appendix 3: Administration and Scoring Key for DLSI can be used as a guide.

FUNCTIONAL FEATURES OF THE DRUG LIFESTYLE

Whereas the structural division of lifestyle theory centers on the individual components of the drug or other lifestyle, the functional branch clarifies the dynamic process of lifestyle development and change. Accordingly, the present discussion focuses on four features of lifestyle development: existential fear, styles of fear management, life tasks, and developmental stages.

Existential Fear

Existential fear is advanced as the primary organizing motive for behavior within the framework of lifestyle theory. As such, it serves as the impetus for all subsequent acts, decisions, and thoughts. The concept of existential fear is founded on two assumptions: (a) that all living organisms possess a survival or life instinct and (b) that this instinct clashes with the reality of a continually changing environment. This conflict creates imbalance or dissonance within the organism, which the organism then attempts to rectify by engaging in activities designed to support survival. These activities may be largely inherent or instinctual, as in the case of plants and simple multicellular organisms, or may be a combination of both instinctual and learned processes, as in the case of *homo sapiens* and other primates. In humans, the conflict that arises between the instinct to survive and a constantly changing environment gradually becomes transformed into existential fear as the organism develops the ability to conceptualize existence. This is the point at which the primordial conflict between survival and environmental change becomes an expression of the person's life condition; hence, the term, existential fear. It is proposed that one's existence cannot be understood, or even acknowledged, until one is able to form an appreciation of nonexistence. Over time, this fear becomes increasingly more personalized, passing through three major experiential filters. This process will be examined in greater detail in the Life Tasks section, but first, we must consider the three primary styles of fear management.

Styles of Fear Management

The three styles of fear management, according to lifestyle theory, are despair, adaptation, and lifestyle. Despair entails being overwhelmed by fear to the point that one becomes suicidal, psychotic, or severely depressed. Consistent with the evolutionary roots of lifestyle theory, the second fear management style is called adaptation. Persons using this approach adjust their thinking and behavior according to information supplied by the environment as a way of comprehending, predicting, and living within the parameters of that environment. People who handle fear with a drug or other lifestyle are following a blueprint of rules, roles, relationships, and rituals that have been established by some external "authority." A lifestyle reduces existential fear by affording the individual a false sense of sameness and low environmental variability. Lifestyles are highly reinforcing because of their ability to temporarily reduce discomfort and fear; they are deceptive, however, in that for all the short-term relief they provide, they create large reservoirs of long-term stress. Lifestyle theory argues that the longer one hides within the seemingly protective confines of a lifestyle, the more dependent one becomes on the lifestyle to manage everyday problems and concerns.

Accommodation and assimilation are concepts originally devised by Piaget (1963) to explain human cognitive development. Accommodation entails constructing a new cognitive representation of an experience (referred to as a schema) in order to code information for which no current mental symbol exists. Conversely, assimilation involves incorporating new information into an existing cognitive schema. These two concepts help clarify the differences between the three styles of fear management. Despair in the face of existential fear subsumes a moderate degree of accommodation, but because this style of fear management is low in assimilation, any information acquired through this method is poorly organized and largely useless in helping the individual cope with life's problems. Managing existential fear with a lifestyle, on the other hand, follows a converse pattern in which assimilation is high and accommodation low. The purpose of a lifestyle, thus, is to force new information into existing schemas, even if the information does not adequately fit the existing schema, and keep new cognitive representations to a minimum. The adaptive approach to fear management differs from the other approaches in that it effectively integrates assimilation and accommodation as a way of achieving a more thorough understanding of the surrounding environment.

Life Tasks

As discussed previously, there are three primary categories of risk for future drug abuse: (a) weak socialization to conventional definitions of drug use, (b) idiosyncratic responses to internal and external stimuli, and (c) strong socialization to deviant definitions of drug use. Another way to conceive of these three risk factors is as life tasks that help shape a person's response to existential fear. Lifestyle theory considers two levels of life task, distinguished by age: early life tasks (0–4 years of age) and later life tasks (5 years of age and older). Failure to socialize to conventional definitions of drug use is thought to reflect problems with the early life task of attachment and later life task of social bonding and empathy. The formation of idiosyncratic responses to internal and external stimuli is hypothesized to be an extension of problems with stimulus modulation (early life task) and internal–external orientation (later life task). Finally, socialization to deviant definitions of drug use is believed to have its foundation in a poor self-image (early life task) and deviant role identity (later life task). An overview of the proposed connections between the three risk categories and the early and later life tasks can be found in Table 2-1.

Lifestyle theory holds that the early and later life tasks act as filters through which existential fear passes and takes shape over the course of a person's life. Issues involving the later life task of social bonding/empathy are believed to transform fear into a concern for social acceptance. Behavioral strategies adopted by people who learn to fear social rejection include withdrawing into a world of superficial relationships, avoiding all expressions of intimacy, and rejecting others before others have a chance to reject them. All of these paths potentially direct one toward drug lifestyle activities, although it should be noted that there are myriad exceptions to this general rule. Abandonment of the drug lifestyle, on the other hand, might be encouraged by instructing clients in more effective life stress management and interactions with others. Beyond stress management and social skills training, however, the client must come to terms with the fact that to attain intimacy he or she must be willing to risk the possibility of rejection.

Table 2-1 Proposed Connections Between Risk Categories and Early and Later Life Tasks

Risk category	Early life tasks	Later life tasks
Failure to socialize to conventional definitions of substance use	Attachment	Social bonding/empathy
Idiosyncratic responses to internal and external stimuli	Stimulus modulation	Internal–external orientation
Socialization to deviant definitions of substance use	Self-image	Role identity

Secondary and tertiary fears that arise when existential fear is filtered through experiences relevant to the internal–external orientation life task center around the issue of control. Preliminary evidence suggests that drug abuse may be associated with an external life orientation in that substance misuse may be an attempt by some individuals to exert control over the environment to compensate for feelings of worthlessness, powerlessness, and fear (McClelland, Davis, Kalin, & Wanner, 1972; Wexler, 1975). Drug abuse can also be construed as a method of achieving "external" control over oneself through the drug's ability to create a predictable change in mood. The person operating on fear that has passed through the internal–external orientation filter is looking for an external solution to an internal problem. Effective intervention, consequently, requires that the client come to realize that the long-term solution to his or her problems resides within him or herself.

The role identity life task may also interact with existential fear to create certain secondary and tertiary fears. Much of the existential fear that filters through the role identity life task either branches off into a generalized preoccupation with one's identity or breaks down further into tertiary fears of failure, success, and fear. People who commit themselves to the drug lifestyle often define themselves on the basis of activities they have engaged in as part of that lifestyle. Hence, self-labeling is one way drug abusers manage role identity–influenced existential fear. Labeling oneself a "drug addict" or "dope fiend," although capable of reducing identity-based fears in the short run, actually serves to add fuel to these fears in the long run by encouraging entrenchment in a drug-based identity. For successful disengagement from the drug lifestyle to take place, clients must be prepared to critically evaluate their self-perceptions and work toward the rapprochement of personal goals and environmental contingencies in the formation of a new and more productive role identity.

Developmental Stages

Noted elsewhere (Walters, 1994c) is the presence of three behavioral transition points in a person's use and abuse of substances: initiation, escalation, and cessation. Initiation marks the onset of drug use, escalation a significant rise in the severity and/or intensity of drug use, and cessation the termination of drug use. I have organized these transition points into stages (Walters, 1994c) and propose here a four-stage sequence of drug lifestyle development. The four stages are labeled the pre-drug lifestyle stage, the early drug stage, the advanced drug stage, and the stage of burnout and maturity.

Pre-Drug Lifestyle Stage   The pre-drug lifestyle stage is inhabited by persons who have abused drugs but have not yet formed a preliminary commitment to the drug lifestyle. Incentives for drug use during this stage include peer acceptance, curiosity, excitement, and the pursuit of pleasure (Walters, 1994c). It is postulated that the overriding goal of pre-drug lifestyle substance use is self-enhancement, and as such, experimentation with a wide variety of different substances is quite common during this stage. Research shows that well over half of the individuals who enter pre-drug lifestyle stage activities do not proceed to the next stage (Johnston, O'Malley, & Bachman, 1991). Consequently, this stage gives rise to a higher rate of voluntary attrition than does any other stage.

Early Drug Stage   There are three indicators of increased involvement in a drug lifestyle: commitment, preoccupation, and identity. People functioning at an early stage of drug lifestyle involvement forge a preliminary commitment to the drug lifestyle in terms of the goals they pursue. Moreover, they show signs of increased preoccupation with drug-related activities and a growing sense of identification with the drug lifestyle ideal. It is also not uncommon for there to be a shift in motivation with the onset of this stage, whereby the stress-reducing (coping) properties of drug use supersede the self-indulgent (enhancement) properties in directing a person's drug-seeking activities. As use begins to escalate, there is a corresponding reduction in the number of different substances consumed, or at least preferred; however, many clients never realize a true drug of choice. Attrition during this stage is less than that which occurs during the pre-drug stage but is higher than the rate observed during the advanced stage.

Advanced Drug Stage   Drug-related commitments, preoccupations, and identifications are at their height during the advanced stage of drug lifestyle development. Incentives for drug use during this stage evolve from a person's efforts to eliminate negative emotions that have filtered through the early and later life tasks and become expressed as a growing fear of intimacy, loss of control, and/or debilitating self-doubt. A firm commitment to drug lifestyle goals is patently evident in clients functioning at an advanced stage, and as a result, they are probably more dangerous to themselves (from overdose, suicide) and others (inadvertently through drunk driving and crime) than at any other stage in the drug lifestyle sequence. Few people voluntarily drop out of the lifestyle at this point because there is a high level of commitment, preoccupation, and identification with the drug lifestyle ideal.

Stage of Burnout and Maturity   The final stage in the drug developmental sequence is comprised of two distinct, yet interrelated processes: burnout and maturity. Burnout refers to the reductions in physical strength, stamina, and pleasure derived from drug use that accrue with advancing age and the accumulated negative effects of the drug lifestyle. A change in values or goals that encourages a person to question his or her continued involvement in the drug lifestyle is referred to as maturity. Hence, whereas burnout is largely physical, maturity is primarily psychological. What clinicians need to realize is that although burnout is inevitable, maturity is not. The goal of intervention, therefore, is to stimulate client maturity so that it might accompany the natural burnout process. Burnout, in the absence of maturity, will oftentimes result in continued drug use and place the individual at increased risk for future relapse.

It should be noted that a client may regress to an earlier stage in the lifestyle development sequence at any time. As a case in point, a client who burns out on cocaine, without achieving concurrent maturity, may return to the early stage of drug lifestyle development, often with a new primary drug of abuse, such as alcohol, marijuana, or heroin. A second point clinicians need to be mindful of is that the age range for each stage varies considerably from client to client. Thus, whereas the majority of individuals in the pre-drug lifestyle stage are adolescents or young adults, some older individuals also work their way into this stage. Likewise, age 40 is employed as a general demarcator of the initiation of burnout, but there are many individuals who burn out well before or well after age 40. Variability in the onset of burnout can be traced to innate physiological factors, variations in the pattern of usage, different routes of drug administration, and the type of drug abused, because certain drugs, such as cocaine, lend themselves to more rapid burnout than others, such as alcohol or heroin. These factors need to be

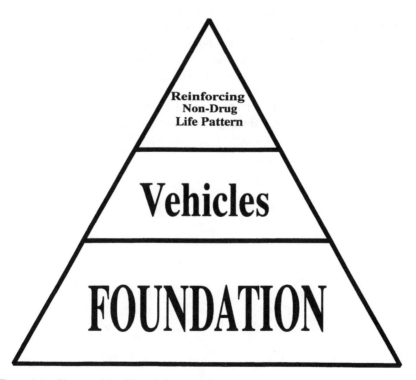

Figure 2-1   Phases of the lifestyle intervention process.

considered in planning, constructing, and implementing an effective program of behavioral change and relapse prevention.

CONCLUSION

An introduction to the goals of lifestyle intervention from both the structural and functional perspectives is now necessary because these goals will be used to organize the subsequent chapters. The three structural goals of lifestyle intervention are to teach clients how to more effectively manage various life conditions, make better life choices, and modify self-defeating cognitions. The three functional goals of lifestyle intervention are to arrest the drug lifestyle; to instruct clients in basic social, coping, and thinking skills; and to encourage resocialization. These three functional goals correspond with the three phases of lifestyle intervention depicted in Figure 2-1. Hence, the goal of the foundation is to arrest the lifestyle, the goal of the vehicle is to teach skills, and the goal of the reinforcement of a non-drug life pattern is to effect resocialization. To integrate the structural and functional goals of lifestyle intervention, Chapter 3 will address the first goal of functional intervention (arresting the lifestyle); Chapter 4 will speak to the second goal of functional intervention (skills training) and the first goal of structural intervention (conditions management); Chapter 5 will consider the second goal of functional intervention (skills training) in conjunction with the second goal of structural intervention (choice development); Chapter 6 will entertain the second goal of functional intervention (skills training) in combination with the third goal of structural intervention (cognition modification); and Chapter 7 will cover issues relevant to the third goal of functional intervention (resocialization). The rationale for spending an entire chapter on theory is that lifestyle intervention follows directly from lifestyle theory. This will become evident during the course of the next several chapters.

Chapter 3

Arresting the Lifestyle

The first step in any program of change, whether the intervention is aimed at crime, gambling, or drugs, is arresting the lifestyle. Unless the lifestyle is temporarily suspended, intervention will be ineffective because people actively engaged in the drug lifestyle generally possess minimal motivation for change. In working with substance abusers, I have found that the most common catalyst in the change process is a crisis of sufficient magnitude to motivate the individual to temporarily suspend lifestyle activities. To be effective, then, a program of change must begin by encouraging the termination of one's active involvement in drug use activities. Additionally, the arresting process must be of suitable duration to allow for more substantive changes in thinking and behavior during the latter stages of intervention. Extension of the arresting process requires preliminary interventions designed to expose clients to ideas and information that run counter to such lifestyle-supporting mechanisms and beliefs as externalization, fatalism, and powerlessness. This may be accomplished with reattribution training and development of an introspective attitude. A discussion of the three major components of a suspended drug lifestyle follows.

INTRODUCTION OF A CRISIS

Interviews with people who have abandoned the drug lifestyle without benefit of formal treatment indicate that a crisis often triggers the person's decision to stop using drugs (Biernacki, 1990; Ludwig, 1985; Tuchfeld, 1981; Vaillant & Milofsky, 1982; Walters, 1995b). Lifestyle theory asserts that a crisis may radiate from either an internal or external source. An internally derived crisis is exemplified by the growing sense of disgust that occurs when people begin to realize that drug use has prevented them from achieving many of their long-term goals. This is referred to as "hitting bottom" in traditional drug treatment circles. Crises may also be provoked by an external source, such as an ultimatum from one's spouse, employer, or probation officer. Hence, the client is informed that unless the drug use stops, he or she risks losing his or her marriage, job, or freedom. Being notified of a medical condition that has been aggravated by one's misuse of chemical substances or seeing an associate die from a drug overdose are other external events potentially capable of stimulating temporary desistance. In many cases, the internal and external pressures that produce a crisis dissipate over time, so that an individual may temporarily suspend his or her involvement with drugs, only to resume drug use once the crisis abates. Thus, it is necessary to sustain the arresting process beyond the initial crisis.

Crises are categorized not only by source (internal versus external), but also by motivation. Two broad categories of motivation for abandoning the drug lifestyle have been proposed: approach-oriented motives and avoidance-oriented motives (Walters, 1995b). Approach-oriented motives direct the individual to abandon the drug lifestyle in favor of participation in activities incompatible with the misuse of drugs. This may entail a change in values and goals, a desire for more than what the drug lifestyle can offer, or the assumption of new responsibilities, such as those associated with being a spouse or parent. Avoidance-oriented incentives for drug use cessation derive from a person's efforts to escape the pain and suffering created by his or her misuse of substances and involvement in the drug lifestyle. Hence, pressure from significant others to seek assistance, a growing awareness of a deteriorating medical condition aggravated by the use of drugs, and a feeling of having hit bottom are avoidance-oriented motives for desisting from drug use. Approach-oriented and avoidance-oriented motives may be either internal or external (see Table 3-1), and all four combinations (internal approach-oriented, external approach-oriented, internal avoidance-oriented, external avoidance-oriented) must be considered in constructing a comprehensive program of change for clients with previous commitment to the drug lifestyle.

☑ SKILL   Directing the Crisis

Several of the more popular systems of family therapy advocate introduction of a crisis designed to disrupt dysfunctional family transactional patterns and stimulate

Table 3-1   Examples of Crises Broken Down by Source and Motivation

Motivation	Source	
	Internal	External
Approach-oriented	Change in values or goals Want more out of life	Assumption of new responsibilities Being a good role model for others
Avoidance-oriented	Sense of having "lost everything" "Hitting bottom"	Ultimatum from spouse Shock of seeing someone die of overdose

reorganization along more functional lines. A crisis, for persons engaged in the drug lifestyle, means that the individual experiences the negative consequences of his or her lifestyle. Although it may be difficult, problematic, or even unethical to create artificial crises in clients, natural crises abound in situations where people are committed to the drug lifestyle. Normally, the effect of a crisis dissipates rapidly and the individual returns to the lifestyle out of frustration, habit, or boredom. Crises, however, are the first step in the change process; without them, the client would have little motivation for change. Short of waiting for one of these crises to materialize, a therapist can intervene by highlighting the natural crises in a person's life and identifying those holding the greatest potential to assist with the temporary suspension of lifestyle activities. Defining, directing, and recognizing crises serve as critical steps in initially arresting the drug lifestyle.

☑ ASSESSMENT   The Inventory of Negative Consequences

By highlighting certain natural crises in a person's life, Appendix 4: Inventory of Negative Consequences can be used by clinicians to identify key issues and experiences that could conceivably orchestrate a temporary cessation of drug use. The client is asked to list the people who have been hurt by his or her use of substances, the opportunities he or she has missed because of his or her use and abuse of drugs, the possessions and relationships lost as a direct result of substance misuse, and the embarrassing situations he or she has encountered as a conse-quence of involvement in drug-related activities. Clients should indicate their current level of discomfort (low, moderate, high) for each of the consequences listed on the form, so that the therapist can pinpoint crises that have a high probability of assisting clients with the arduous task of temporarily suspending lifestyle activities. The Inventory of Negative Consequences is designed to identify the perceived negative consequences of drug use potentially capable of creating a crisis of sufficient magnitude to motivate the client to enter the early stages of the change process. Consequences viewed by clients as most disturbing (items rated as highly distressing rather than moderately or minimally distressing) should be made the focal point of the therapist's future interventions in this area.

☑ PLAN

Intervention begins with a review of the results obtained from the Inventory of Negative Consequences. Although group-based intervention is normally the preferred route in working with those who have chosen the drug lifestyle, this preliminary phase of the change process is probably most effective if conducted individually. This is because many of the issues and situations that contribute to the initiation of a crisis, such as the people one has hurt or the embarrassing situations one has encountered as a consequence of one's use of substances, are not the kinds of things most clients are willing to discuss in front of a group of strangers. Therapists who are willing to listen to their clients, yet are unwilling to allow themselves to be confused, controlled, or manipulated by their client's behavior, typically enjoy the greatest measure of success in working with substance abusing populations.

The previous paragraph insinuates that if intervention is to be effective, some degree of relationship building must take place, even as the crisis unfolds. The formation of a trusting relationship between the therapist and client cannot be overemphasized in interventions with clients who have entered into the drug lifestyle. The therapeutic value of trust can be traced to the fact that it provides the client with the opportunity to explore his or her perceptions and express his or her views in a nonthreatening, supportive environment. Incorporating family and close friends in the early phase of intervention may also be helpful because of the trust that may still exist between the client and these individuals (at least from the client's point of view). Family-based interventions or group "confrontations" involving the client's family and closest friends may therefore be of some utility in defining a crisis for clients who may otherwise be unwilling to take an honest look at the negative consequences of their drug use.

A crisis is typically the first step in arresting the lifestyle. However, crises come and go, often without inspiring meaningful or lasting change. For this reason, the momentary arresting process initiated by the crisis must be expanded so that the client has the opportunity to learn the skills that will eventually bring about long-term cognitive, behavioral, and lifestyle changes. Removing the individual from a drug-infested environment can sometimes act to prolong the arresting process beyond the point at which the crisis no longer sustains continued desistance from drugs. Confinement in a hospital bed or jail cell may serve a similar purpose; but as anyone who has ever worked in these settings can attest, it is impossible to keep drugs out of the hands of those who would use them, whether the person is confined in a highly structured inpatient drug treatment program or a maximum security penitentiary. Although removal from a drug-infested environ-ment may be helpful to clients interested in extending the arresting process, other less drastic and potentially more effective strategies are also available, two of which—the attribution triad and introspection—are discussed in this chapter.

THE ATTRIBUTION TRIAD

Attributions are the causal inferences people draw about another person's thoughts and motivations from observing that person's behavior. Intellectual aspirations may be attributed to someone seen walking down the street with several textbooks tucked neatly underneath his or her arm, just as athletic inclinations may be ascribed to a person working out on the nautilus machine at a local gym. Even more important than the attributions we make of others are the attributions we make of our own behavior. Thus, we might attribute our conduct to personal effort or to the influence of some external force such as fate or luck; likewise, we might perceive these factors as global, stable, and unchangeable, or as specific, unstable, and malleable (Weiner, 1974). Lifestyle theory holds that there are three personal attributions that serve as preconditions for change. By holding that change is necessary, possible, and attainable, these three personal attributions, labeled the attribution triad, promote change by extending the arresting process and creating a positive attitude toward change. These three attributions are a belief in the necessity of change, a belief in the possibility of change, and a belief in one's ability to effect change.

☑ SKILL Belief in the Necessity of Change

During the early stages of intervention, it is quite common for clients to deny responsibility for the negative events of their drug use. Regardless of the number of items a client lists on the Inventory of Negative Consequences, he or she is likely to have an excuse for each one. Therefore, in asking clients to complete the inventory, the therapist is laying the groundwork for interventions directed at instilling in the client a belief in the necessity of change. Nonetheless, a great deal more work will probably still need to be done on this particular attribution. Belief in the necessity of change entails acknowledging the presence of a problem, accepting personal responsibility for that problem, and understanding that the problem will continue to exist unless the individual makes certain changes in his or her thinking and behavior.

☑ ASSESSMENT Locus Test

Appendix 5: Locus Test measures the degree to which the respondent perceives certain experiences as a consequence of outside forces or his or her own decision making. A five-point rating scale is used, with higher scores signifying greater attributions of self-determination. Because the Locus Test is comprised of only five items, the highest score a respondent can receive on this scale is 25. It is recommended that clinicians develop their own norms for this measure because scores, and the specific meanings attached to them, tend to vary from setting to setting. In my own clinical work with substance abusers, I have found scores below 18 to be indicative of an external world-view that frequently interferes with the formation of a belief in the necessity of change. Scores between 18 and 21, on the other hand, indicate a trend toward externalized thinking that should probably be targeted for change during the early phases of intervention.

☑ PLAN

If the results of the Inventory of Negative Consequences, the Locus Test, and the clinician's own personal appraisal suggest that the client lacks a belief in the necessity of change, then intervention is indicated. The present model advocates a three-step procedure. The first step in developing a belief in the necessity of change is to educate the client on matters of choice and personal responsibility. This is the didactic portion of the intervention. Whether the intervention is con-ducted via lecture, discussions, readings, or all three, the point that needs to be stressed is that accountability is imperative for success. Following didactic review of the personal responsibility issue, the next step is to highlight the client's contributions to his or her current situation. This might be accomplished by having the client compile a list of the problem situations he or she has encountered in the recent past, and then asking the client to identify the common denominator across situations. The answer is quite simple: in nearly all cases the only common denominator is the client. The third step in assisting clients with the formation of a belief in the necessity of change is to address and challenge thinking styles that typically minimize personal accountability, most notably mollification and senti-mentality (see Chapter 6 for more information on how to challenge these thinking styles). Clients exhibiting a strong belief in the necessity of change are a step or two ahead of their peers, a fact that can be exploited by the astute therapist for the purpose of stimulating change in other areas of a client's life.

☑ SKILL   Belief in the Possibility of Change

The second precondition for change is a belief in the possibility of change. An acknowledgment of the need for change is no guarantee that the client views change as a possibility in his or her own life. Some people are of the opinion that leopards do not change their spots, tigers do not change their stripes, and people do not change their behavior. Lifestyle theory argues that there can be no change without belief in the theoretical possibility of change. Whereas the necessity and possibility of change are obviously related, they are far from identical. Research, in fact, highlights the importance of acknowledging the possibility of change and attributing this change to one's own actions, rather than to forces outside oneself. Davison, Tsujimoto, and Glaros (1973), as a case in point, discerned that attributing reduced insomnia to one's own efforts was more effective in maintaining initial treatment gains than attributing the initial gains to an optimal dosage of sleeping medication. Belief in the necessity of change consequently reinforces a belief in the possibility of change, but because these beliefs are functionally independent they must be addressed separately in any program of treatment intervention.

✔ ASSESSMENT   Rational Emotive Imagery and the Change Thermometer

Albert Ellis (1970) developed a technique known as rational emotive imagery whereby the therapist asks the client to recall a recent event in which he or she felt particularly angry, depressed, frustrated, or afraid. Using Appendix 6: Change Thermometer, the client charts his or her emotional response by identifying the initial level of emotion he or she experienced during the episode in question. This is accomplished by circling the number on the thermometer that corresponds to the individual's initial reaction. Once the initial level of emotion has been identified, the client is instructed to move down the thermometer, number by number. For instance, if the client's initial emotional level was 9, then he or she should be instructed to drop to level 8, then to level 7, and so on, down the scale. At the end of the exercise the therapist asks the client how far he or she descended the scale and requests a description of the methods he or she employed in accomplishing this task. Most clients are able to achieve a reduction of at least three or four points, and oftentimes a change in thought or perception precedes the decrease in negative affect. This exercise not only demonstrates that change is possible, but also points to a potential avenue (i.e., modification of one's thinking) through which such change might be realized.

✔ PLAN

Clients who persist in being skeptical about the possibility of change, even after participating in the rational emotive imagery exercise, may benefit from listening to the accounts of former substance abusers who have since recovered from their drug use difficulties. Arranging for former clients to visit with and speak to new program participants may be a particularly effective way of demonstrating the possibility of change. By sharing their experiences with persons unfamiliar with the change process, former clients and program graduates not only serve as role models for novice program participants, but also reinforce their own commitment to a non-drug lifestyle. Both parties consequently benefit from such an arrangement. Whether acquired directly, through experiences set up in exercises such as the one described in the preceding paragraph, or vicariously, following exposure to the personal accounts of former clients who have abandoned the drug lifestyle, a belief in the possibility of change is a necessary precondition for change, with implications for the final leg of the attribution triad—namely, belief in one's ability to effect change.

✔ SKILL   Belief in One's Ability to Effect Change

Believing that change is possible is not particularly helpful unless one also has confidence one's or her ability to enact change. Hence, an additional precondition for change is a belief in one's ability to effect change and manage the types of temptations and risky situations that invite relapse. This component of the attribution triad is based on Albert Bandura's (1982) self-efficacy concept. Self-efficacy is defined as a cognitive evaluation of one's ability to cope with a specific high-risk situation. Self-efficacy measures often predict who will relapse and frequently pinpoint the circumstances under which relapse occurs (Condiotte & Lichtenstein, 1981). There is additional evidence to suggest that self-efficacy is situation-specific, as represented by the results of a study in which subjects displaying weak self-efficacy in alcohol-related situations were significantly more likely to relapse than subjects exhibiting strong self-efficacy in alcohol-related situations; however, there were no outcome differences for groups divided on the basis of their perceived self-efficacy in non-alcohol-related situations (Rist & Watzl, 1983). These findings indicate that professing a belief in one's ability to effect change and demonstrating confidence in one's ability to manage drug-related situations and temptations are pivotal prerequisites for change.

✔ ASSESSMENT   Estimated Self-Efficacy in Avoiding Drugs

The assessment procedure provided in Appendix 7: Estimated Self-Efficacy in Avoiding Drugs gauges the respondent's confidence in his or her ability to avoid situations that could possibly encourage and precipitate relapse. This measure is designed to provide a general estimate of self-efficacy and to identify specific situations in which relapse may occur. Part A deals with negative affect, Part B with positive affect, Part C with drug-related cues, Part D with drug availability, and Part E with interpersonal situations and pressures. The totals for each section are then divided by the number of items in the section to yield an average score per item. The total score can either be divided by 20, to produce an average score per item, or be treated as a simple sum, with a range of 0 to 80, higher scores indicating greater self-efficacy. Scores above 75 are typically interpreted as evidence that the individual has never had a serious problem with drugs, has effectively abandoned the drug lifestyle, or suffers from superoptimism. Scores ranging from 66 to 75 may reflect a realistic level of self-efficacy in an individual who has had significant problems with drugs in the past. Scores between 56 and 65, on the other hand, signal a potential problem with self-efficacy, whereas scores below 56 indicate a serious lack of self-efficacy that demands therapeutic attention. The average self-efficacy scores for items within each of the five subscales can also be evaluated to identify potential targets for intervention.

☑ PLAN

Marlatt and Gordon (1985) have discussed several options that therapists may wish to pursue in addressing low self-efficacy. They include development of a good working relationship with the client, avoidance of the weak will attribution, division of tasks into manageable units, and provision of ample feedback and positive reinforcement. As has been mentioned previously in this text, there is no substitute for a good working alliance between the client and therapist. Clinicians must avoid the inclination to become robot-like dispensers of intervention techniques and instead seek to become therapeutically involved with their clients. Second, the argument that substance abusers have problems with drugs because they are morally weak or lacking in will power is neither true nor particularly helpful in forming a working relationship with clients. Lifestyle theory avoids the moral argument, choosing instead to conceptualize drug abuse as a learned process that is amenable to change through the development of specific skills. Separating tasks into manageable units is a third recommendation offered by Marlatt and Gordon, and one that works its way into the present book in discussions on choice-based intervention (see Chapter 5). Providing clients with heavy doses of feedback and positive reinforcement is a fourth avenue through which self-efficacy might be addressed and eventually enhanced.

Situations for which clients demonstrate low self-efficacy need to be treated as targets for intervention. In fact, interventions for each of the five areas that might potentially reflect low self-efficacy, as assessed by the Estimated Self-Efficacy in Avoiding Drugs measure (Appendix 7), are covered in this manual. Negative emotional reactions such as depression, boredom, anger, and despair can be handled with the aid of the emotions management techniques described in Chapter 4. Positive affective states capable of stimulating relapse are probably most amenable to interventions directed at the thinking styles described in Chapter 6, particularly superoptimism. Lack of self-efficacy in confronting drug-related cues is probably best managed through cue avoidance and cue exposure procedures, whereas poor self-efficacy in response to a rise in the availability of drugs requires implementation of access reduction techniques. Both sets of strategies are discussed in Chapter 4. Finally, a lack of confidence in one's ability to resist interpersonal temptation and the pressure to use drugs requires social skill and assertiveness training (see Chapters 4 and 5). The situational specificity of the self-efficacy concept provides clinicians with a plethora of targets for intervention, most of which involve instructing clients in one or more skills. The theory behind the method is that as people increase their skill in these areas and begin to experience success and reinforcement in using these skills, they gradually begin to believe in their ability to effectively manage high-risk situations.

INTROSPECTION

Before exploring the role of introspection in treatment, it is important that this term be defined to avoid confusing it with related concepts. Introspection is an attitude characterized by an open evaluation of one's thoughts, feelings, and actions. Lifestyle theory contends that introspection subsumes an inward focus, as opposed to the outward preoccupation of the drug lifestyle. The reader may recall from Chapter 2 that the drug lifestyle, like most lifestyles, is geared toward external power and control. The introspective attitude, on the other hand, converges around thoughts, plans, and expectancies, many of which have gone unchallenged for years. This attitude, like the attribution triad, is believed to be an important precondition for change. Introspection is also like the attribution triad in the sense that its influence extends well beyond the arresting stage of intervention. In other words, an introspective attitude potentially facilitates future phases of therapeutic change, as well as encouraging extension of the arresting process.

There are several concepts with which introspection is commonly confused. One such concept is remorse. Remorse is defined as anguish stemming from one's repentance for past misconduct. Although related to introspection, substantial differences nonetheless exist. Whereas remorse implies sorrow for one or more past acts, introspection encompasses a more general attitude in which the individual surveys the major consequences of his or her lifestyle, accepts responsibility for these consequences, and demonstrates a willingness to change his or her behavior in order to avoid these negative consequences in the future. Sensitivity is another term that is sometimes confused with introspection. Sensitivity connotes responsiveness to external conditions or stimulation, particularly other people's feelings, whereas introspection assumes responsiveness to one's own inner thoughts, feelings, and behaviors. People committed to the drug lifestyle may display sensitivity to another person's feelings, but rarely do they demonstrate genuine introspection. This is because the honesty of introspection is incompatible with the deception that fuels the drug lifestyle. Insight is a third concept that should not be confused with introspection. Whereas insight describes the ability to discern the "true" nature of a situation, introspection is a much less ambitious effort to honestly evaluate one's thoughts, feelings, and actions. Change, it is argued, can occur in the absence of insight, but not in the absence of introspection.

Partitioning introspection into its component phases and skills as a way of teaching it to clients presents several challenges to therapists, not the least of which is a lack of understanding as to how to go about defining and measuring this concept. For the purpose of training clients to be more introspective, lifestyle theory defines introspection as the ability to visualize the negative consequences of one's actions via internalized processes stored as memories, images, and thoughts. There is some evidence that autogenic training or self-hypnosis (Bagdy, 1984), transcendental meditation (Eppley, Abrams, & Shear, 1989), and the psychedelic drug LSD (DiLeo, 1982) may be helpful in encouraging the formation of an introspective attitude. Employing a more traditional, cognitive-behavioral approach, lifestyle theory advocates imagery training and self-monitoring as a way of teaching introspection. Such skills, it is believed, can be used to sustain the arresting process initiated by various crises and facilitate later stages of intervention. The three beliefs that serve as the cornerstones of the attribution triad can also be conceptualized as aids in the development of an introspective attitude. Hence, by instructing clients in the attribution triad, the therapist is actually assisting with the early development of an introspective attitude.

☑ SKILL Imagery

To appreciate the role of imagery in sustaining the arresting process we must comprehend the nature of the foundational stage of lifestyle intervention. The foundation is designed to promote a sense of disgust with one's past drug-related activities and current drug-related thinking. As such, it is the primary mechanism through which a lifestyle is initially arrested. Imagery, because it can be used to invoke a sense of disgust with one's past and current behavior, may figure prominently in the construction of this foundation. By picturing the people he or she has harmed and the opportunities missed as a consequence of involvement with drugs, the client may be able to generate sufficient disgust to prolong the arresting process initiated by a crisis. This would imply that the foundation can be constructed on images such as those produced in the Inventory of Negative Consequences (Appendix 4). Using responses from the Inventory of Negative Consequences to assemble a foundation requires that these images be as specific as possible. It should not be assumed, however, that all clients possess adequate imagery skills. For this reason, imagery skills must be assessed, and, if necessary, taught and expanded.

☑ ASSESSMENT Imagery Exercise

After instructing the client to assume a relaxed posture, the therapist can use the following instructions to conduct an exercise that may be useful in evaluating a client's imagery skills:

> Close your eyes and draw a simple two-dimensional box with four equal sides in your mind. (10-second pause.) Now add a third dimension to this image. Make the box

three-dimensional by adding depth. (10-second pause.) Were you able to successfully convert the square into a cube? If not take another 10 seconds to get a good image of a cube in your mind. (10-second pause.) Now run your hand over the cube. Is the surface rough or smooth to the touch? (10-second pause.) Does it feel warm, hot, cold? Or maybe you can identify a specific temperature. (10-second pause.) What color or combination of colors is your cube? (10-second pause.) Is it solid or transparent? (20-second pause.) Put you nose up to the cube. What does it smell like? (10-second pause.) Put the cube in your mouth. What does it taste like? (20-second pause.) Imagine what the cube would sound like if you dropped it on the floor. (20-second pause.) Now complete the Imagery Exercise Questionnaire (Appendix 8).

People with strong imagery skills should be able to complete each step of the exercise. This means that in addition to constructing an image of a cube, manipulating it in their minds, and assigning it a color, clients should be able to experience the cube using all five senses: sight, sound, touch, smell, and taste. For clients who have difficulty perceiving the cube through one or two senses other than sight, focused training designed to enhance the image-generating capacity of the weaker sensory modalities may be advisable. A complete regimen of imagery training, however, is required in situations where clients have trouble just visualizing the cube or experiencing it in three or more modalities. The Imagery Exercise Questionnaire is reproduced in Appendix 8.

☑ PLAN

Imagery training consists of specialized instruction in the formation, recruitment, and manipulation of mental images for the purpose of managing stress, establishing goals, acquiring social skills, mentally rehearsing alternative behaviors, and eliciting pleasurable emotional responses. In the second edition of a handbook entitled *Visualization for Change,* Patrick Fanning (1994) offers several exercises designed to assist clients and therapists with the development of strong visual imaging skills. Fanning also considers how one might go about creating the proper atmosphere for employing these visualization skills. In other sections of the book, which is recommended for clinicians interested in constructing a comprehensive program of imagery skill training, Fanning discusses ways in which imagery might be used to enhance creativity, manage stress, and solve problems. He also proposes the following guidelines in the use of visualization techniques. Fanning advises therapists to instruct clients to lie down, close their eyes, and relax. The next step is for the client to create and manipulate sense impressions, followed by intensification of both the relaxation and sensory responses. By accentuating the positive, suspending judgment, exploring resistance, utilizing affirmations (belief that something is already so), and assuming responsibility for their lives, clients can achieve deeper visualization. Encouraging patience, practice, and the use of relaxation aids, such as soft music and the sound of the surf, may also improve visualization skills, according to Fanning.

The primary use of imagery in extending the arresting process is visualizing the harm created by one's involvement in the drug lifestyle. Visualizing the disappointment on the face of a young child whose Christmas has been ruined by a parental drug binge, imagining the lost opportunities of a life dedicated to drugs, and seeing the pain inflicted on one's spouse as a consequence of one's own drug-related or drug-influenced behavior are all ways that imagery might be used to devise a foundation for change, the phase of intervention wherein the initial arresting and extension of that process take place. Of major significance in concocting these images is using as many different sense modalities (sight, sound, touch, smell, taste) as possible. The more senses that can be creatively incorporated into an image, the more vivid the recollection and, ultimately, the more powerful the effect on subsequent behavior. This section details how imagery might be used to construct a foundation for change; in future chapters we will examine how imagery can be used to cope with stress, practice social skills, and challenge drug-related thinking.

✔ SKILL Self-Monitoring

Self-monitoring is a method by which a person surveys and records his or her observable behavior and such private events as cognitions. There is evidence that self-monitoring alone may be sufficient to bring about a significant change in behavior (Emmelkamp, 1986). For instance, Skutle and Berg (1987) discerned that the self-monitoring activities of a group of heavy drinkers led to a reduction in alcohol intake based simply on feedback supplied by the self-observation of drinking behavior. This is referred to as the reactivity of the self-monitoring method. The reactivity of self-monitoring hinders research on the reliability and validity of this procedure, but it is clearly advantageous from a clinical intervention point of view. Self-monitoring may assist a client in abandoning the drug lifestyle by training the client to monitor and record inner processes (thoughts and feelings) as well as overt behavior toward the development of an introspective attitude. It must be pointed out, however, that the relationship between self-monitoring and introspection is, in all likelihood, bidirectional because people who self-monitor their drinking behavior for reasons of increased intrinsic control tend to be more successful in curtailing their use of alcohol than people who self-monitor alcohol usage in response to external pressure (Greenfield, Guydish, & Temple, 1989). It may very well be, then, that instruction in self-monitoring may both facilitate and be facilitated by a developing introspective attitude.

✔ ASSESSMENT Self-Monitoring of
Drug-Related Thoughts and Behaviors

Using Appendix 9: Self-Monitoring of Drug-Related Thoughts and Behaviors, clinicians can obtain a sample of a client's self-monitoring skills. This form is divided into two parts—behaviors and thoughts—each of which covers four drug-related items. Procedure dictates that clients note each time they enact one of the behaviors or thoughts listed on this form, by making a small check mark in the box for the day on which the thought or behavior occurs. To avoid the problem of differential recall, entries should be made as soon as possible after the behavior or thought has been enacted. The reader may well ask why this form focuses on drug use behavior and drug-related thinking when these are the issues for which the client is seeking treatment. Lifestyle theory counters that new clients will nearly always be preoccupied with drugs, and that there is little that can be done to eliminate these preoccupations in the early stages of intervention. However, clinicians can take full advantage of their clients' preoccupations in this area by using them to initiate a process of self-focusing designed to foster an introspective attitude and assist clients in abandoning the drug lifestyle and its associated preoccupations. There is no formal scoring system for this procedure. Nevertheless, in cases where clients have difficulty completing the task or record fewer than three observations in more than half the boxes, training in self-monitoring may be required.

☑ PLAN

Self-monitoring necessitates disruption of a person's normal routine. If the client has trouble self-monitoring, as suggested by the results of the Self-Monitoring of Drug-Related Thoughts and Behaviors procedure, then specialized training and/or instruction may be necessary. One way to enhance a client's self-monitoring skills is by making the procedure as disruptive and intrusive as possible (e.g., having the client hold a hand counter and click off each time he or she engages in a drug-related behavior or entertains a drug-related thought). Diaries are another method with the capacity to improve a client's self-monitoring skills. By encouraging clients to make entries in a diary or journal the therapist is providing them with a structured format through which they might learn to self-focus and monitor their thinking and behavior. It is critical, however, that these diaries be reviewed regularly with the therapist; otherwise, the client may tend to lose interest in the procedure over time. Self-monitoring is a potentially effective intervention at several different points in the change process. It can be a mechanism for encouraging greater self-observation of thoughts and behaviors, the ultimate goal being to shift the client's attention away from external events and onto internal processes—a prerequisite for the creation of an introspective attitude.

CONCLUSION

The arresting of the drug lifestyle involves more than identifying and directing a crisis. A crisis may initiate the arresting process, but this process must be expanded through development of attributions of necessity, possibility, and efficacy and a general attitude of introspection. The notion of arresting the drug lifestyle is akin to a salesperson getting a "foot in the door." The salesperson realizes that if given the opportunity to explain the product, he or she has a better than average chance of selling that product. If, however, the salesperson is unable to accomplish this first step, then there is virtually no chance of a sale being made. A similar situation exists when intervening with substance-abusing clients. There is little opportunity for change if a client is unwilling to momentarily suspend lifestyle activities. The realization of a crisis and extension of the arresting process through reattribution training and formation of an introspective attitude are a therapist's way of getting a foot in the door in anticipation of more substantive changes in thinking and behavior as intervention proceeds.

The attributions and introspective attitude described in this chapter, rather than being all-or-nothing phenomena, are more accurately portrayed as dimensions along which clients vary. As such, it is possible for two individuals to harbor a belief in the necessity of change, but for one individual's belief to be stronger and more effective in extending the arresting process than that of the other individual. The goal of the foundational phase of intervention, as the reader may recall, is to temporarily arrest the lifestyle by terminating current involvement in lifestyle activities. This is accomplished by highlighting naturally occurring crises, promoting attributions of responsibility, hope, and confidence, and overseeing the development of an introspective attitude, while simultaneously challenging the externalization, fatalism, and powerlessness that characterize the drug lifestyle. The change process begins as soon as lifestyle activities momentarily cease. It continues with the aid of the attribution triad and evolution of an introspective attitude, which not only expand the arresting process, but also assist with the development of skills designed to manage lifestyle-promoting conditions, choices, and cognitions. The attribution triad and introspective attitude, therefore, serve to bridge the gap between the first and second phases of intervention.

Before moving on to the next phase of the change process (skill development), mention should be made of one other change strategy with implications for both expansion of the arresting process and later stage intervention: the initial change contract. By highlighting the natural consequences of a client's behavior and creating an avenue through which commitment to change might be accomplished, the behavioral contract is capable of promoting a budding sense of responsibility in program participants. Research, in fact, demonstrates that contingency management, of which behavioral contracting is a major component, can be used effectively in the treatment of substance abusing clients (Budney, Higgins, Delaney, Kent, & Bickel, 1991). The behavioral contract used by proponents of the lifestyle approach outlines the responsibilities of each of the three major groups involved in interventions with substance abusers: the client, the therapy team, and the client's support system (e.g., family, friends). Appendix 10: Sample

Behavioral Contract delineates the responsibilities of each party to the agreement and provides places for the client, therapy team representative, and major support group members to sign the agreement. Like the attribution triad and introspective attitude, the initial change contract can be useful in extending the arresting process, thereby setting the stage for more substantive changes to take place during the second and third phases of intervention.

Chapter 4

Skill Development:
Condition-Based Strategies

According to lifestyle theory skills are sequential building blocks for behavior and, along with instinctual responses, are the primary avenue through which an organism acts on its environment. Whether in infancy, childhood, adolescence, or adulthood, skills create the opportunity for increased behavioral control and self-determination. However, people engaged in a lifestyle pattern of drug-seeking behavior frequently lack many fundamental skills because preoccupation with the drug lifestyle tends to impede psychological and emotional development. Lack of skill also increases a person's risk of relapse. Hence, in situations where the drug lifestyle has been temporarily arrested, the probability is high that the individual will return to the lifestyle out of boredom, fear, or habit if he or she does not acquire the social, coping, and life skills necessary for responsible living. Although skill development is fundamental to both the first (foundation) and second (vehicle) phases of lifestyle intervention, it assumes a bolder visage in the second phase. In other words, specific skills may facilitate realization of the first or arresting phase of treatment, but skill development is the intervention during the second phase. The skills taught to clients can be broken down into the previously discussed concept known as the three Cs: conditions, choice, and cognition. The present chapter deals with condition-based strategies of intervention.

As mentioned in the overview of lifestyle theory in Chapter 2, conditions fall into two general categories. Historical–developmental conditions are internal and external factors that influence whether a person will choose to begin engaging in drug lifestyle activities by enhancing or restricting the person's options in life. Current–contextual conditions, on the other hand, are internal and external factors that increase or decrease a person's chances of engaging in a specific drug use episode. The relapse prevention literature lists unpleasant mood states (Bradley, Phillips, Green, & Gossop, 1989; Litman, Stapleton, Oppenheim, Peleg, & Jackson, 1983; Marlatt, 1978), drug-related cues (Bradley et al., 1989; Litman et al., 1983), urges and temptations (Bradley et al., 1989; Marlatt, 1978), drug availability and withdrawal symptomatology (Bradley et al., 1989), social pressures (Marlatt, 1978), interpersonal conflict (Bradley et al., 1989; Marlatt, 1978), and cognitive factors (Bradley et al., 1989; Litman et al., 1983) as the primary precipitants of relapse in persons previously committed to the drug lifestyle. With the exception of cognitive factors, which will be discussed in Chapter 6, the majority of these influences are, in actuality, current–contextual conditions. These conditions are organized into four general categories for the purposes of the present discussion—negative affect, drug-related cues, drug availability, and interpersonal situations and pressure—and each will be explored in an effort to identify viable avenues of condition-based intervention.

Before reviewing the four current–contextual conditions that serve as potential targets for intervention, the more general issue of assessment needs to be addressed. The Estimated Self-Efficacy in Avoiding Drugs form (Appendix 7), described in Chapter 3, can be used by clinicians to pinpoint the current–contextual conditions most likely to encourage a return to the drug lifestyle. In fact, four of the five areas assessed by the estimated self-efficacy procedure conform to the four categories of current–contextual condition described in this chapter. The fifth section, positive affect, is examined in Chapter 6 as part of a discussion on potential treatment strategies for entitlement and superoptimism. From the results of the Estimated Self-Efficacy in Avoiding Drugs measure, the therapist can identify the current–contextual conditions that are of particular concern with a specific client. If the client's average section score on this measure is below 3.5 it may be advisable to consider this area a potential target for therapeutic intervention. An average section score below 3.0, on the other hand, identifies an area unquestionably in need of attention. The four current–contextual conditions most frequently cited by clients attempting to account for a recent relapse into drug use will be discussed in separate sections. Each section— negative affect, drug-related cues, drug availability, and interpersonal situations and pressure—will consider the identified skill deficit, relevant assessment procedures, and proposed intervention strategies.

NEGATIVE AFFECT

Emotions such as anger, frustration, fear, depression, and boredom have been shown to correlate with abusive drinking in adults (Brennan & Moos, 1990) and have been linked to a high rate of relapse in persons released from treatment (Brown, Vik, McQuaid, Patterson, Irwin, & Grant, 1990). Negative affect, in fact, is often the single most frequently mentioned incentive for both drug use escalation and subsequent relapse. However, the results of a study by Hall, Havassy, and Wasserman (1990) call into question the nature of the negative affect–relapse relationship. Through interviews with newly treated and released alcoholics, opiate addicts, and cigarette smokers, Hall et al. determined that stress and negative affect failed to correspond with relapse in the weekly descriptions of relapsing subjects, but were often viewed as important in the retrospective (at the end of 12 weeks) accounts of these same subjects. This suggests that clinicians need to be cautious in interpreting the long-term retrospective accounts of their clients because these reports may be colored by the client's attempts to rationalize or make sense of his or her most recent relapse. In reconciling the results of the Hall et al. investigation with clinical reports holding stress to be a major precipitant of relapse, it may be advisable to consider the results of a study by Marlatt, Kosturn, and Lang (1975), in which a qualified relationship was observed between negative affect and drug use. Specifically, Marlatt et al. observed that heavy drinkers provoked to anger by an annoying confederate consumed more alcohol than unprovoked drinkers, but only in situations where they were not provided with the opportunity to retaliate against the confederate. Hence, drug use may be associated with stress only in situations where people fail to perceive alternatives to drug use in response to stress.

☑ SKILL   Stress Management

The outcome of the Marlatt et al. (1975) study implies that negative affect may lead to increased drug use only in situations where clients fail to consider alternative stress management strategies. From this, one might speculate that relaxation training, aerobic exercise, and related procedures may serve as alternatives to drug use for the purpose of alleviating and managing stress. After all, negative affect is, in many cases, the direct outgrowth of poorly managed stress, and stress is the consequence of an interactive network encompassing a person's environmental situation and his or her interpretation of and response to that situation. Lifestyle theory readily admits that people often have minimal control over their environments, but that people are capable of exerting maximum control over their own thinking and behavior. When people fail to exert proper control over their thoughts and actions, uncontrolled stress frequently ensues. Ineffective stress management, consequently, is one of the cardinal behavioral features of the drug lifestyle, i.e., stress-coping imbalance. Stress management is one way a person might learn to more effectively cope with life stress and eliminate the problem of stress-coping imbalance.

✔ ASSESSMENT   Lifestyle Stress Test

Appendix 11: Lifestyle Stress Test is an inventory of 20 situations the respondent is asked to rate using a four-point scale. A rating of 0 signifies that the respondent has never experienced the situation; a rating of 1 indicates that the respondent rarely experiences the situation; a rating of 2 implies that the respondent occasionally experiences the situation; and a rating of 3 denotes that the respondent frequently experiences the situation. Ratings are made for two time periods: the month the respondent was most heavily involved with substances and the past 30 days. If the two time periods overlap (i.e., share some of the same days) it is advisable to wait several days or weeks before administering this measure so that data may be obtained from two independent time periods. As mentioned previously, there is no substitute for local norms in the use and interpretation of results obtained from measures like the Lifestyle Stress Test. For this reason, it is recommended that clinicians become familiar with the instrument in their own clinical setting before attaching too much significance to the observed results.

The Lifestyle Stress Test yields a total score and two subscale scores— personal sources of stress and interpersonal sources of stress—for each of the two time periods. The personal sources of stress score is obtained by summing the ratings for the ten odd-numbered items (i.e., 1, 3, 5, 7, 9, 11, 13, 15, 17, 19), whereas the interpersonal sources of stress score is obtained by summing the ten even-numbered items (i.e., 2, 4, 6, 8, 10, 12, 14, 16, 18, 20). The total score provides the best estimate of a person's stress level for each of the two time periods, but a comparison of the two subscores does a better job of clarifying the principal source of stress in a person's life: personal (e.g., financial concerns, fear of losing control, unrealistic expectations) versus interpersonal (e.g., noise-induced tension, interpersonal conflict, communication problems). General guidelines for the total score are as follows: <15, respondent is denying a problem with stress or is effectively managing his or her stress; 15–24, respondent is experiencing a mild problem with stress; 25–34, respondent is experiencing a moderate problem with stress; ≥35, respondent is experiencing a serious problem with stress. When interpreting the subscale scores for the Lifestyle Stress Test these ranges should be divided in half because there are half as many items for each of the two subscales (i.e., 10 versus the 20 that comprise the total score).

✔ PLAN

In drawing up a change plan designed to address the problem of stress, clinicians should begin by consulting the client's scores on the Lifestyle Stress Test. The total score and a comparison of the personal and interpersonal subscores are not the only factors that need to be considered when interpreting results from the

Lifestyle Stress Test; scores on individual items can also provide valuable information. As a case in point, a client may achieve an overall score of 14 on the Lifestyle Stress Test, yet register the maximum score (i.e., 3) for three or four individual items. This indicates that the total score, scores for the two subscales, and the individual items rated highest by the client, should all be reviewed when formulating a change plan for stress-related problems. These three indices furnish an estimate of a subject's overall level of stress, the probable source of this stress (personal versus interpersonal), and specific targets for intervention, respectively. Together, these three data points converge to yield a change plan with possibilities for the alleviation of negative affect and instruction in basic stress management technique. Although the overall stress level and specific targets for change are vital to effective intervention, the first step in devising a change plan for stress-related issues and concerns is to determine the primary source of a client's stress, personal or interpersonal.

If the assessment results identify personal sources of stress as the principal origin of a client's psychological discomfort, attention should turn to techniques designed to reduce tension. Biofeedback (Denney, Baugh, & Hardt, 1991), meditation (Gelderloos, Walton, Orem-Johnson, & Alexander, 1991), and progressive muscle relaxation (Marlatt & Marques, 1977) have all achieved some measure of success in drug treatment settings, presumably by reducing the stress that may encourage problematic drug use. Progressive muscle relaxation is probably the easiest of these techniques to apply. In this procedure, clinicians train clients to alternately tense and relax certain muscle groups, usually starting with the feet.[1] Hence, the therapist instructs the client to tightly curl his or her toes, hold the tension for 5 or 10 seconds, and then release the tension for 15 to 20 seconds. This same procedure is then used to tense and relax the ankles (heels down, toes up), calves (toes down, heels up), thighs and knees (bring feet under chair), stomach (tighten abdominal muscles), chest and back (push chest out), shoulders (shrug shoulders), upper arms (arms bent at elbow, touching shoulders), forearms (arms straight out, hands pointing up), fingers and hands (tightly clenched fists), neck (bury chin in chest), jaw (bite down), mouth (lips pursed), eyes (tightly shut), and forehead (wrinkle forehead). Once all muscle groups have been tensed and relaxed, the therapist may introduce pleasant images (walking through a wooded area, resting comfortably on a sandy beach), with or without the assistance of an audiotaped recording of background noise or music, so that the client may achieve an even more profound state of bodily relaxation.

Cognitive control, exercise, diet, and time management are other avenues through which personal sources of stress might be identified and alleviated. Cognitive control entails thinking more rationally in order to minimize the thinking errors that sometimes create stress. Because these procedures are cognitive in nature, they will not be discussed at length in this chapter, but will be addressed as

---

[1]Therapist should make certain client does not suffer from any medical conditions that would be aggravated by the tensing of muscles before using this procedure.

part of a wider survey of cognitive strategies in Chapter 6. Physical exercise may be efficacious in reducing both personal and interpersonal sources of stress, but is best suited for managing personal sources of stress. Murphy, Pagano, and Marlatt (1986) discerned that aerobic exercise was more effective than meditation or a placebo control condition in managing the urge to drink. A person's diet can also influence his or her stress level and should be incorporated into a comprehensive program of stress management. The results of at least one study suggest that poor nutritional habits are linked to greater levels of subjective stress (Posner, Leitner, & Lester, 1994). Time management skills can be very valuable for managing personal sources of stress, in that poor scheduling is oftentimes at the heart of such problems. Learning to prioritize one's activities, leave sufficient time to complete tasks, and develop a timetable for longer projects can reduce many of the stresses of everyday living.

Interpersonal sources of stress require a slightly different approach than personal sources of stress. Hence, if a client's stress can be traced to interpersonal factors, social skills training is often the intervention of choice. The group of social skills that is often most helpful in managing such stress is assertiveness; the client is taught to stand up for his or her rights without being aggressive. Assertiveness training has been shown to be effective in work with substance abusers; but only when refusal skills (Chaney, O'Leary, & Marlatt, 1978) and role playing (Ingram & Salzberg, 1990) are included. Anger management skills (Novaco, 1975) are a second group of social skills relevant to interpersonal sources of stress. Although anger management training may be helpful in mastering the anger and frustration regularly observed in persons who abuse drugs, lifestyle theory considers most anger to be a reflection of fear. As such, fear-based models of intervention, as described in Chapter 6, figure prominently in interventions directed at a client's anger. Communication skills are a third group of social skills potentially capable of ameliorating interpersonal sources of stress. In fact, one group of investigators found that communication skills training was even more efficacious than an intrapersonal coping skills procedure in reducing problematic drug use (Monti et al., 1990). Communication skills training has the added benefit of being less bound by educational level, anxiety, and initial behavioral skill than more traditional treatment approaches (Rohsenow et al., 1991).

DRUG-RELATED CUES

Experienced drinkers exposed to exteroceptive (environmental) cues associated with a lounge or bar displayed a stronger urge for alcohol after consuming either ethanol or an ethanol-like placebo (inert substance) than drinkers imbibing these substances in environments where no alcohol-related exteroceptive cues were present (McCusker & Brown, 1990). Furthermore, clients enrolled in alcohol rehabilitation programs who exhibit anxiety and craving in the presence of alcohol-related exteroceptive cues are more apt to relapse than clients who fail to record a physiological response to these cues (Binkoff et al., 1986). The urge to ingest opiates (Childress, McLellan, & O'Brien, 1986) and cocaine (Childress, McLellan, Ehrman, & O'Brien, 1987) may also be attributed to the effect of exteroceptive cues on a user's autonomic response. Like exteroceptive cues, interoceptive (internal) cues may instigate a craving for drugs and encourage relapse. This is illustrated by the so-called reinstatement paradigm, whereby behaviors previously conditioned to a chemical substance and subsequently extinguished reemerge when random noncontingent (unrelated to behavior) injections of the "training" compound are introduced into the subject's bloodstream (Preston, Bigelow, Bickel, & Liebson, 1987). Drug-based rituals are another category of interoceptive cue with the capacity to encourage relapse. It is argued that the intersection of interoceptive and exteroceptive cues in time and space provides particularly fertile soil for the formation of drug use patterns.

☑ SKILL   Cue Control

Extricating oneself from the interoceptive and exteroceptive cues that have been linked to one's past use of chemical substances necessitates learning how to control these cues. The first lesson clinicians need to learn is that cues set the stage for a drug use episode by arousing a desire or urge, on the part of the user, to seek out and ingest certain chemical compounds. The power of interoceptive and exteroceptive cues to encourage drug use can therefore be reduced, if not eliminated, by pairing these cues with a negative or nonreinforcing stimulus or by eliminating these cues from the client's environment. This represents the two major categories of cue control: cue exposure and cue avoidance. However, before these procedures can be discussed, we must first identify a means of reliably assessing the impact of drug-related cues on a person's current emotional and physiological state.

☑ ASSESSMENT   Drug-Related Cues Checklist

Appendix 12: Drug-Related Cues Checklist can be used to chart the specific physical and psychological changes a person experiences when exposed to a drug-related cue. Clients should be instructed to record the physical and psychological symptoms that arise in response to the target stimulus; the target stimulus should be a short videotape depiction of drug use or a drug replica (material that looks, smells, or tastes like an abusable substance). Once clients have recorded their reactions to the target stimulus in Column 1 of the checklist, they should indicate their level of identification with the film or the perceived authenticity of the drug replica by circling the corresponding number (1 to 5) at the bottom of the page. Videotape depictions of drug use are particularly effective target stimuli, in that they often portray drug-related behaviors and rituals, in addition to the actual use of a drug. However, the clinician may need to acquire a library of 20 or more 3- to 5-minute videos in order to cover the range of substances, routes of administration, and other characteristics that influence the degree to which clients identify with a videotape depiction of drug use. If a drug replica is employed, the sight, touch, smell, or even taste of the substance can serve as the activating stimulus. As an adjunct to the Drug-Related Cues Checklist, clinicians might want to include certain physiological measures of autonomic arousal, such as heart rate, muscle tension, or galvanic skin response, in their assessment. Cues and situations for which clients mark more than one item or demonstrate a significant increase in physiological arousal are cues with the power to precipitate relapse and probably warrant therapeutic attention.

☑ PLAN

Perhaps the simplest form of cue control is the avoidance of drug-related stimuli. This is illustrated by the so-called geographic cure, whereby a drug abuser escapes from a drug-infested environment and moves to a new city, town, or neighborhood. Although much maligned in traditional drug treatment circles, there is something to be said for geographic change as an intervention for habitual drug use. When we compare a 90% rate of relapse in heroin addicts who are detoxified and returned to the environments in which they acquired their habits (Cushman, 1974) with a 12% relapse rate for heroin-addicted servicemen who were detoxified in Vietnam prior to returning to the United States (Robins, Davis, & Goodwin, 1974), we can see the potential value of geographic change for persons previously involved in the abuse of opiates. The remarkably low rate of relapse experienced by Vietnam veterans can be explained, in part, by the fact that these individuals returned to an environment (exteroceptive cues) very different from the one in which they had acquired their heroin habit (Siegel, 1988). In addition, many of the interoceptive cues (e.g., anxiety and fear) that may have supported the abuse of opioids while the individual was in Vietnam, were no longer present once the service member returned to the United States. This implies that cue avoidance may be a powerful vehicle for eliminating drug-related interoceptive and exteroceptive cues. Cue avoidance need not be as drastic as moving to another city, state, or country; it may be as simple as staying away from the taverns one once drank in or the street corners where one used to cop drugs.

    Common sense dictates that cue avoidance is the preferred cue management strategy in situations where it is possible. However, cue avoidance is not always a realistic or feasible alternative. Hence, the therapist may want to consider a second option, cue exposure, in situations where cue avoidance is not possible. Cue exposure involves presenting the cue (whether the sight or smell of a drug replica or a videotape presentation of drug use) while simultaneously preventing the client from ingesting drugs. Repeatedly presenting the cue in the absence of a drug effect leads to extinction of the conditioned emotional response to the cue. In other words, the cue gradually loses its ability to produce a drug urge or craving. Using the procedure outlined in the Assessment section, we can present the videotape or drug replica repeatedly until the individual's subjective and physiological responses start to dwindle. It may be necessary to conduct as many as fifteen to twenty sessions, each session consisting of five or six separate trials, before the more powerful cues begin to show signs of extinction. A coping version of the cue exposure procedure is also available, whereby the videotape is paused or the drug replica removed when the client begins to experience discomfort (as measured by self-report and/or physiological response). As soon as the client successfully alleviates the tension or discomfort through relaxation or another coping strategy, the tape is continued or the replica reintroduced, until the discomfort is again experienced or the client successfully completes the task. For maximum clinical efficacy, therapists are advised to incorporate realistic environmental cues in the extinction procedure (Childress, McLellan, Ehrman, & O'Brien, 1988) and to use cognitive control techniques, such as imagery (distraction) as much as possible (Cooney, Baker, & Pomerleau, 1983).

Aversion therapy is similar to extinction, but rather than pairing the cue with an absent drug response, the aversion model connects drug-related cues to a negative or aversive stimulus. Hence, a videotape presentation of a person injecting heroin may be paired with a noxious odor; the smell of burning crack cocaine may be linked to an aversive noise; and the taste of alcohol may be coupled with electric shock. Aversive conditioning has been shown to produce moderately effective results in the treatment of alcohol abuse (Liskow & Goodwin, 1987), although covert sensitization (Cautela, 1967) may be the preferred route in the use of the aversive paradigm because it employs an image-based aversive stimulus instead of a physical one and may be just as effective as the standard aversion model. In performing covert sensitization, the therapist pairs the image of alcohol or some other drug with an aversive, nauseating, or repugnant image. A therapist working with an alcohol abusing client may have the individual imagine bringing a large glass of alcohol, saturated with small particles of feces or vomit, to his or her lips, with the intent of reconditioning nausea to the drug-related mental cue. When employing this procedure it is essential that clients achieve a sense of relief and rejuvenation from getting as far away from the image-based drug stimulus as possible. Empirical research supports the utility of covert sensitization in treating alcoholics (Miller & Dougher, 1989) and persons interested in terminating their use of tobacco (Goldberg, Zwibel, Safir, & Merbaum, 1983).

DRUG AVAILABILITY

Quite obviously, drugs cannot be used if they are unavailable. Access, then, is a necessary precondition for the use and abuse of drugs, and reduced access is one avenue of program intervention. Crowley (1988) observed a relationship between availability and substance abuse in comparing a Colorado ski community with the Colorado state average on pharmaceutical prescriptions for abusable substances such as cocaine, benzodiazepine, and methaqualone and the percentage of adults classified as "involved and dysfunctional" substance abusers. Crowley observed that pharmaceutical prescriptions for abusable substances were 2 to 17 times more prevalent and diagnoses of "involved and dysfunctional" substance abuse four times more frequent in the Colorado ski community than in other areas of Colorado. Additional evidence suggests that availability is an important facilitating condition during both the early and advanced stages of the drug lifestyle. Simpson and Marsh (1986), for instance, determined that heroin addicts rated the accessibility of heroin high on their lists of reasons for initial opiate usage, whereas Meyer and Mirin (1979) ascertained that the availability of opiates was a prime precipitant of relapse in a group of long-term opiate users. In addressing availability, therapists must find ways to reduce clients' access to drugs and their opportunities to engage in drug lifestyle activities.

☑ SKILL   Access Reduction

Reducing the availability of drugs may follow either a wide-band (society/ community) or narrow-band (individual) philosophy. Wide-band access-reducing strategies normally encompass system-wide policies that reduce the availability of substances or restrict opportunities for drug use. The 1972 East Coast heroin shortage, which precipitated a marked reduction in drug use and drug-related crime, was the direct result of increased interdiction and other wide-band access-reducing intervention policies (Research Triangle Institute, 1976). Similarly, limiting the availability of alcohol by increasing the price of distilled beverages has been found effective in lowering alcohol-related traffic fatalities as well as deaths attributable to cirrhosis (Moore, 1984). Although narrow-band access-reducing strategies are somewhat more limited than wide-band procedures, they will be the principal topic of discussion in the present section because, unlike wide-band methods of intervention, narrow-band strategies can be used with individual clients.

☑ ASSESSMENT   Access to Drug Use

Dividing conditions with high relapse potential into people, places, and things, an approach first popularized by the self-help group, Alcoholics Anonymous (1980), is believed to be an efficient way of identifying vehicles capable of reducing a client's access to drugs and limiting his or her opportunities for drug lifestyle involvement. The Appendix 13: Access to Drug Use form partitions access-relevant conditions into the people, places, and things associated with one's past misuse of chemical substances. In completing this form, clients should be instructed to list the people, places, and things they perceive as linked, in some way, to their previous misuse of substances. This can then be used by the therapist to identify potential avenues of access reduction for these clients.

☑ PLAN

Dividing access-promoting current–contextual conditions into people, places, and things supplies clinicians with a vehicle for pursuing intervention and effecting change. Persons currently involved in the use of substances are obviously the kinds of people a client recovering from a drug abuse problem should avoid, but this is not the only group of individuals the client needs to steer clear of if he or she wishes to limit access to drug use opportunities. People who sell drugs or encourage a client's use of substances by permitting him or her to escape the negative consequences of his or her lifestyle also need to be avoided. The latter pattern has traditionally been termed enabling because it is believed that such persons enable or assist substance abusers by shielding them from the negative repercussions of their drug-related activities. Eliminating potential enablers from one's life is sometimes easier said than done, because some of those individuals may be family members. For this reason, it is unrealistic to expect clients to avoid all people who use drugs, sell drugs, or encourage their use of drugs by allowing them to elude the negative consequences of their behavior. However, the degree to which clients are able to limit their contact with such individuals corresponds with their ability to avoid future relapse.

The places that need to be avoided in reducing one's access to drugs and drug use opportunities are the environments in which drug use has occurred in the past or where the client is likely to encounter drug users, drug dealers, or people who might enable his or her use of substances. Some of the places that should be avoided, such as bars, crack houses, and discos, are obvious. Other drug-promoting environments are much less obvious, although no less important in providing opportunities for drug use; these environments might include parks, gambling houses, or even the local community center. Instead of patronizing establishments that increase one's access to drugs, the client should be encouraged to seek out environments where drug use is uncommon. Environments more conducive to the facilitation of non-drug living include school, work, church, cultural events, and settings where people generally do not use drugs, legal or otherwise. Identifying and avoiding locations where drug use is commonplace and seeking out environments where drug use is infrequent is a relatively simple, yet potentially productive, way of reducing one's access to drugs.

The things clients need to avoid in order to reduce their opportunities for drug lifestyle involvement are the drugs themselves, assorted drug paraphernalia, and ready access to cash. Limiting one's access to abusable substances in order to reduce opportunities for future substance misuse is self-evident. However, drug paraphernalia (syringes, rolling papers, spoons) must also be eliminated because they encourage substance use by providing opportunities for drug ingestion. Unfettered access to money is another factor capable of facilitating the drug lifestyle by providing access to abusable substances. Faupel and Klockars (1987) noted that a rise in discretionary income is generally followed by an increase in the use of drugs by people addicted to heroin. Limiting a person's access to ready cash consequently blocks one channel through which drug use generally flows. This might be accomplished by encouraging the client to avoid carrying large sums of money and arranging for a spouse or relative to assist with the financial management of a client's personal funds.

Obviously, if someone wants to use drugs, that person will find a way to gain access to an abusable substance. Access reduction simply makes drug use less convenient by raising the costs of substance use and eliminating common pathways to drug involvement. When drug abusers enter prison many stop using drugs, only to start up again once they are released. This can be attributed, in large part, to the many hassles associated with drug use in a prison setting. The price of drugs acquired in prison is anywhere from two to ten times their cost on the street, surveillance is normally increased through random urinalyses, and a drug-intoxicated state is often incompatible with the desire to remain alert and avoid conflicts with other inmates. Many of these deterrents are no longer in effect, however, upon release from prison, and so if one has not made substantial changes in his or her thinking and behavior, there is a strong likelihood that drug use will reoccur. Access reduction is designed to achieve what prison appears to accomplish naturally: namely, to make drug use less convenient. Another way to conceive of access reduction is as a procedure for inserting buffers between the individual and his or her opportunities for drug use and drug-related activity. At any time, one may overstep these boundaries and use drugs, but the buffers aid those who possess a commitment to change.

INTERPERSONAL SITUATIONS AND PRESSURE

Because the drug lifestyle is largely a matter of socialization, it is little wonder that interpersonal influences play an important role in the initiation, maintenance, and reactivation of drug use patterns. Marlatt and Gordon (1980) noted that the single most powerful precipitant of relapse in a group of heroin addicts was social pressure from other drug users. Accordingly, those individuals who felt verbally coerced into using drugs or who voluntarily associated with known drug users were at greatest risk for relapse. This points to the fact that no man or woman is an island and that all people have a basic need for contact with their fellow human beings. The behavioral characteristic of interpersonal triviality illustrates precisely how drug users satisfy this need: specifically, by entering into superficial relationships with other drug users. Lifestyle theory proposes that in escaping the drug lifestyle one must avoid people who use drugs and seek to establish relationships with non-drug users. One study, in fact, has indicated that support from family and friends who did not use drugs predicted superior outcomes in persons released from an inpatient alcohol rehabilitation program, independent of the patient's history of prior treatment (Booth, Russell, Soucek, & Laughlin, 1992). As the reader has probably already gathered, the people with whom clients associate exert a powerful influence over these clients' opportunities for drug use.

✔ SKILL   Modification of Interpersonal Relationships

Lifestyle interventions aimed at the modification of interpersonal relationships fall into two general categories or clusters of skills: (a) avoidance of persons currently involved in the use of drugs and (b) generation and fostering of long-term relationships with persons who do not abuse drugs. Avoiding drug users and resisting the pressure to use drugs comes under the heading of resistance skills training. The client must learn to confront and manage the pressures that can be brought to bear on a currently abstaining individual to reenter the drug lifestyle. Social skills training, the second category of interpersonal modification, is the primary vehicle through which the client might eventually acquire the skills necessary for development of intimate long-term relationships with people who do not abuse substances.

✔ ASSESSMENT   Interpersonal Influence Scale

Appendix 14: Interpersonal Influence Scale is comprised of 10 multiple-choice items. For odd-numbered items the "a" option is scored 1, the "b" option 2, and the "c" option 3. For even numbered-items the "a" option is scored 3, the "b" option 2, and the "c" option 1. The individual items are then summed to produce a total score with a range of 10 to 30. Clinicians are encouraged to develop their own norms for this measure, but the author's own experience suggests that scores between 15 and 20 portend potential problems with interpersonal influence, whereas scores between 21 and 30 signal a clear and present tendency to be influenced by the opinions of others. The Interpersonal Influence Scale is designed to assess conditions relevant to the avoidance of drug-related interpersonal situations; social skill measures, such as those outlined in Chapter 5, can be used to assess a subject's potential ability to relate to non-drug users.

✔ PLAN

Jean Shope and her colleagues at the University of Michigan Medical School in Ann Arbor have developed a social pressure resistance training program that may be of some assistance to clinicians interested in teaching clients refusal and social resistance skills (Shope, Dielman, Butchart, Campanelli, & Kloska, 1992). Although the original program was conceived as an alcohol prevention measure for fifth and sixth graders, the general procedure seems applicable to a wider range of age groups, substances, and stages of drug involvement. The curriculum consists of four initial 45-minute sessions, each conducted 1 week apart, and three booster sessions, also conducted 1 week apart, 1 year after the final initial session. Topics such as the physical and psychological effects of drugs, the consequences of drug misuse, and the pressures that encourage people to use drugs are discussed in the first session. Awareness of advertising pressure and advice on how to resist such pressure are the topics explored in the second session. The third session instructs clients in skills that can be used to resist various interpersonal influences and pressures and the final session provides clients with opportunities to role play refusing peer requests to use drugs. The three booster sessions review and reinforce skills learned in the four initial sessions and supply clients with additional practice and role-playing opportunities. To obtain more detailed information on how this program might be implemented, the reader should consult the original article by Shope et al. (1992).

Social skills, interpersonal communication, and the ability to negotiate with others are often lacking in persons who habitually use substances. Consequently, therapists may want to consider these skills in formulating a program of relationship enhancement for drug abusing clients. Any number of techniques might be used to encourage development of these skills, but instruction, modeling, role playing, and feedback are the procedures most commonly employed. These techniques will be the primary focus of the Option Expansion section of the next chapter, and therefore will not be discussed in great detail here. Instead, the present section will concentrate on the development of social perspective taking skills. Research indicates that substance abusers often have great difficulty viewing events from the perspective of another person (Pernanen, 1976). In other words, role-taking and empathy skills are generally lacking in people who abuse drugs. For this reason, training in social perspective taking should be considered within the context of a comprehensive program of intervention. Using situations such as those outlined in Appendix 15: Suggested Role Plays for Social Perspective Taking, the therapist can have clients assume the perspective of someone who has been victimized, disappointed, or inconvenienced by the actions of a drug user. Videotaping the role play may be particularly helpful in that this gives the client the opportunity to evaluate his or her skill in adopting the perspective of another. Role playing and feedback should be used liberally in exercises designed to augment, develop, and direct a client's ability to empathize and experience another person's point of view.

CONCLUSION

It should be clear from this review that substantial overlap exists between the various procedures one might employ in confronting drug lifestyle-supporting current–contextual conditions. Assertiveness training, for instance, is applicable to both negative affect and interpersonal pressure, whereas the avoidance of people engaged in drug-related activities not only qualifies as a cue control technique, but may also prove beneficial in reducing drug availability and drug-related interpersonal sources of conditional influence. Mention should also be made of the overlap between the strategies and treatment procedures employed in the modification of drug-related choices and cognitions, as described in Chapters 5 and 6, respectively. This overlap should therefore be considered when designing a program of intervention for substance-abusing clients. Not only will this make the interventions that much more efficient, but it will also assist in eventually clarifying the interrelated nature of the different component features of the drug lifestyle.

Despite the wide array of techniques potentially capable of managing the current–contextual conditions that support the drug lifestyle, we must not lose sight of the fact that no matter how the pie is sliced, people are not passive recipients of environmental influence, but rather, active decision makers. The fact of the matter is that unless the client is willing to cooperate with the change program and actively supports the procedures outlined in this manual, intervention will prove meaningless and ineffectual. There is nothing innately therapeutic about these procedures and techniques in situations in which clients are unwilling to vigorously pursue and support the change process. The client, and only the client, can make the decision to learn and use the skills described in this book. The drug lifestyle can be reversed only in situations where the client makes an explicit commitment to change—a commitment that has its foundation in choice and decision making. Accordingly, the choice process should be emphasized in one's interventions with clients and will serve as the main topic of discussion in the next chapter.

Chapter 5

Skill Development: Choice-Based Strategies

Choice assumes a prominent position in the lifestyle approach to intervention in that lifestyle theory considers choice a necessary precondition for change. As such, choice plays a pivotal role in the construction of change plans, the selection of strategic goals, and the configuration of an organized program of intervention. Choice and decision making are also intimately involved in the development of a client's commitment to change. In the conclusion of Chapter 4, it was noted that the techniques described in this book are useless in situations where the client is unwilling to make a commitment to change. It would be logical to assume, then, that commitment to change must be present before a meaningful change in behavior can take place. Experience suggests that commitment is something most substance abusers have at least passing familiarity with, in that commitment to drug-using norms and ideals is a cardinal feature of the drug lifestyle. Therefore, a major goal of lifestyle intervention is helping clients replace their prior commitment to the drug lifestyle with a growing commitment to change. It should be noted, however, that commitments, regardless of whether drugs or change are being referenced, take time to develop. Interventions designed to encourage and maintain a commitment to change are consequently the first order of business in a review of choice-based intervention as an intervention for substance abuse.

Prochaska and DiClemente (1988) have proposed a four-stage model of change with relevance to the present discussion. The first stage of the Prochaska–DiClemente model, pre-contemplation, is characterized by denial. The second stage, contemplation, gives rise to a growing suspicion that something is wrong, but the individual feels ambivalent and lacks the knowledge to correct the problem. It is during the third, or action, stage that the individual begins to modify his or her problematic behavior. The final stage, maintenance, requires stabilization of behavioral patterns established during the action stage. Prochaska and DiClemente's contemplation stage coincides with the arresting phase of lifestyle intervention. Accordingly, crises, the attribution triad, and an introspective attitude may help stimulate a preliminary commitment to change. The action stage of the Prochaska–DiClemente model, on the other hand, requires instruction in alternative behaviors, opportunities for practice, constructive feedback, and social support designed to minimize fear and insecurity. One way the therapist might stimulate action is by encouraging clients to perform one behavior incompatible with the drug lifestyle each and every day, toward an eventual goal of forming a preliminary commitment to change. To be effective, these actions should be incongruent with the goals and ideals of the drug lifestyle. The maintenance stage of the change process requires an appreciation of, and preparation for, high-risk situations, regular evaluation of goals and values, and consideration of major identity issues.

The thesis of this chapter is that before substance abusers can permanently abandon the drug lifestyle, they must learn to make better choices. Vehicles designed to teach clients how to make better choices fall into two general categories: (a) increasing a client's options in life and (b) enhancing the client's ability to evaluate life options. The first set of procedures, option expansion techniques, are meant to increase the number of alternative solutions a person entertains in a specific problem situation. One obvious limitation of the typical decision-making approach adopted by most substance abusers is a paucity of perceived alternatives to the problems of everyday life. It is believed that most people, not just substance abusers, restrict themselves to a small number of options, which in the end, reduces their chances of identifying the optimal solution. One way to make better choices, then, is to expand one's range of options. The second procedure, competence enhancement, is designed to augment and reinforce a client's ability to productively evaluate available options in his or her life. Substance abusers are well practiced in the art of taking shortcuts, and most have learned to handle stress through drugs. This insinuates that change can be both initiated and maintained by a comprehensive evaluation of alternative solutions. Before considering skills capable of expediting either the option expansion or competence enhancement approaches to improved decision making, we must examine a procedure that incorporates features of both approaches, namely, interpersonal problem solving.

PROBLEM SOLVING

It has been reasonably well established that training in interpersonal problem solving promotes positive change in persons previously dependent on alcohol (Chaney et al., 1978), tobacco (Sjoberg & Johnson, 1978), and heroin (Platt, Perry, & Metzger, 1980). The overriding objective of the problem-solving approach is to teach clients to define and manage problems in as organized and systematic a fashion as possible. The standard problem-solving program follows five basic stages: general orientation, problem definition, generation of alternatives, evaluation of alternatives, and verification (D'Zurilla & Goldfried, 1971). The general orientation stage is marked by development of a positive attitude toward change and inhibition of the natural human tendency to act impulsively under stress. In the second, or problem definition, stage the client defines the problem in terms that are clear, precise, and measurable. During the third stage, the client is instructed to generate alternative solutions to the problem. Then the client must evaluate each alternative, select the optimal alternative, and put the proposed solution into effect. This is followed by verification wherein the client evaluates whether the problem has been solved. If the problem has been satisfactorily resolved, the problem-solving sequence is terminated. If, however, the problem persists despite the client's best efforts to apply the problem-solving method to his or her situation, then the client should be directed to repeat the five-step procedure.

There are several key skill-building applications that may prove invaluable in conducting problem-solving training. Modeling is one such application. Therapists should not only model the correct procedure to follow in managing interpersonal problems, but also model how to implement the various alternative solutions or options. Monti et al. (1990), for instance, determined that the modeling of social-communication and problem-solving skills strengthened the impact of a standard social-communication and problem-solving training program in a group of alcohol-dependent Veterans Administration inpatients. Behavioral rehearsal or role playing is a second potential adjunct to problem-solving training. Rehearsing various alternative solutions, particularly if the problem is interpersonal in nature, affords the client an opportunity to experience the viability of a particular solution in a real-life situation. Sjoberg, Samsonowitz, and Olsson (1978) observed that behavioral rehearsal enhanced the therapeutic effectiveness of interpersonal problem-solving training in a group of alcohol-dependent subjects. Given the apparent success of interpersonal problem-solving training in substance-using populations, identifying and highlighting the active ingredients of the problem-solving approach is recommended. Although all five stages contribute to problem resolution, stages three (generation of alternatives) and four (evaluation of alternatives) are particularly amenable to innovation. For this reason, the remainder of this chapter will be divided into discussions of option expansion (generation of alternatives) and competence enhancement (evaluation of alternatives) strategies.

OPTION EXPANSION

There are several procedures potentially capable of expanding a person's range of life options. During the third stage of the problem-solving sequence, subjects are encouraged to suspend judgment and list as many different solutions to the problem as possible. This process, also known as brainstorming, has been found to produce more high-quality solutions than evaluating the alternatives as they are being enumerated (Thorn, 1987). This suggests that creativity is an avenue through which options might be expanded. It is also possible to increase options by developing social-communication, life, and occupational-educational skills. People who facilely communicate with others, are able to effectively manage their finances, and have at their disposal a wealth of marketable job skills, are in a better position to realize success than persons who do not possess these faculties. This is because social-communication, life, and occupational-educational skills arm the individual with additional life options. The effective communicator can talk his or her way out of a potential conflict situation rather than being propelled into a violent exchange with the antagonist; the individual with good financial management skills will have more options at the end of the month than someone who spends money frivolously; the skilled worker has a wider array of job opportunities than someone who lacks marketable job skills. Each of these general skill groups will be discussed in an effort to determine precisely how expanding a person's options in life can facilitate change in persons previously committed to the drug lifestyle.

☑ SKILL   Lateral Thinking

Problem-oriented thinking generally falls into one of two categories: convergent or divergent. Convergent or vertical thinking connotes the paring down of alternatives designed to identify an optimal solution. Divergent or lateral thinking, on the other hand, is directed at extending one's range of options by considering as many different solutions to a problem as possible. Whereas vertical thinking is selective, lateral thinking is generative (de Bono, 1977). Formal schooling tends to emphasize vertical over lateral thinking, which may help explain why creativity and innovation often decline as one proceeds through grammar school and high school, into adulthood. The accentuated cognitive rigidity and decreased adaptability that may evolve from neglect of lateral thinking clearly interferes with effective problem solving (Eysenck, 1964). More to the point, cognitive rigidity and weak means–ends thinking have been observed with regularity in the behavior of both drug abusers (Ryan & Butters, 1983) and criminals (Kipper, 1977). Results from the Kipper investigation imply that the problem is one of application, however, rather than comprehension, in that the criminal offenders who participated in this study understood the abstract terms and concepts presented to them, but had trouble effectively using this information. Therefore, it is vital that clients be trained not only in lateral thinking, but also in how to apply this information in real-life situations.

☑ ASSESSMENT Multiple Options Analysis

The Multiple Options Analysis (Appendix 16) is a series of eight problem situations to which the respondent is asked to supply as many alternative solutions as possible in 1 minute. In administering this assessment to clients, clinicians should read Item 1 and then allow clients 1 minute to list as many potential solutions to the problem (up to a total of nine) as come to mind, regardless of their practicality. This procedure should be repeated for the remaining seven items. Instructions and items for the Multiple Options Analysis can be found in Appendix 16. Most people are able to generate anywhere from five to seven options per problem, although not all of the alternatives are something a person might necessarily want to implement. It is important, in conducting this exercise, to stress with clients that it is the quantity, rather than the quality, of alternatives that is being evaluated. Hence, we are looking for the total number of possible solutions the client is able to generate in 1 minute. Clients who produce an average of five or more options to each item possess adequate lateral reasoning skills. A possible lateral thinking deficit is suggested by an average score of 3 to 4, and a serious lateral thinking deficit is implied when the average score is below 3.

☑ PLAN

Training in lateral thinking can be initiated with the aid of several techniques introduced by de Bono (1977, 1981). For instance, de Bono (1977) proposed that the therapist/trainer present various geometric designs, ambiguous pictures, and written stories to clients and then ask them to generate alternative perceptions, descriptions, and interpretations for these varied stimuli. In a similar vein, de Bono suggested using practical exercises to illustrate precisely how one might learn to suspend judgment, restructure perceptual patterns, and challenge accepted ideas as a way of becoming more creative in managing problem situations. As a way of facilitating recall for key elements of the problem-solving procedure, de Bono (1981) has coined several acronyms, two of which (PNI and CAF) may be particularly helpful in teaching lateral thinking skills. PNI refers to the thorough exploration of the Positive, Negative, and Interesting aspects of an idea or concept, which should be done before decisions are rendered. The acronym CAF (Consider All Factors) serves to remind the client that effective problem solving will occur only if he or she inhibits the natural tendency to react emotionally or impulsively to a new idea. Despite a lack of long-term follow-up on his program, de Bono (1983) reported some success in enhancing the short-term institutional adjustment of incarcerated delinquents. There is circumscribed support for specific features of de Bono's program, nonetheless, in studies probing the effects of goal-setting, social perspective taking, and impulse control training on drug abuse and criminal behavior.

According to the results of the Kipper (1977) study, the lateral thinking deficits observed in offender and drug-using populations may be more a function of improper application than of poor comprehension. Clients may perceive the gravity of their situations and understand the necessity of generating alternative solutions to a problem, yet have trouble applying this knowledge to their own situations. Impulsivity is a common barrier to application in many client populations. For this reason, self-instructional training (Meichenbaum, 1974), or a related procedure, should be included in any program designed to teach clients creativity and lateral thinking skills. Inadequate opportunity to practice a skill is another reason clients sometimes have difficulty translating knowledge into behavior. Consequently, role playing, behavioral rehearsal, and corrective feedback need to be incorporated into the training of lateral thinking skills. Brainstorming requires that the client learn to inhibit or suspend judgment, while generating alternative solutions to various problem situations. Relaxation, meditation, and self-hypnosis are all techniques capable of creating an atmosphere wherein the client learns to consider all factors, rather than jumping to conclusions or relying on familiar, but ineffective, approaches to problem situations. Regular prompts from the therapist to keep the generation and evaluation stages of the problem-solving sequence separate may also be helpful in encouraging creativity. What this means is that application is a prime consideration when it comes to teaching lateral thinking skills to substance-abusing clients.

☑ SKILL   Social-Communication Skills

The social skill deficits of problem drinkers (Hover & Gaffney, 1991) and illicit drug users (Linquist, Lindsay, & White, 1979) are well documented. Social skills training (SST), therefore, may be an alternative or adjunct to traditional therapy by virtue of its ability to expand a client's range of options in social situations. Although SST has been shown to produce short-term reductions in drug usage (Eriksen, Bjornstad, & Gertestam, 1986), there are questions concerning its long-range effectiveness in drug abusers (Hawkins, Catalano, Gillmore, & Wells, 1989). Giving clients the opportunity to observe models, role play social situations, and receive feedback (Oei & Jackson, 1980), and incorporating a cognitive component in the training program (Oei & Jackson, 1982), however, tend to promote better long-term outcomes. This may be a way, then, of enhancing the long-term effectiveness of social skills training. Incorporating communication exercises in an existing program of SST is another way to improve the long-term efficacy of the social skills approach to substance abuse treatment.

Communication skills training enables the individual to establish or reestablish a positive relationship with significant others, the development of which may open the door to a number of non-drug alternatives. Zucker and Gomberg (1986) report that the families of alcoholics frequently exhibit poor communication, and the results of several additional studies indicate that including the spouse and other family members in treatment elevates a substance abuser's chances for recovery by improving family communication (O'Farrell, Cutter, & Floyd, 1985; Sisson & Azrin, 1986). Even without family involvement, social and communication skills training has been found effective in promoting change in clients with an alcohol abuse history (Chick, Ritson, Connaughton, Stewart, & Chick, 1988). Furthermore, communication skills training may benefit a larger segment of the chemically dependent population than more traditional approaches such as mood management training because the outcome is less dependent on anxiety level, education, substance abuse history, and behavioral skill (Rohsenow et al., 1991).

☑ ASSESSMENT Social-Communication Skills Checklist

Appendix 17: Social-Communication Skills Checklist covers social-communication skills that are performed on a daily basis by most people. Clients should be instructed to check off the skills they perform infrequently or feel particularly uncomfortable executing, so that the therapist may identify potential areas of social-communication deficit. These deficit areas can then be explored further through role-playing exercises. The relative skill of the client during the role play is evaluated using Appendix 18: Role Play Rating Scale. The Role Play Rating Scale, which can be filled out by the therapist or by other group members, allows raters to assess the adequacy of a person's verbal and nonverbal behavior during a role play. This information can then be incorporated into a feedback loop designed to apprise the client of his or her social-communication skill level and document any changes that may occur in these skills over the course of the program.

☑ PLAN

Of prime consideration in deciphering the connotation of a client's poor performance or nonperformance of social-communication skills is determining whether the individual lacks the social-communication skill in question or simply is inhibited in expressing the skill because of anxiety or environmental constraint. Having clients role play assorted social interactions, such as those outlined in Appendix 19: Suggested Social-Communication Role Plays, in a relaxed, nonthreatening therapeutic milieu is one way to distinguish between anxiety or environmental constraint and lack of skill. If poor performance or nonperformance of a social skill can be attributed to anxiety or environmental constraint, then emphasis should be placed on the alleviation of social anxiety or the removal of environmental barriers to behavioral performance so that the client is free to engage in the social behavior of his or her choosing. If nonperformance or poor performance can be traced to a lack of social skill, then a five-step social skills training procedure is recommended. Before discussing this training program, however, it is important to understand that the problem is often a result of both anxiety or environmental constraint and lack of skill, and so both areas may need to be addressed with clients.

The first step in the social-communication skills training program is learning to identify relevant verbal and nonverbal social cues. One way to promote awareness of social cues is to expose clients to a short segment taped from a television show with the sound turned off. Situation comedies are good for this purpose because this brand of entertainment makes frequent use of exaggerated expressions of emotion. After showing the film clip, therapists should encourage clients to describe what they believe was going on in the scene. Once the sound has been reinstated, therapists should discuss with clients how verbal cues contribute to the comprehension of nonverbal cues and various social transactions. Once social awareness has been achieved, the next step in the process is providing clients with instruction in the targeted social skill. It is during this stage that the social skill is reduced to its component subskills. The third step in the skill acquisition process is furnishing clients with the opportunity to practice the targeted skill. Because behavioral rehearsal and role playing assume a major role in the acquisition of social skills, it is recommended that social-communication skills training take place in a group setting. The fourth step of the training program entails furnishing clients with coaching, feedback, and reinforcement. The final step in the social-communication skills training process involves generalization. This encompasses both response generalization (employing a number of different social skills in the same social situation) and stimulus generalization (employing the same social skill across a number of divergent social situations) with the aid of between-sessions consultation, review of role play tapes, and homework assignments that allow clients to practice these skills in real-life situations (Linehan, 1993).

As the reader may have gathered, role playing is indispensable to the ultimate success of social-communication skills training. To be optimally effective these role plays should be supplemented by instruction, modeling, feedback, and cognitive restructuring. Role playing is not the only approach useful in teaching social-communication skills, however. Social-communication skills can also be taught through therapeutic games. Although many adults view games as the exclusive province of children, therapeutic games may have a place in programs for adult substance abusers. There is nothing written in the annals of treatment theory to indicate that therapy must be boring or tedious to be effective. The situation may, in fact, be quite the opposite, in that games have the potential of providing insight and a perspective that would otherwise be unavailable if the individual relied exclusively on a traditional treatment model. Therapeutic games have the capacity to teach certain basic life lessons, one of which is that situations are rarely as grave or hopeless as we often make them out to be. Lifestyle theory contends that taking oneself and one's situation too seriously frequently contributes to a growing sense of hopelessness and futility, both of which inhibit meaningful long-term change. Possessing the capacity to laugh at oneself may therefore be a defining character-istic of persons who are healthy, productive, independent adults. For this reason, several therapeutic games that may be helpful in improving the social-communi-cation skills of substance abusing clients are listed in Table 5-1.

✔ SKILL Life Skills

Purchasing a car, renting an apartment, and shopping for food are skills most of us take for granted. However, drug abusers are generally intimidated by these every-day responsibilities because they frequently lack the requisite life skills. Training in life skills may therefore be of some assistance in addressing the problems of persons committed to the drug lifestyle in that it could conceivably supply the individual with a wider array of options and make it less likely that he or she will enact the cutoff ("fuck it") in response to the frustrations of everyday living. Life skills training has been found effective in reducing tobacco use, marijuana smok-ing, and problem drinking in junior high students in studies with follow-ups as long as 3 years (Dusenbury & Botvin, 1992). Moreover, instruction in occupa-tional skills, money management, and food preparation led to improved program participation and skill performance in a group of drug-involved offenders enrolled in a prison-based skills program, although the long-term effects of this program on

Table 5-1 List of Therapeutic Games

Game	Skill covered	No. of players	Ages
Anger Control Game	Anger control	2–4 players	6–14
Conduct Management Game	Impulse control	2–4 players	7–18
Let's Get Rational	Rational thinking	2 or more	16–adult
Never Say Never	Problem solving	2 or more	7–adult
Personal Power POW	Risk taking	2–6 players	10–adult
Problem Solver	Problem solving	2–6 players	10–16
Self-Concept Game	Self-esteem	2 or more	7–14
Self-Control Game	Self-control	2 or more	6–14
Social Skills Game	Communication (cooperation)	2 or more	6–14
The Ungame	Communication (verbalizing/listening)	2 or more	5–adult

Note. The construction of this table does not constitute endorsement of any of the products listed, but is designed to provide clinicians with an increased number of options for use in improving the social-communication skills of substance-abusing clients. For prices and additional information, the reader should contact The Center for Applied Psychology, Inc., P.O. Box 61586, King of Prussia, PA 19406.

recidivism are unknown at this time (Field, 1985). This would imply that another way people could potentially increase their options in life is by developing basic life management and self-care skills.

☑ ASSESSMENT   Index of Life Skills

Clients should be instructed to complete Appendix 20: Index of Life Skills by checking off the life skills they feel confident and competent performing. These skills are organized into 10 basic areas or themes and overlap slightly with some of the skills discussed in the Social-Communication Skills section. The 10 sections are entitled personal hygiene, clothing maintenance, food skills, housing, job skills, transportation, money management, leisure-time activities, telephoning skills, and dating skills. Skills listed on the index that the client does not check off are potential targets for intervention. Before arranging for treatment, however, it is important that the results be discussed with the client in order to rule out alternative explanations for why they are not performing these activities (e.g., debilitating anxiety, environmental constraints, misunderstanding of the instructions).

☑ PLAN

Training seminars need to be established for clients with skill deficits in the areas assessed by the Index of Life Skills. Providing life skills training to individual clients is both expensive and impractical. The clinician is therefore advised to make arrangements for specialized staff or consultants to perform life skills training in groups, because the demands on a single therapist can be prohibitive. A major consideration in acquiring staff for this purpose is identifying persons who have worked, or currently work, in the field or area in which training is being sought. Hence, a dietician should be hired for food skills training, a person with business expertise for a course on money management, and an authority on interpersonal communication for a program of dating skills instruction. The goal of intervention is to provide the substance-abusing client with the skills necessary to manage the pressures and responsibilities of everyday living without having to resort to the use of drugs. The end result is a client who is goal-directed, accountable, and self-confident.

☑ SKILL   Occupational and Educational Skills

Work and academic skills could potentially augment a person's options in life by providing him or her with increased opportunities for employment and personal advancement. Whereas research supports the power of job training to bring about positive changes in persons previously addicted to drugs (Gueron, 1980), the effect may vary as a function of minority status and drug history. Minority subjects, presumably because they are at greater disadvantage in finding employment (Beck, 1981), and persons with the heaviest prior commitment to the drug lifestyle, perhaps because they never acquired rudimentary work skills in the first place (Jeffrey & Woopert, 1974), may profit the most from job training and occupational assistance. The ability of education to reduce relapse in persons who previously abused alcohol and other drugs remains an unanswered question (Mulford, 1970). However, there is evidence that positive outcomes may be attainable if arrangements are made for transition to a community-based academic program upon one's release from jail or inpatient treatment (Seashore, Haberfield, Irwin, & Baker, 1976) and if training in problem solving, moral development, and cognitive self-management accompanies the academic curriculum (Ayers, Duguid, Montague, & Wolowidnyk, 1980).

✔ ASSESSMENT   Review of Academic and Occupational Skills

The Review of Academic and Occupational Skills is outlined in Appendix 21. This form should be completed by the clinician following an educational/occupational interview with the client. The first section of the interview should be used to inquire about the client's academic and occupational status and experience. From this, the interviewer can attain a general sense of the client's educational history, record of vocational training, and past employment. In the second part of the interview, the clinician asks the client to list his or her academic and occupational goals and objectives. Although this interview rarely takes longer than 10 or 15 minutes to complete, the results can be extremely helpful in identifying academic and occupational areas of strength, weakness, and interest.

✔ PLAN

Similar to instruction in life skills, academic and occupational skills training requires the services of educational and vocational specialists. Most clinicians have neither the time nor expertise to offer competent educational or vocational programming to their clients. Therefore, as denoted in the section on life skills, there is a need for an integrated program of intervention that employs service providers with different areas of expertise. If the clinician does not have the luxury of a comprehensive program of treatment intervention, then he or she will need to consult with one or more outside educational and vocational specialists. Information supplied by the Review of Academic and Occupational Skills may serve as a starting point, but in many cases these specialists will want to conduct their own interviews and may require that the client complete a battery of aptitude, achievement, and vocational interest tests. Clinicians therefore need to keep in mind that even though they may not conduct the occupational/academic portion of the intervention, they are still responsible for ensuring that the client's needs in this area are being addressed by a competent professional.

COMPETENCE ENHANCEMENT

Once the individual options have been delineated, the next task confronting the problem solver is evaluating each option. The founding premise of rational choice theory is that the individual conducts an exhaustive and systematic review of alternative solutions, followed by selection of the optimal solution (Becker, 1968). However, contrary to the optimistic predictions of rational choice theorists, the decisions most people make, regardless of whether they abuse drugs, are impulsive (Fattah, 1982), perseverative (Einhorn & Hogarth, 1978), and expedient (Corbin, 1980) rather than methodical, innovative, and efficient. Results of studies addressing the decision-making competence of substance abusers (Bennett, 1986) are particularly incompatible with Becker's notion of decision making as a rational, organized process. This does not mean that humans are incapable of solving problems in a logical and proficient manner, only that, antithetical to the contentions of rational choice theorists, the human decision-making enterprise is more often guided by convenience than by reasoned judgment. The purpose of this section is to explore ways in which therapists might encourage greater competence on the part of their clients in evaluating various life options.

At the heart of the human decision-making process is the cost–benefit analysis in which the client compares the advantages and disadvantages (pros and cons) of each alternative solution. This approach is generally all that is required for problems without a compelling emotional overlay. The cost–benefit analysis is frequently not enough, however, in managing problems with an emotional overlay. Consider, for instance, deciding how to respond to a fight with one's spouse. Although alternatives such as "talk it out" or "take time to think it through" may be viewed as reasonable options by someone with a history of substance abuse, the values normally assigned to the positive and negative consequences of each alternative tend to vary only slightly. The same may not be true of the alternative "go out and get high." Whereas the number of negative perceived consequences of drug use may, in fact, exceed the number of positive perceived consequences in the mind of someone who uses drugs, the negative consequences will probably be assigned significantly less value because they tend to be more distant in time (hangover, further conflict with spouse) than the positive consequences (tension reduction). This demonstrates that a cost–benefit analysis of options may be inadequate to the task of effectively evaluating options for problems that arouse strong emotions. It is therefore recommended that the therapist attempt to neutralize the emotional overlay that sometimes interferes with effective decision making by taking into account priorities, values, expectancies, and goals.

✔ SKILL   Values Clarification and Skill Development

Values are the general standards, ideals, and qualities regarded by an individual as desirable or beneficial, whereas rules are the customs, directives, and practices that support these values. Priorities are the behavioral application of these rules and reflect the impact of values and rules on the decision-making process of the individual. By examining a client's priorities, the therapist is in a position to form a deeper appreciation of the values and rules on which that individual's life is based. Ideally, values should set the general tone of one's life; rules are then devised to support and actualize these values; and behavioral priorities spring from the rules and direct the individual toward activities congruent with his or her value system. The drug lifestyle, however, disrupts this orderly process by re-arranging people's priorities, supplying them with alternative rules, and distancing them from their values. This is such a slow, insidious process that the individual may be unaware of the changes gradually taking place in his or her value system. By the time the lifestyle enters the advanced stage, the person is largely divorced from his or her values. One avenue of treatment intervention, therefore, involves realigning one's behavior with one's values. In situations where the lifestyle process began at an early age, or where the individual was raised to accept "deviant" values, however, a simple values–behavior realignment may not be sufficient. Under such circumstances, the individual may require training in certain value skills.

A course in values clarification affords the client the opportunity to realign his or her behavioral priorities with his or her values. Linkenbach (1990) has im-plemented a values clarification program at the Center for Alcohol Education in Fort Collins, Colorado, to assist clients with the actualization of life options and the development of decision-making abilities. Treatment is conducted in a non-threatening environment where empowerment and values reorientation come to replace the powerlessness and confused priorities of the drug lifestyle. Brown and Peterson (1990) have also emphasized values reorientation and spirituality in their approach to substance abuse treatment. These authors supply data to support their claim that value change and value–behavior congruence are vital to the recovery process. Values clarification appears to be an important adjunct to change pro-grams for substance-abusing clients because of its ability to challenge drug-involved priorities and reinforce values that support desirable behavior (Rokeach, 1983). Value skill development may be necessary, however, in situations where the individual has adopted a deviant set of values.

✔ ASSESSMENT   Values Inventory

The Values Inventory can be found in Appendix 22. It is comprised of 20 general priorities that respondents rate on a four-point scale designed to measure the relative value the respondent places on each priority (0 = no value, 1 = low value, 2 = moderate value, 3 = high value). The 20 general priorities are rated for three time periods, each represented by a different column. In Column (a) the respondent estimates the value he or she placed on each priority during the period of heaviest drug use; in Column (b) the respondent records his or her current evaluation of the 20 priorities; and in Column (c) the individual records his or her future ideal ratings. The ratings are then summed for each time period. Items 1, 5, 9, 13, and 17, when added together, produce a social value cluster score; Items 2, 6, 10, 14, and 18 a work value cluster score; Items 3, 7, 11, 15, and 19 a visceral value cluster score; and Items 4, 8, 12, 16, and 20 an intellectual value cluster score. The Values Inventory is one of the more complicated assessment devices found in this book and, as such, therapists are advised to take the time to fully explain the instructions to clients, answer questions, and provide supervision and assistance when needed. The actual scores on the four value cluster scales are less important than their overall relationship. Problems are suggested by a lack of balance between the value cluster scales, indicating that one value cluster is perceived by the individual as significantly more important than the other value clusters.

✔ PLAN

Lifestyle theory postulates the presence of four primary value clusters. The social value cluster reflects the perceived value of interpersonal relationships (family, friends) and themes (sharing, love). The work value cluster assesses the perceived value of honest labor and accomplishment as represented by such priorities as job, productivity, and achievement. The visceral value cluster measures the pull for sensory experience (pleasure, excitement) and immediate gratification (sex, power). This is often the dominant value cluster in persons committed to the drug lifestyle, although denying this aspect of one's experience can be just as damaging as allowing it to predominate; again, balance is the key to a healthy value system. The final cluster of values, those that are concerned with intellectual understanding, reflect an interest in the pursuit of education, truth, and knowledge. In some cases, the act of clarifying one's values and observing the unbalanced configuration of priorities that normally characterize the drug lifestyle, or incongruence between one's current priorities and future ideal, is sufficient to motivate the person to realign his or her priorities and values. This, of course, assumes that the individual possesses a solid system of values that has simply been disrupted by his or her involvement with drugs. For some clients, however, especially those who began using drugs during childhood or early adolescence, certain fundamental value skills may be lacking.

It is impossible to tell from the results of the Values Inventory whether a low score on a value cluster represents misdirected priorities that can be remedied by instruction in values clarification or whether it signals a more serious lack of prior instruction in value skills that can be addressed only through training. Only through continued interaction with a client can this be deciphered with any degree of confidence. Brown and Peterson (1990) have offered a model of values clarification training that may be useful to clinicians hoping to assist a client with values–behavior realignment. After assessment of the client's values with a measure similar to the Values Inventory, Brown and Peterson advocate instruction in the delineation, definition, and clarification of value systems and training in how to identify inconsistencies between one's behavior and values. Next, the client should be encouraged to engage in daily self-monitoring of value–behavior inconsistencies and discuss the results with the clinician during weekly therapy sessions. According to Brown and Peterson, it is vital that the client compare his or her value system with the value systems of successfully recovering individuals to guard against self-deception and the configuration of a value system with obvious relapse-promoting potential. However, because value systems and recovery tend to vary from individual to individual, it is recommended that clients be encouraged to compare their value systems against more reliable criteria; namely, the criteria of balancing the four value clusters and congruence between the current and future evaluation of the 20 priorities of the Values Inventory. The final phase of Brown and Peterson's values clarification intervention is continued evaluation and updating of the client's self-monitoring efforts and self-confrontation of any inconsistencies observed between the client's stated values and behavior.

Value skill deficits require more than a brief course in values clarification; in a majority of cases, skill deficits require skills training and development. To facilitate the process of value skill acquisition, lifestyle theory introduces eight value skills: honesty, relatedness, disclosure, responsibility, industriousness, sentience, concurrence, and erudition. Figure 5-1 illustrates the proposed relationship between the eight value skills and four value clusters. Honesty assumes a lack of deception in one's dealings with others, but quite obviously, honesty with oneself is a prerequisite for honesty with others. Relatedness, on the other hand, portends an abiding interest in interpersonal relationships and the welfare of others. Disclosure, with roots in the social and work value clusters, shows evidence of multichannel communication (e.g., listening, sharing perceptions and ideas, negotiating) and rejection of single-channel communication (e.g., using language to manipulate, intimidate, or control others). Responsibility emphasizes accountability and the meeting of obligations, whereas industriousness reflects acceptance of the work ethic and a belief in the value of diligence. Sentience, the value skill that falls at the center of the visceral cluster, is the quality or condition of being aware of one's feelings and sensations. Concurrence, because it crosses the line between the visceral and intellectual value clusters, emphasizes sensitivity to environmental change and flexibility in the face of conflicting or contradictory environmental input. The final value skill, erudition, is defined by the active pursuit of under-

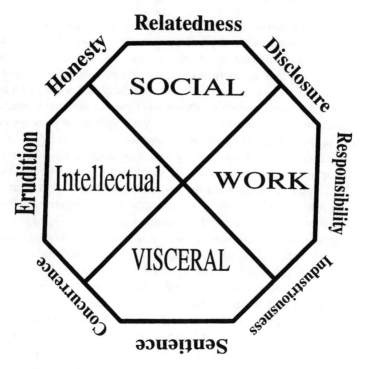

Figure 5-1 Relationship presumed to exist between the eight value skills and four value clusters.

standing and the desire to acquire new knowledge. Suggested interventions designed to build and strengthen these value skills are outlined in Table 5-2.

☑ SKILL Goal-Setting

Similar to value systems, goal networks are comprised of three fundamental components. Whereas value systems link values, rules, and priorities, goal networks incorporate goals, expectancies, and consequences. In developing a goal network, it is important to understand that consequences are the perceived potential outcome of a specific behavior, expectancies are the perceived likelihood of a consequence's occurrence, and goals are the objectives a person pursues. Hence, consequences are the perceived long- and short-term costs and benefits of a particular course of action, whereas expectancies are the person's estimate of the likelihood that each consequence—positive short-term, negative short-term, positive long-term, negative long-term—will occur. The long- and short-term goals that direct people's behavior stem from the perceived consequences of their actions and their evaluation of each consequence's perceived probability. For instance, even if overdose and death are viewed as potential outcomes of heroin

Table 5-2 Proposed Interventions for Value Skill Deficits

Value skill	Suggested interventions
Honesty	Advise client of the importance of honesty and how dishonesty supports the drug lifestyle; teach client the difference between fact and fiction and how to identify self-deception; reinforce client when he or she tells a verifiable truth.
Relatedness	Provide instruction in basic social skills; remove barriers to social interaction (e.g., anxiety, irrational thoughts, lack of self-confidence); encourage involvement with others by reinforcing successive approximations to the target behaviors.
Disclosure	Demonstrate the value of multichannel communication; provide instruction in basic listening skills; teach client how to negotiate; establish an environment in which client feels comfortable sharing his or her "secret" thoughts and ideas.
Responsibility	Teach client the value of responsibility and the role of accountability in future success; break down tasks into manageable units; show the consequences of behavior through behavioral contracts and other forms of contingency management; reinforce responsibility when it occurs.
Industriousness	Demonstrate the value of hard work for building good psychological and medical health; reframe work as an expression of one's humanity with the capacity to inject meaning into one's life; provide job skills training; provide opportunities for working in areas that are of interest to client.
Sentience	Educate client about the importance of understanding and using internal messages such as feelings and sensations; provide sensitivity training; instruct in breathing exercises and other forms of deep muscle relaxation, yoga, and meditation.
Concurrence	Help client appreciate the reality of change and that physical and psychological survival depends on a person's ability to adapt; teach client how to suspend judgment and attend to information supplied by the environment (including other people) rather than jumping to conclusions; assist client in learning to entertain multiple options toward a goal of increased cognitive flexibility.
Erudition	Stress and illustrate the value of knowledge in meeting the demands of everyday living; establish opportunities for new learning that are fun and rewarding; encourage and reinforce self-initiated attempts to acquire new information.

use, and it is established that the individual values his or her life, these negative consequences may be given little serious consideration if they are perceived to have a low probability of occurrence.

Rohsenow, Beach, and Marlatt (1978) have argued that the expected consequences of drinking, subjective value of these consequences, anticipated probability that these consequences will occur, and each consequence's perceived immediacy determine whether a person will consume a quantity of alcohol in a particular situation. Leigh and Stacy (1994) add that, in general, the negative consequences of substance misuse do not exert as much influence over behavior as the positive consequences, because the latter tend to be more immediate. When subjects are led to believe that they have consumed an alcoholic beverage, regardless of whether the drink actually contains ethanol, they demonstrate an expectancy effect. This effect has been shown to be stronger for social behaviors such as aggression (Lang, Goeckner, Adesso, & Marlatt, 1975) and sexual interest (Briddle et al., 1978) than for physical actions such as body sway and reaction time (Marlatt & Rohsenow, 1980). It has been noted that alcohol abusers who attach positive expectancies to drinking and drunkenness are more prone to relapse than alcohol abusers who hold negative expectancies of drinking and drunkenness (Eastman & Norris, 1982). Escalation of drug use (Fromme & Dunn, 1992) and out-of-control drinking (Berg, Laberg, Skutle, & Ohman, 1981) have also been attributed to the influence of expectancies on human decision-making behavior. Interestingly, Darkes and Goldman (1993) found that an expectancy challenge, which involved demonstrating to subjects that they are unable to reliably distinguish between the behavior of persons who have consumed alcohol and the behavior of persons who have consumed a placebo, led to a reduction in the subsequent use of alcohol on the part of a group of moderate to heavy drinking college males.

☑ ASSESSMENT   Expectancies Grid

Using Appendix 23: Expectancies Grid, the clinician can have the client chart the perceived positive short-term consequences of drug use in box (1), the perceived negative short-term consequences of drug use in box (2), the perceived positive long-term consequences of drug use in box (3), and the perceived negative long-term consequences of drug use in box (4). Once all of the perceived consequences have been listed, the client should rate each consequence on a scale from 1 to 10 (1 representing a very low likelihood of occurrence and 10 a very high likelihood of occurrence) to signify his or her expectancies for each consequence. First, the client should rate the expectancies he or she had of substance use during the period he or she was most heavily involved with drugs, placing the rating in parentheses to the right of the consequence. Then, using the same 10-point rating scale, but a different color pen or pencil, the client should estimate his or her current expectancy of each consequence in the event he or she were to abuse drugs again. Results obtained from the Expectancy Grid can be helpful in unmasking a client's expectancies concerning the consequences of regular drug use. An increase in the expectancies for the negative long-term consequences of drug use or a decrease in the expectancies for the positive short-term consequences of drug use should be viewed as a sign (provided the client is not simply manipulating the results) that the client is laying the groundwork for a more competent evaluation of alternatives.

☑ PLAN

One way to modify expectancies is to extend a client's time horizon. The time horizon is an estimate of a person's future orientation and ability to anticipate the possible intermediate- and long-range consequences of his or her actions (Wilson & Herrnstein, 1985). The normal developmental progression is for the time horizon to extend as a child develops. Hence, older children are generally less impulsive and more willing to delay immediate gratification than younger children (Mischel, 1974). Unfortunately, many people who abuse drugs, particularly those who have been involved in the drug lifestyle for a protracted period of time, suffer from short time horizons. Whether an abbreviated time horizon is the cause of drug abuse, a consequence of it, or both, is uncertain. What is clear, however, is that the decision to use drugs invites a conflict between the positive short-term effects and negative long-term consequences of this behavior. What the reader needs to understand is that the positive short-term consequences of drug use normally hold dominion over the negative long-term effects in people who abuse substances, perhaps because many such individuals possess a short time horizon. As with the value clusters, the goal of lifestyle intervention is to encourage clients to pursue behaviors that balance short-term pleasure and long-term considerations.

Goal-setting is one procedure potentially capable of addressing the problems introduced by a short time horizon. The first step of goal-setting training is to ask the client to define his or her long-range goals. Once the long-range goals have been identified, the individual establishes short-range (from a minute to a few days) and intermediate-range (more than a few days but shorter than the long-range goal) objectives that tie directly into each long-range goal. Short- and intermediate-range goals become the steps the client takes to achieve his or her long-range goals. Next, the perceived consequences of specific objectives and the expectancy of realizing each consequence are examined. Hence, the client must consider the anticipated positive and negative short- and long-term consequences of the various short-, intermediate-, and long-range goals he or she is pursuing. Although such an activity may seem tedious, it can be extremely helpful in identifying specific behaviors capable of aiding clients in the realization of their life goals and ambitions. It should also be noted that modeling and role playing can be invaluable in solidifying the acquisition of effective goal-setting strategies (Lochman, Burch, Curry, & Lampron, 1984). In summary, goal-setting starts with the identification of a long-range goal, continues with the establishment of a system of short- and intermediate-range goals that tie into the individual's long-term objectives, and culminates with the selection of specific behavioral strategies that follows from an evaluation of the perceived consequences and expectancies of each goal.

CONCLUSION

As this chapter illustrates, there are two primary pathways through which clinicians might influence the choice process. One pathway necessitates increasing the client's options in life. This can be accomplished by helping clients increase their range of available alternatives by teaching them creativity, social-communication, life, and academic-occupational skills. The second pathway through which therapists might influence their clients' decision-making processes is founded on techniques that instruct clients in the proper manner of evaluating currently available options. This not only necessitates paying closer attention to the costs and benefits of individual alternative solutions, but also requires the incorporation of priorities, values, expectancies, and goals into one's judgments. What lifestyle theory attempts to demonstrate in placing such an emphasis on choice is that despite the influence of the environment on the behavior of individuals, the person remains at the vortex of all program interventions. The client will not change until he or she chooses to change. To this end, lifestyle theory seeks to empower clients, rather than emphasizing powerlessness in the face of drug-related temptation; the manner in which this is accomplished requires implementation of procedures that allow clients to begin to take control of their lives.

Choice-based intervention serves the interests of both empowerment and self-confidence. As the client experiences success in applying the skills discussed in this chapter, self-esteem and self-confidence should rise accordingly. However, the efficacy of choice-based intervention is enhanced when accompanied by modeling, role playing, and cognitive restructuring. Emulation of a modeled behavior facilitates change by providing the client with the requisite guidance. In modeling the behavior of a trained professional, the client learns the proper technique for engaging in the targeted behavior and the skills necessary to overcome common roadblocks to behavioral performance (e.g., anxiety). Role playing or behavioral rehearsal is essential for skill development as well, and is particularly helpful for learning social-communication skills. This points to the fact that in order to master a skill, one must regularly practice that skill. Finally, cognitive restructuring presents individual clients with the opportunity to challenge several classes of self-defeating ideation that generally stand in the way of a person experimenting with a new behavior. Cognition, it would seem, is an invaluable tool in working with clients. As such, the next chapter will focus exclusively on cognition-based intervention strategies.

Chapter 6

Skill Development:
Cognition-Based Strategies

Cognition is the mental process through which knowledge is acquired, developed, and applied. As such, it is synonymous with thinking and interfaces with the drug lifestyle on several different fronts. The first two Cs, conditions and choice, incorporate elements of cognition, but the nature of the cognitive activity involved differs qualitatively from that which supports the third C. As the reader will recall, conditions are the internal and external forces that increase or decrease a person's options in life. However, it is the person's perception of these conditions, not the conditions themselves, that exert the greatest measure of authority over the person's conduct. To the extent that perception is colored by cognition, conditions can be conceptualized as possessing a clear cognitive component. Choice is even more distinctly cognitive, because key parameters of the decision-making process (i.e., deliberation, evaluation, and problem solving) have their foundation in human cognition. What distinguishes the first two Cs (conditions and choice) from the cognitive operations that subserve the third C is that the former tend to be more restricted, circumscribed, and anchored to specific environmental events and behavioral responses. The free-floating cognitive thinking patterns that support the third C of lifestyle theory will consequently be the focus of the present discussion.

Because humans possess the capacity to think, they often rely on these cognitive abilities to cope with their constantly changing environment. This is why survival becomes increasingly less physical and progressively more psychological as one moves up the phylogenic ladder. The free-floating cognitions that characterize the third C of lifestyle theory are especially crucial in managing environmental change. However, before we can comprehend the cognitive mechanism that supports survival we must understand the two primary functions of human cognition. One function is constructive, the other defensive. Kelly (1955), in proposing a theory of personal constructs, argued that people function much like scientists, to the extent that they establish and test hypotheses as a way of envisioning, comprehending, and anticipating their surroundings. Lifestyle theory maintains that free-floating cognition plays a major role in the development of these constructs and that it promotes survival by arming the individual with the ability to predict, construe, and understand his or her environment. Constructive thinking involves accommodation, in which cognitive structures or schemas are modified to account for previously unsymbolized environmental information (Piaget, 1963). However, environmental information can also be assimilated into existing cognitive structures. This is where the defensive function of cognition comes into play. Human organisms, according to lifestyle theory, seek to protect themselves against informational overload by incorporating novel environmental information into existing schemas. The well-functioning individual strikes a healthy balance between the accommodative and assimilative functions of free-floating cognition.

The constructive function can be divided into four subcategories, with the mythical category being the most primitive. Mythical constructions are most prominent in children, but can also be observed in adults. Because myths are based on untested assumptions, they are classified as pre-scientific. In contrast to myths, in which causal inferences are drawn from associations in time or space, empirical constructs, the next category of constructive thinking, require the derivation and systematic testing of hypotheses. Teleological methods of evaluation, however, are even more advanced than empirical methods. Thus, whereas the empirical approach contemplates the "what" of natural relationships, the teleological method ponders the "why" of such relationships, particularly as this relates to the end goals of one's investigation. Teleological thought is more sophisticated than the empirical method, but is not the highest level of constructional development available to humans. That honor is reserved for epistemological constructs, where the focus shifts to the nature, origins, and limits of human knowledge. Tracing the history of physics, we can see that it began with mythical formulations in which gods and demons controlled the fate of humankind. This eventually gave way to an empirical analysis of natural relationships, teleological investigations and goal-directed theorizing, and an epistemological probe into the limitations of science, as represented by Einstein's work on relativity, the Heisenberg uncertainty principle, and recent developments in the science of chaos.

Whereas the constructive function of cognition is motivated by accommodative interests, the defensive function is driven by the desire to assimilate new information into existing cognitive schemas. In this way, assimilation serves to flesh out the schemas created by accommodation. Because the capacity of the human brain is limited, it is unable to attend to, process, and store all information to which it is exposed. The filtering of "extraneous" information is the responsibility of the defensive function of human cognition. Insofar as awareness normally initiates the information processing sequence, denying awareness of information incompatible with or irrelevant to one's self-system is often a person's first line of defense. Coding and symbolizing information that has been attended to is the next step in the information processing sequence; experiences incompatible with the self-system can be deflected at this level by distorting or modifying their symbolization. Once information is coded it must be stored. Improper storage can lead to diversion whereby the individual externalizes, displaces, or projects personally relevant information onto related and unrelated objects and situations. The final step in the information processing sequence is retrieval of stored information. Here, properly symbolized and stored experiences incongruent with one's current awareness can be channeled into arguments and activities that do not clash with the self-system. This is referred to by proponents of the lifestyle approach as justification.

Denial is the most primitive or basic defensive function, whereas justification is the most sophisticated. Sophistication is measured by the number of operations required to prevent information incompatible with one's self-system from disrupting one's current self- and world-view. It should be noted, however, that the defensive function contributes as much to cognitive growth and development as the constructive function. Defensive maneuvers serve to assimilate and digest new environmental information in ways that potentially complement and sustain constructive operations, for without the defensive function the organism would be inundated with a steady stream of new information. Problems arise when the organism becomes overly reliant on one of these two functions. A theme echoed throughout this book is that lifestyle theory places a premium on balance; it can be stated with some degree of authority that achieving a workable compromise between the creation of new schemas and the expansion and protection of these schemas is the key to cognitive growth and development. Difficulties arise when either the constructive or defensive functions predominate, or when the individual comes to rely on lower level constructions (mythological) and defenses (denial, distortion) to the detriment of more sophisticated constructions (teleological, epistemological) and defenses (justification). The purpose of this chapter is threefold: (a) to teach clients how to identify and correct common constructional errors and distortions; (b) to educate clients about common defensive maneuvers and discuss how these stratagems might be evaluated and, if necessary, eliminated; and (c) to consider the role of uncomfortable affect (e.g., existential fear) in the initiation and progression of the drug lifestyle and identify tactics useful in managing these feelings.

THE CONSTRUCTIVE FUNCTION OF COGNITION

Denoff (1988) determined that irrational thinking accounted for 17% of the variance in a drug abuse frequency measure attained by a group of juveniles enrolled in a residential substance abuse treatment program. Catastrophizing and approval-seeking self-talk were particularly prevalent in this group. Probing the relationship between cognition and alcohol abuse, Rohsenow and his colleagues determined that irrational beliefs correlated with problem avoidance, alcohol-related craving, and relapse in a group of Veterans Administration inpatients (Rohsenow et al., 1989). To the extent that a meaningful connection exists between constructive errors and substance misuse, cognitive therapy is a major vehicle of intervention for persons previously committed to the drug lifestyle. There are numerous versions of cognitive therapy available to clinicians; several of the more popular models include Ellis' (1970) system of irrational beliefs, Beck's (1976) review of automatic thoughts, Meichenbaum's (1974) self-instructional approach, and Maultsby's (1975) method of evaluating debilitating self-talk. Beck's automatic thoughts and distortions are particularly relevant to the constructional errors discussed in this chapter. Accordingly, they will serve as the framework for the present discussion.

☑ SKILL   Identifying and Correcting Constructional Errors

In their work with depressed patients, Beck, Rush, Shaw, and Emery (1979) identified six automatic thoughts and distortions that may be helpful in conceptualizing the constructional errors commonly displayed by substance abusing clients. One of these distortions is a stimulus set and the other five are response sets. The stimulus set distortion, selective abstraction, is defined as the tendency to focus on a small detail to the exclusion of other salient features of the stimulus situation. The five response set errors delineated by Beck et al. are arbitrary inference, dichotomous reasoning, magnification/minimization, overgeneralization, and personalization. Arbitrary inference entails forming a conclusion without supporting evidence or in the face of contradictory evidence. Dichotomous or black-and-white reasoning involves segregating one's experience into mutually exclusive bipolar categories (e.g., good–bad, weak–strong, win–lose). Magnification and minimization occur when a person either overestimates or underestimates the significance of a particular event. Overgeneralization arises when the individual draws an inference from an isolated event and then applies this inference to related and unrelated situations. People who catastrophize, that is, view things as terrible, awful, or hopeless ("my life is over") in response to relatively minor setbacks and other adversities, are operating on the basis of both magnification and overgeneralization. Personalization encompasses the tendency to inappropriately and unjustifiably relate external events to oneself.

☑ ASSESSMENT   Self-Monitoring of Constructional Errors

Self-monitoring is one procedure through which constructional errors might be accessed and identified. The therapist should instruct the client to record the number of times he or she engages in each of the six constructional distortions listed in Appendix 24: Self-Monitoring of Constructional Errors. This form provides a daily record of self-monitoring for 1 week. Multiple forms should be used when longer periods of self-monitoring are required. Prior to employing this procedure, therapists should define the six constructional errors for clients and provide concrete examples of each. Selective abstraction is at work when an individual presumes that the "straight life" is boring, based on the accounts of a handful of "straight" people who are occasionally bored with their lives. Arbitrary inference is contained in the comments of students who conclude that they are "stupid" when their report cards reflect As and Bs. Dichotomous reasoning results when a person divides the members of his or her therapy group into givers and takers and then acts on this artificial dichotomy. Quitting one's job in response to a minor reprimand from one's boss is an example of magnification. The converse of magnification; minimization, is observed when a person ignores clear signs of an impending heart attack. The client who labels him or herself an "addict" or "dope fiend" on the basis of a subset of behaviors (substance use) is overgeneralizing, whereas the client who believes that the new federal guidelines for drug offenders were devised specifically with him or her in mind is personalizing.

☑ PLAN

Beck et al. (1979) have recommend a five-step procedure to correct constructional errors. The first step in the Beck et al. procedure is to train clients in the use of the self-monitoring technique. This can be accomplished with the aid of the Self-Monitoring of Constructional Errors assessment procedure described in the previous section. The second step in challenging constructional errors is educating clients about the connection between thinking, affect, and behavior. Albert Ellis' (1970) A-B-Cs of emotion may be helpful in this regard, with A representing the activating event, B the belief the individual has concerning the activating event, and C the consequent emotions and behaviors that stem from the person's interpretation of the activating event. The rationale for acquainting clients with the A-B-Cs of emotion is to expose the relationship between cognition, affect, and conduct. Once clients appreciate the connection between thoughts, feelings, and behavior, the next step is to guide them through an evaluation of evidence compatible and incompatible with their monitored thoughts. To maximize the effectiveness of this procedure therapists should model the stages for clients and provide assistance when needed. This is similar, in many ways, to the cost–benefit analysis described in Chapter 5. The fourth and fifth steps of the Beck et al. procedure involve devising more reality-oriented interpretations of the event in question and identifying and altering the dysfunctional beliefs that led the client to distort his or her perception of the event in the first place.

There is little doubt that cognitive approaches can play a pivotal role in intervening with substance-abusing clients (see Miller, 1992). It is imperative, however, that the therapist take each client's level of cognitive sophistication into account when selecting cognitive techniques for use with specific clients. Thought stopping (Wolpe, 1969) is a simple cognitive strategy in which subvocal commands such as "stop" and the snap of a rubber band worn around the wrist are used to disrupt the cognitively based urge to use drugs or engage in a drug-related constructional error. This strategy may assist with the management of urges and simple constructional errors, but is limited in that it fails to provide the client with alternative constructions. A somewhat more sophisticated procedure, cognitive rehearsal (Beck et al., 1979), requires that the client imagine each step that must be performed in accomplishing a task, anticipate and confront the constructional errors that, if left unchallenged, would impede his or her performance, and visualize being rewarded for successful completion of the task. A third procedure, rational restructuring, involves challenging dysfunctional patterns of ideation. The rational challenge that is at the heart of this procedure can be implemented in several different ways. Maultsby's (1975) procedure may be the most practical. Using the five questions listed in Table 6-1, Maultsby encourages clients to consider whether a specific belief satisfies minimal criteria for rational thought, and, if not, to replace it with a more rational alternative. Maultsby asserts that if at least three of the criterion questions can be answered in the affirmative, then the thought is rational. However, if fewer than three of these criteria are satisfied, the thought is classified as irrational. It has been the author's experience that drug lifestyle-supporting thoughts rarely satisfy even one of the five criteria for rational thinking.

Table 6-1   Maultsby's Five Criteria for Rational Thinking

1. Does the thought meet with objective reality?
2. Does the thought serve to protect my life and health?
3. Does the thought lead me to achieve my short- and long-range goals?
4. Does the thought help me avoid conflict with others?
5. Does the thought make me feel the way I want to feel?

Adapted from Maultsby, M. C. (1975). *Help yourself to happiness through rational self-counseling.* New York: Institute for Rational Living.

☑ SKILL   Reframing Perceptions and Thoughts

Viewing a glass filled to the midpoint with water, one could legitimately conclude that the glass was either half empty or half full. Although these two interpretations are both accurate, the emotional consequences are hardly identical. Whereas the half empty interpretation may promote an attitude of dissatisfaction, pessimism, and gloom, the half full interpretation may engender contentment, optimism, and hope. How we frame our thoughts and perceptions, as this example clearly illustrates, can have a wide-ranging effect on our emotional reactions and world-view. Cognitive reframing is particularly apropos when it comes to interpreting slips and lapses. Marlatt and Gordon (1985) contend that a slip attributed to external, unstable, specific, and controllable factors is less likely to lead to relapse than a slip attributed to internal, stable, global, and uncontrollable factors. Hence, attributing a slip to fatigue, a lack of effort, or bad decision making is considered less serious than attributing a slip to an inborn disease or defect over which the person has no control. If a slip can be reframed as a learning experience and not a fatal blunder, then the individual has a better chance of preventing the slip from escalating into a full-blown relapse.

Marlatt and Gordon (1985) postulate that adhering to a philosophy of total abstinence may actually encourage relapse by framing slips as failures, a process known as the abstinence violation effect (AVE). Evidence in favor of the AVE has been obtained from studies in which clients expressing strong beliefs in the necessity of total abstinence experienced higher rates of relapse after an initial lapse or slip than clients less dedicated to a philosophy of complete abstinence (Collins & Lapp, 1991; Curry, Marlatt, & Gordon, 1987). Other studies, however, fail to provide support for Marlatt and Gordon's AVE hypothesis (Birke, Edelmann, & Davis, 1990; Brandon, Tiffany, & Baker, 1986). Although data on the AVE are inconclusive, the manner in which a client cognitively frames a slip or lapse may have a far-reaching effect on how he or she copes with it, which in some cases may influence the individual's propensity for relapse.

☑ ASSESSMENT   Lapse Versus Relapse

The Appendix 25: Lapse Versus Relapse questionnaire asks respondents to register their agreement or disagreement with a series of 12 statements. These statements are designed to measure the client's interpretation of lapses and beliefs about the eventual likelihood of relapsing from a single episode of drug use. The six constructional errors discussed in the previous section are also represented on this questionnaire: selective abstraction (Item 2), arbitrary inference (Items 6 and 11), dichotomous reasoning (Items 4 and 5), magnification (Item 1), overgeneralization (Items 1, 3, and 10), and personalization (Item 7). The Lapse Versus Relapse questionnaire is relatively easy to score, with "agree" responses to Items 1, 4, 6, 7, 10, and 11 and "disagree" responses to Items 2, 3, 5, 8, 9, and 12 being summed to yield a total score that may range between 0 and 12. Total scores of 4 to 6 suggest a potential problem with the way the client frames lapses, whereas scores of 7 or higher signal the presence of a serious problem with the framing of lapses and a belief in the inevitability of relapse following a slip or lapse.

☑ PLAN

Reframing and lateral thinking have a great deal in common. With both, the goal is to generate alternative perceptions and explanations for specific stimuli and events. Perceptual reframing can be dramatized by having the client describe the cube in part (a) of Figure 6-1. Some people frame their perception as if they were standing above and slightly to the right of the cube (b), others frame their perception as if they are standing below and slightly to the left of the cube (c), and still others alternate between these two perceptions. What this exercise illustrates is that objects and situations can frequently be viewed from several different, but equally accurate, perspectives. Buchanan (1992) offers another example of perceptual reframing. He suggests writing "IAMNOWHERE" in large block letters on a two-foot piece of cardboard, briefly flashing the sign in front of clients, and asking them to write down what they perceived was written on the cardboard. Many clients perceive the message "I am nowhere," whereas others indicate that they organized the letters into the sentence "I am now here"; however, very few people report seeing both messages. This not only demonstrates the possibility of multiple perceptions, but also suggests that the manner in which a person frames various life circumstances can have an important effect on his or her mood and behavior. The message "I am nowhere" clearly promotes a different mental and emotional set than the message "I am now here," a fact that substantiates the value of reframing in therapy.

Like perceptual reframing, cognitive reframing entails a reformulation of one's point of view. As discussed previously, a critical reframing issue is the client's interpretation of slips and lapses. Based on the work of Marlatt and Gordon (1985), it is hypothesized that clients who reframe a slip or lapse as a learning experience are in a better position to manage slips and lapses than clients who view them as signs of failure. The first step in the cognitive reframing process, whether the emphasis is on a slip or other relapse-relevant behavior, is to explore the negative aspects of the client's conduct. Once this is done, the next step is to have the client survey the positive features or possibilities. This is the proverbial silver lining found in every dark cloud. When the silver lining has been identified, the final step is to decide which interpretation, positive or negative, is more liable to provide the client with the opportunity to achieve long- and short-term goals, avoid conflict with others, and feel the way he or she wants to feel (abbreviated Maultsby criteria). Some clients may view cognitive reframing as nothing short of self-deception. However, what the client needs to understand is that there is always more than one way to interpret a stimulus, behavior, or event,

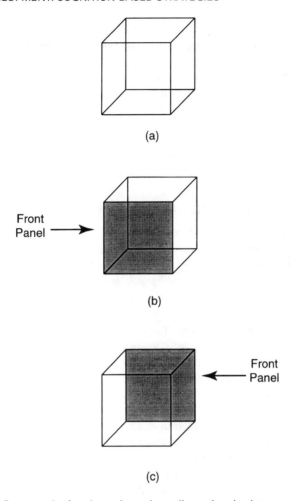

Figure 6-1   Perceptual reframing using a three-dimensional cube.

and adopting one that is more conducive to future success makes a great deal more sense than adopting an interpretation that keeps one depressed, angry, or enmeshed in a destructive lifestyle.

Drug-related cues, as discussed in Chapter 4, can be handled through various cue control procedures. This might be accomplished by avoiding the cue stimulus or extinguishing the emotional response associated with the cue by repeatedly presenting it in the absence of a drug effect. Reframing or reinterpreting the cue is a third way to achieve cue control. Take, for instance, the interoceptive (anger, frustration) and exteroceptive (bar setting, sight of drug) cues associated with a person's past misuse of substances. Reframing these cues as harbingers of self-destruction, rather than as forerunners of pleasure, may go a long way in assisting someone interested in abandoning the drug lifestyle. Drug-related cues can also be reinterpreted by clients as a sign or signal to which they should pay close attention; in other words, specific drug-related cues may be reframed as alarms that activate a coping mindset and alert the individual to potential areas of risk or vulnerability that need to be addressed. In this way, reframing may be helpful in reinforcing a client's self-confidence in the face of drug-related cues and situations. Although a relatively simple procedure, reframing can be used to reinterpret perceptions, thoughts, behaviors, and cues in ways that enhance a person's ability to manage high-risk situations and avoid relapsing into drug use patterns.

THE DEFENSIVE FUNCTION OF COGNITION

As mentioned previously, the defensive function of cognition plays as integral a role in promoting the psychological health and adjustment of the human organism as the constructive function. Problems arise, however, when the natural balance between the constructive and defensive functions breaks down and the individual comes to depend on either function to the exclusion of the other. Overreliance on the accommodative properties of constructive cognition can result in a system overwhelmed by new information and concepts, whereas overreliance on the assimilative properties of defensive cognition generally inhibits system growth and development. As the individual comes to depend on the defensive function, experiences that cannot be incorporated into existing schema are either denied, distorted, diverted, or organized inappropriately. The end result is a rigid set of thinking styles designed to justify, buttress, and reinforce the person's lifestyle. The purpose of the defensive function in a well-balanced cognitive system is to protect the organism from the barrage of environmental information that frequently impinges on it; the purpose of the defensive function in an unbalanced system, as is the case with someone who commits him or herself to the drug lifestyle, is to protect the lifestyle. The inflexible cognitions that evolve from an overactive defensive system divert the person from the path of adaptation onto a road of lifestyle recitation by severely limiting the scope, range, and activity of his or her accommodative skills. The eight defensive thinking styles believed to be at the heart of the drug lifestyle include mollification, cutoff, entitlement, power orientation, sentimentality, superoptimism, cognitive indolence, and discontinuity (see Chapter 2).

☑ SKILL   Challenging the Eight Thinking Styles

Because the eight thinking styles were defined and discussed in Chapter 2, a brief review is all that is required here. Mollification is the term lifestyle theory uses to describe the tendency to exonerate one's drug use and the negative consequences of such use by offering excuses and rationalizations, transferring blame for one's use onto others, or shifting one's attention to various societal injustices. The cutoff is a mechanism the individual uses to rapidly eliminate deterrents to drug use, the phrase "fuck it" perhaps being the most popular cutoff in substance-abusing populations. The third thinking style, entitlement, gives the individual permission to use drugs through an attitude of privilege, uniqueness, or necessity. The power orientation, on the other hand, betrays a person's efforts to maintain control over his or her environment and affective state through the use of mind-altering substances. Sentimentality affords the individual an opportunity to think well of him or herself through the performance of assorted good deeds, whereas super-optimism entails an overestimate of one's chances of avoiding the negative consequences of the drug lifestyle. Lazy, shortcut thinking is a hallmark sign of cognitive indolence, the seventh thinking style associated with lifestyle patterns of drug abuse, and lack of consistency suggests the presence of discontinuity. It is important to understand that many of these defensive thinking styles incorporate specific constructional errors, such as the minimization observed in mollification and the dichotomous reasoning that contributes to the development of discontinuity. This illustrates the overlap that exists between the constructive and defensive functions of free-floating ideation.

☑ ASSESSMENT   Psychological Inventory of Drug-Based Thinking Styles

Appendix 26A: Psychological Inventory of Drug-Based Thinking Styles (PIDTS) is an 80-item inventory that yields scores on two validity scales—confusion and defensiveness—and eight thinking style scales—mollification, cutoff, entitlement, power orientation, sentimentality, superoptimism, cognitive indolence, and discontinuity—each scale comprised of eight items. Respondents are instructed to circle the number that best represents their level of agreement with each of the 80 statements: "1" = disagree, "2" = uncertain, "3" = agree, "4" = strongly agree. Items are then summed by scale according to the scoring criteria outlined in Appendix 26B: PIDTS Scoring Key. All eight items on each of the thinking style scales are scored in the same direction: disagree is weighted 1, uncertain 2, agree 3, and strongly agree 4. Four of the eight items on each of the validity scales are scored in the same direction as the thinking style scales, but the other four items are scored in the reverse direction; i.e., disagree is weighted 4, uncertain 3, agree 2, and strongly agree 1. This is signified in Appendix 26B: PIDTS Scoring Key with a (+) sign after items that are scored in the standard direction and a (−) sign after items that are scored in the reverse direction. Once the raw scores have been calculated for each scale they should be converted into T-scores using the table found in Appendix 26C: T-Score Conversions for PIDTS Scales. These T-score conversions were derived from a sample of 125 Veterans Administration substance abuse outpatients, the characteristics of which are described in greater detail in Walters and Willoughby (1995). Test-retest and internal consistency coefficients for the 10 PIDTS scales are listed in Table 6-2.

In interpreting the results of the PIDTS, it is important to keep in mind that this instrument is designed to identify the unique pattern of thinking styles for individual substance abusers. Because many of the items assume past use and abuse of substances, it should not be administered to persons who have never misused drugs. Hence, the PIDTS is reserved for clients with a current or prior history of substance misuse. Scores that fall one or more standard deviations above the mean (i.e., T-scores of 60 or higher) are considered significant, as are scores that fall one or more standard deviations below the mean (i.e., T-scores of 40 or lower). After ruling out the possibility of reading difficulties, lack of cooperation, serious emotional disorders, exaggeration of problems (T-scores on Confusion >60), and extreme defensiveness (T-scores on Defensiveness >60), the therapist should identify the highest ranking thinking scale at or above a T-score of 60. This is normally considered the client's core thinking style. The second highest ranking thinking scale score at or above a T-score of 60 is also interpreted, as is the third highest score, provided it is at a T-score of at least 60 and is no more than 5 T-score points below the second highest scale. The two or three highest scales on a profile are believed to reflect the thinking styles a respondent habitually employs and should be considered cogent targets for intervention. Scales with T-scores of 40 or below may signal potential areas of strength that can be incorporated into a client's change plan, assuming his or her score on the defensiveness scale does not exceed a T-score of 55.

Table 6-2   Test-Retest Reliability and Cronbach's Alpha Coefficients for the Ten PIDTS Scales

Scale	Two-Week Test-Retest Reliability (N = 40)	Twelve-Week Test-Retest Reliability (N = 40)	Cronbach Alpha (N = 122)
Confusion (Cf)	.68	.74	.26
Defensiveness (Df)	.30	.48	.01
Mollification (Mo)	.72	.67	.66
Cutoff (Co)	.70	.75	.78
Entitlement (En)	.74	.58	.61
Power orientation (Po)	.67	.59	.73
Sentimentality (Sn)	.65	.34	.45
Superoptimism (So)	.59	.60	.72
Cognitive indolence (Ci)	.61	.66	.74
Discontinuity (Ds)	.70	.64	.77

Note. Test-retest reliability was measured using the Pearson Product Moment Correlation (*r*). These data were derived from a sample of 125 Veterans Administration substance abuse domiciliary inpatients.

☑ PLAN

For clients who exhibit a propensity to mollify their actions, intervention should focus on issues of personal responsibility and choice. Confronting common rationalizations for smoking with factual information about the health hazards of tobacco use has been found effective in reducing the smoking behavior of persons enrolled in smoking cessation classes (Reed & Janis, 1974). One of the problems with mollification, however, is that it generally interweaves truths, half-truths, and utter falsehoods into a single rationalization. It may be true that alcohol, a legal drug, is more physically harmful than an illicit substance such as marijuana or perhaps even heroin. However, to use this to justify the ingestion of marijuana or heroin is self-deceptive, not to mention self-destructive. Just because alcohol is potentially more damaging to a person's body than either marijuana or heroin does not mean that marijuana and heroin are innocuous substances. Clients who rely on mollification must come to realize that to use other people's mistakes or societal injustice as an excuse for their own wrongdoing is both irrational and self-defeating.

Persons who regularly enact the cutoff to defend their lifestyles may suffer from poor impulse control. Developing self-control and identifying ways in which to effectively manage uncomfortable feelings such as anger, depression, and boredom are consequently pivotal goals in helping these clients change. Training clients in basic stress management may be particularly efficacious in containing cutoff-related thoughts and impulses. The implosive nature of the cutoff can also be addressed through instruction in emotions management (Ross & Fabiano, 1985) and anger control (Novaco, 1975). The principal objective of such interventions is to teach clients to recognize the cues associated with loss of control and provide them with alternative coping strategies so that they are better able to manage their feelings and cope with frustrating circumstances without resorting to the use of drugs. Once the individual gets to the point of cutting off there is usually nothing that can be done to preclude one from using drugs. Consequently, interventions directed at the cutoff must be preventive in nature so that the client is in a position to manage the frustrations that often fuel implosive thinking before they have a chance to ignite the actual cutoff response.

The rational challenge may be the most effective change strategy for clients who exude an attitude of entitlement. Identifying and disputing beliefs the client has about privilege, ownership, uniqueness, and necessity would appear to be particularly efficacious with this type individual. In addition, it may be helpful to teach clients to distinguish between wants and needs. One way to implement such training is by having the client list all of his or her needs on a sheet of paper, after which the therapist reviews the list with the client in an effort to determine whether the items on the list are actually needs or simply wants masquerading as needs. A particularly virulent strain of entitlement is the use of one's "addiction" to justify continued use of chemical substances: i.e., the "I can't help myself" gambit. Therapists must see this thinking for what it is—helplessness in the service of the drug lifestyle—and seek to challenge it at every turn. This is also one of the reasons why lifestyle theory does not subscribe to the addiction model of substance misuse.

Drug abuse is one avenue open to people who feel thwarted in achieving power and control (Penk, Robinowitz, & Fudge, 1978). The control such individuals seek is nearly always external and therefore they often leave themselves vulnerable to zero-state feelings because full environmental control eludes all human beings. Intervention, consequently, needs to focus on developing self-control and encouraging a shift in attitude on the part of clients so that they begin to view self-discipline as a more realistic and satisfying goal than external power. People who continue to value external control over self-discipline are subjecting themselves to a steady stream of zero state-feelings. Because self-discipline takes time to develop, clinicians may want to supplement self-control training with a program of response prevention, although caution needs to be exercised in conducting such interventions. Response prevention involves provoking zero-state feelings in clients and then preventing them from power thrusting in a physically or verbally aggressive manner while simultaneously guiding them through the frustration with the aid of alternative coping strategies such as relaxation, imagery, and rational thinking.

Sentimentality may also respond to a rational intervention. It may be useful to have the client partition a piece of paper into two columns, listing in the left-hand column the positive behaviors he or she has enacted over the course of his or her drug lifestyle and in the right-hand column the negative behaviors resulting from his or her involvement in this lifestyle. The therapist can then use this to challenge the perception that the client was a "good person" while in the lifestyle because rarely do the items in the left-hand column compensate for the items in the right-hand column. An additional intervention for sentimentality is reviewing with clients the differences between sentimentality and true caring and concern. Thus, where sentimentality is a self-centered attempt to make oneself look good, true caring and concern is focused primarily outside oneself. A way of differentiating between the two is to understand that true caring and concern normally constitutes making sacrifices and giving up things that are truly meaningful to the person, something that cannot be said of the selfish maneuvers associated with sentimentality. Clinicians should address sentimentality but temper their interventions with the knowledge that sentimentality may be the client's only means of defense against feelings of guilt and self-loathing.

Clients who achieve elevated scores on the superoptimism scale frequently act as if they can escape the negative consequences of the drug lifestyle indefinitely. The fact that they are now in a hospital or jail cell, or attending an outpatient drug program should, in some way, challenges this belief, but if the individual's superoptimism is strong, such crises often have little impact on the person's thinking. Confronting the irrational assumptions that normally underpin a client's superoptimistic attitude is customarily required before the client can begin challenging the overall pattern of superoptimism observed in his or her thinking and behavior. In so doing, the client can be trained to anticipate the positive and negative consequences of his or her actions and learn to evaluate the likelihood of each consequence's occurrence. Expectancies and goals, as discussed in Chapter 5, figure prominently in such an approach. The feedback clients receive from persons who have experience in the drug lifestyle, but are further along in the treatment process, can also be helpful in dispelling many of the myths and misconceptions that contribute to superoptimism. This is why proponents of lifestyle theory recommend that the majority of interventions conducted with persons committed to the drug lifestyle take place in a group setting, preferably with clients who are at different stages in the change process.

Cognitive indolence interferes with vigilance, critical reasoning, and long-term planning. Lack of vigilance has been observed in treated heroin abusers who eventually relapse (Litman et al., 1983) and may explain the subpar performance of chronic marijuana users on various problem-solving measures (Yamaguchi & Kandel, 1984). Cognitive indolence opens the door to shortcuts, which invariably lead to failure. Interventions for persons earning elevated scores on the cognitive indolence scale include interpersonal problem-solving training and goal-setting, but should also address the client's critical reasoning skills (Ross & Fabiano, 1985). The first step in improving critical reasoning, according to Ross and Fabiano, is instruction in the mechanisms used by advertisers to persuade people to purchase specific products. After this, the client is taught to understand the schemes that draw people to certain products and arguments. Next, the client is briefed on strategies that might be used to identify inferences and assumptions, while learning to discriminate between facts and opinions. The fourth step of the procedure outlined by Ross and Fabiano is teaching clients how to be open-minded and avoid jumping to conclusions by carefully scrutinizing a problem, effectively organizing their analysis, and clearly communicating their results. The final step in the critical reasoning training procedure is learning how to argue persuasively by attending to the salient cues in a situation, anticipating alternative arguments, and developing the social skills necessary to construct a convincing argument.

The final thinking style, discontinuity, is probably the most difficult of the eight thinking styles to address therapeutically. In contrast to content-oriented thinking patterns such as mollification, sentimentality, and superoptimism, discontinuity is mediated by thought processes. Accordingly, the problem of discontinuity must be approached using highly structured procedures and techniques. Feedback from others, particularly those with experience in the lifestyle, is vital to the success of any intervention directed at discontinuity and illustrates once again the value of conducting programming in groups. Feedback can also be obtained through self-monitoring of thoughts. Having the client construct a diary of his or her thinking on specific issues and subjects supplies clinicians with a mechanism through which discontinuity and inconsistency of thought might be observed, scrutinized, and eventually ameliorated. Conversations structured around a concrete issue or theme, in which the therapist directs the client back to the issue at hand whenever he or she deviates from the theme, may also prove effective in working with such clients. Finally, the compartmentalization that often fosters discontinuity (dividing experiences into "me" and "not me," also known as the Jekyll and Hyde syndrome) can be rectified by encouraging the client to work toward incorporating these disparate experiences into a single concept.

AFFECT-ORIENTED INTERVENTION

It has been observed that depression and anxiety often improve following participation in a course of cognitive-behavioral intervention, purportedly because the client experiences increased self-confidence and greater success in interpersonal situations and relationships as a consequence of intervention (Kazdin, 1975). Such experiences may reduce negative affect by arousing a sense of mastery, empowerment, and self-efficacy. If cognitive-behavioral forms of intervention fail to assist a client in resolving certain affective difficulties, then these issues must be addressed directly. There is one emotional issue, however, that should be broached with clients regardless of the success of one's cognitive and behavioral interventions—the issue of existential fear. Existential fear is construed by lifestyle theory as the primary incentive for all behavior, including movement into the drug lifestyle. Lifestyle theory holds that regardless of whether we are cognizant of the fear, it has a major effect on our lives. The present discussion will concern itself with interventions conceived for the purpose of assisting clients in managing existential fear.

✔ SKILL   Confronting Existential Fear

As discussed in Chapter 2, the fear that gives rise to a person's retreat into the drug lifestyle is reflective of that person's existential condition, in particular the conflict that normally arises between the instinct to survive and the reality of a constantly changing environment. Existential fear is, in essence, a fear of change. Because existential fear is a dynamic process that is highly responsive to environmental contingencies, it is in a constant state of motion, change, and self-modification. The early and later life tasks described in Chapter 2 are believed to act as filters through which existential fear passes and becomes transformed. As the reader will recall, the social domain gives birth to the early life task of attachment and the later life task of social bonding or empathy. It makes sense, then, that problems affecting these particular life tasks will tend to steer the fear into intimacy-related concerns. The physical domain is composed of the early life task of stimulus modulation and the later life task of internal–external orientation. Existential fear that has been shaped by problems in the physical domain is believed to pattern itself around issues of control. Finally, concerns that arise out of the psychological domain life tasks of self-image and role identity cast existential fear in a light dominated by insecurity and self-doubt. Experiences and incidents occurring outside the framework of the early and later life tasks shape a person's experience of existential fear further; this, in turn, yields a truly unique expression of a client's existential condition.

✔ ASESSMENT   Fear Checklist

Appendix 27: Fear Checklist is administered to clients in an effort to ascertain the nature and character of their existential fear. The checklist is comprised of 18 items arranged in three columns. A confirmatory factor analysis conducted on the original 24-item version of this measure using a sample of 78 prison inmates enrolled in group or individual therapy revealed the presence of three underlying factors—bonding, orientation, and identity—but also demonstrated that an 18-item version of the checklist more closely fit the proposed model (with slight modifications made to two items). To complete the Fear Checklist, the client simply marks off the items that have been a source of personal concern for him or her, after which the total number of checks per column are recorded in the boxes provided at the bottom of the form. The bonding box, consequently, represents the number of attachment and social bonding–related fears acknowledged by the respondent (Items 1, 4, 7, 10, 13, and 16), whereas the orientation box shows the total number of fears experienced that touch on the early life task of stimulus modulation and the later life task of internal–external orientation (Items 2, 5, 8, 11, 14, and 17). The identity box, on the other hand, is a tabulation of fears that relate most closely to the self-image and role identity life tasks (Items 3, 6, 9, 12, 15, and 18). A comparison of the three scores affords the therapist a snapshot of the issues (intimacy, control, identity) that may have helped shape the client's personal experience of existential fear. Obtaining a complete picture of the fear, however, will require additional procedures.

One way in which client encounters with existential fear can be explored in greater detail than is possible through review of the Fear Checklist is with the construction of a Fear Portrait. All that is required for this exercise is a sheet of unlined paper and set of colored pens or pencils. The therapist then instructs the client to draw fear as he or she experiences it. A Fear Portrait not only furnishes the therapist with a glimpse of the client's personal encounter with existential fear, but also gives the client an opportunity to put his or her fears onto paper. This, in turn, allows the client some semblance of mastery over the previously debilitating fear. Some clients will refuse to participate in this exercise. The therapist should respect clients' concerns in this regard, but seek to make the task as nonthreatening as possible so as to encourage maximum participation. The therapist can point to research showing that art therapy has been found effective in the treatment of substance abuse (Moore, 1983) and that the present exercise is simply an extension of this often neglected approach to intervention. Treating the exercise as a break from the normal therapy routine may also enlist the cooperation of clients who may at first be hesitant. Lifestyle theory holds firmly to the belief that interpretation by the therapist should be kept to a minimum because "mind-reading" is one of the behaviors lifestyle theorists are encouraging clients to abandon. For this reason, therapists should, in the vast majority of cases, abstain from interpreting the drawings, but instead guide the client to his or her own interpretation of the meaning behind the portrait.

✔ PLAN

The Fear Checklist and Fear Portrait are designed to clarify the nature of a client's existential fear. Fear-based intervention will obviously need to be conducted on a case-by-case basis because existential fear is a unique expression of a person's life situation. This does not mean that certain general guidelines are unavailable, just that therapists should refrain from treating existential fear as if it were a recipe in a cookbook. One general guideline is that improving clients' adaptive abilities and skills will assist them in managing existential fear. Another way fear might be managed is through resolution of the early and later life tasks. Interventions aimed at key life tasks may prove fruitful, although lifestyle theory maintains that the outcomes of the three early life tasks are largely unmodifiable after age four or five. The later life tasks, on the other hand, are never fully resolved, and as such, their outcomes are regularly altered by various internal and external influences. This also makes the later life tasks amenable to intervention. Therapies aimed at existential fear should therefore concentrate on issues relevant to the negotiation of the later life tasks of social bonding, internal–external orientation, and role identity and the fears of intimacy, control, and identity to which they give rise.

To address the fear of intimacy that evolves from interactions in the social domain of human experience, therapists must direct their attention to the social bonding and empathy processes. The development of social skills and instruction in how to empathize with others are consequently vital in working with clients who display existential fear that has been shaped by intimacy concerns. The ultimate issue in managing intimacy-related concerns, however, is learning how to discriminate between positive risk taking and negative risk taking. Undertaking negative long-term consequences for the opportunity to experience short-term pleasure is commonly referred to as negative risk taking, of which drug use is a prime example. This form of risk taking obviously needs to be reduced if one is to abandon the drug lifestyle. Risking short-term discomforts, such as boredom and rejection, for the opportunity to experience long-term positive outcomes is known as positive risk taking. Lifestyle theory contends that this form of risk taking will help the individual find the path less traveled. Clients struggling with intimacy-related existential fear should be encouraged to examine the individual advantages and disadvantages of positive and negative risk taking, with the understanding that intimacy is available only to those willing to risk the possibility of short-term rejection. Reframing the prospect of rejection as a necessary step in achieving intimacy and supplying clients with strategies designed to reduce and manage social anxiety may be particularly helpful with these clients.

Existential fear that has filtered through issues that touch on the stimulus modulation and internal–external orientation life tasks finds its expression in fears that center around control. The issue of control is of prime significance to people who abuse alcohol and other mind-altering substances. This is because drugs provide such individuals with an avenue through which they might control others as well as manipulate their own physiology. One possible explanation for the continued use of drugs long after it stops being pleasurable is that drug effects are reasonably predictable and, as such, promote a sense of control over one's physical being. Along these lines, it has been reported that many persons who misuse substances are externally, rather than internally, oriented (Wexler, 1975). For clients whose perception of existential fear has been colored by issues of control, intervention should focus on the development of internalization skills and increased interest in self-discipline as a substitute for the individual's prior preoccupation with external forms of power and control. The therapist might also want to share with clients the observation that external control is conceptualized by lifestyle theory as an illusion, because it will eventually elude the grasp of even the strongest and most powerful of individuals. Internal control or self-discipline, on the other hand, is always within the person's exclusive province to achieve.

Clients who struggle with the self-image and role identity life tasks frequently display uncertainty about identity issues, their ability to succeed, and their courage in the face of adversity. These individuals' existential fear may also be prompted by such varied concerns as fear of failure, fear of success, and fear of insignificance. It should be kept in mind, then, that the drug lifestyle furnishes a person with a sense of identity, even if the identity is invariably negative. By intervening through the role identity later life task the therapist can assist the client in constructing a new identity, one that will afford him or her a broader sense of self-efficacy and purpose without leading to the self-destructive consequences of the drug lifestyle. Kelly's (1955) fixed role therapy and other role-playing techniques may be helpful in confronting the fear of insignificance that plagues these individuals. Assisting clients with the acquisition of self-acceptance through inculcation of new skills and interests and the rejection of labels such as "alcoholic," "drug addict," and "dope fiend" may go a long way toward allaying identity-based existential fear. The topic of identity transformation is so fundamental to the prevention of relapse that it will be discussed in greater detail in Chapter 7. It is important for the reader to understand that fear is often concealed by other emotions (e.g., anger, depression). The clinician must therefore avoid being sidetracked by these "surface" emotions and look to the fear that lies underneath.

CONCLUSION

The lifestyle model considers adaptation to be the most effective and reliable avenue of fear management. Whereas the majority of adaptations performed by lower animals are of the physical (e.g., hair growth to protect against the cold) and behavioral (e.g., hibernation) variety, adaptation in humans is predominately psychological. One way to conceive of adaptation in human organisms is as a mental process. Accordingly, cognition is as pertinent to the development of a person's repertoire of adaptive skills as it is to the formation of the drug lifestyle. Thinking guides both methods of fear management. However, the cognitions that support adaptation and the cognitions that support lifestyle recitation differ in their content as well as in their ultimate objectives. For this reason, therapists must do more than offer challenge to the cognitions that support the drug lifestyle; they must also help clients develop a thinking style that promotes, rather than inhibits, adaptive living. Meichenbaum's (1974) self-instructional training may be helpful in this regard. This procedure has been found effective with several different problems and follows a structured, easy-to-follow format that can be readily adapted to substance-abusing populations: (a) Instruct and supervise the client in the construction of coping self-statements; (b) have the client cognitively rehearse behaviors and coping self-statements; (c) actively guide the client through the performance of the behavior in a real-life situation, with simultaneous verbalization of coping self-statements; and (d) teach the client how to establish a program of self-reinforcement. As new self-statements begin to surface, they come to replace the thinking that once succored the drug lifestyle. The construction of a new cognitive system is consequently critical in establishing a climate conducive to change in persons previously committed to the drug lifestyle.

Although cognition plays a pivotal role in substance abuse treatment, there is evidence to suggest that cognition alone may be insufficient to elicit change in most situations. Wilson (1987) states that in the treatment of chronic alcohol abuse, performance-based cognitive-behavioral interventions are often superior to cognitive therapies that rely solely on imagery-based processes and verbal persuasion. These findings insinuate that cognitive intervention should incorporate specific behavioral strategies for maximum clinical effectiveness. Behavioral rehearsal, guided practice, and generalization exercises in which the client enacts cognitively rehearsed behaviors in real-life situations may therefore augment the therapeutic value of cognitive change strategies. Lifestyle theory goes a step further by insisting that pertinent affective issues, existential fear in particular, be considered in conjunction with cognitive and behavioral interventions. Oftentimes, addressing affect, thought, and behavior is said to be necessary in a comprehensive program of intervention; however, therapists are left to their own devices as to how to go about constructing and implementing such a program. By construing intervention as a finite number of general skills organized around five major themes (arresting the lifestyle, conditional vehicles, choice vehicles, cognitive vehicles, resocialization), lifestyle theory seeks to provide clinicians with a format useful in linking various cognitive, behavioral, and affective goals for change. The skills that a client might use in forging a commitment to a new lifestyle will be the principal topic of discussion in the chapter that follows.

Chapter 7

Resocialization and Effective Aftercare

To this point, discussion has focused on the first two goals of lifestyle intervention, i.e., arresting the lifestyle and acquiring skills for the prevention of relapse, in ameliorating the drug lifestyle. In this chapter, however, the attention turns to the third goal of lifestyle intervention: providing effective aftercare, a goal that brings with it the prospect of resocialization. Within the framework of lifestyle theory, the drug lifestyle is believed to be the product of socialization. As the reader may recall, socialization is the process by which a person learns and adopts the actions, attitudes, and norms of a larger social group. Although socialization is ordinarily discussed with reference to a person's indoctrination into conventional society, it is proposed that societally defined deviant behavior is also acquired through socialization. Consequently, lifestyle theorists advocate resocialization as a major objective of aftercare and follow-up programs designed to facilitate a client's escape from the journey that leads nowhere. It is worth noting that resocialization does not constitute conformity to the prevailing social order, which itself may be dysfunctional. Rather, therapists should seek to support their clients' efforts to identify and pursue a life path that supplies them with maximum personal satisfaction through coordination of short- and long-range goals and a consideration of the probable short- and long-term consequences of their actions.

Hirschi (1969), in an effort to clarify the socialization process believed to be responsible for preventing serious delinquency and drug abuse, established involvement, commitment, attachment, and belief as key elements of indoctrination into the conventional social order. In Hirschi's model, involvement entails regular participation in conventional activities; commitment presupposes investment in conformity and the pursuit of conventional goals; attachment embodies the connective bond that forms between the individual and various agents of social control (e.g., parents, school authorities); and belief signifies confidence in the moral validity of societal rules. The lifestyle model retains Hirschi's emphasis on involvement, expands the commitment category, and adds a third category, identification, in its theory of socialization. It is argued that involvement in lifestyle-congruent activities, commitment to lifestyle goals and objectives, and identification with the lifestyle ideal are necessary and sufficient conditions for socialization into that lifestyle. Hirschi was primarily interested in how people came to internalize the norms and values of conventional society and conceived of delinquency and drug abuse as products of poor socialization. Lifestyle theory, on the other hand, contends that acquisition of a drug or criminal lifestyle is the product of socialization to deviant forms of behavior. Hence, socialization to deviant definitions of drug use and failed socialization to conventional definitions of drug use are seen as equally important in the formation of the drug lifestyle.

The drug lifestyle affords its adherents several advantages: (a) It helps structure the affiliated individual's time; (b) it establishes goals for the individual to pursue and work toward; and (c) it supplies the individual with a sense of identity, specifically who he or she is and how he or she fits into the wider social world. As such, the drug lifestyle is characterized by preoccupation with drug use activities (involvement), pursuit of drug-related objectives (commitment), and construction of a drug-centered self-image (identity). Resocialization requires that these three elements be used to effect the person's escape from the drug lifestyle. So that resocialization might assist in identifying the path less traveled, involvement in non-drug activities, commitment to goals incompatible with drug abuse, and identification with something other than the drug ideal are required. Success in resisting future drug use opportunities dictates that the lifestyle be challenged and replaced by socialization to a new way of life. Consequently, the client should be encouraged to move in a direction antithetical to the drug lifestyle and seek to design more constructive self- and world-views. This chapter will address the three core elements of socialization—involvement, commitment, and identification—in an effort to describe precisely how a person might resocialize him- or herself into accepting a life path that furnishes the opportunity to experience an equitable balance between short-term gratification and long-term satisfaction, exploring various avenues through which clients might initiate and foster their involvement in non-drug activities and behaviors.

INVOLVEMENT

The drug lifestyle is defined, in part, by a person's preoccupation with drugs and involvement in drug-related activities. Relationships, activities, and thoughts become increasingly centered on drugs as a person progresses from a pre-, to an early, to an advanced stage of drug lifestyle involvement. If we agree that the number of hours per day remains constant, then it follows that the more time a person spends in drug-related activities, the less time he or she will have to engage in other pursuits (and vice versa). As the drug lifestyle grows, it demands increasingly greater amounts of time and energy, to the point where the individual has little time for anything else. Eventually, he or she will lose either interest or skill in many non-drug behaviors. Daryl Poynter, the character portrayed by Michael Keaton in the movie *Clean and Sober,* encountered just such a dilemma. Upon being released from a drug treatment center, Daryl was left to sit on his couch and pace the floor of his kitchen because his normal routine had been disrupted; in other words, he no longer had drugs to structure his time. Clients must learn to fill their free time with productive activity or risk returning to the drug lifestyle out of boredom or habit. The major goal of intervention, therefore, is to encourage clients to shift their involvement from drug-related activities to behaviors incompatible with the drug lifestyle. One way in which this goal might be achieved is through the development of substitute activities.

☑ SKILL   Substitution

Clients who report having abandoned an alcohol-based lifestyle without treatment frequently attribute their success to the availability and reinforcing value of substitute activities (Ludwig, 1985; Tuchfeld, 1981). Investigating spontaneous remission from alcohol, tobacco, and opiate abuse, Stall and Biernacki (1986) ascertained that substitute activities such as jogging, meditation, and immersion in work led to decreased use of drugs, presumably by encouraging the client to find purpose in his or her life. A major consideration in determining whether a substitute activity will assist in reducing drug lifestyle involvement is the degree to which the activity promotes goals and objectives incompatible with the drug lifestyle. Vaillant and Milofsky (1982) noted that nearly half their sample of "successfully recovered" problem drinkers reportedly engaged in substitute activities, some more positive (e.g., regular attendance at AA meetings, prayer, or meditation) than others (e.g., compulsive eating, use of an alternate substance such as tobacco, marijuana, or tranquilizers). The success of substitution depends on the nature of the activities engaged in and their potential for encouraging or discouraging the resurfacing of old lifestyle patterns.

☑ ASSESSMENT   What Will Be Missed from the Drug Lifestyle

Having clients assemble a list of the feelings, activities, relationships, and other aspects of the drug lifestyle they found most rewarding can serve as the initial step in devising a program of intervention around the issue of substitution. When administering this exercise it is critical that clients specify what it is they believe will be missed from not participating in drug use activities. Common themes expressed during this exercise include the loss of drug-based relationships, disengagement from the drug scene, sacrificing the pleasure that drugs provide, and foregoing drug use as one's primary means of coping with the problems of everyday living. These perceptions of loss generally reflect certain basic emotions, desires, and needs the individual feels incapable of achieving without drugs. Such issues as power and control, instant versus delayed gratification, acceptance, and identity are also frequently expressed during this exercise. Consequently, this list may prove invaluable during the early stages of resocialization because of its ability to encourage the initiation, implementation, and pursuit of substitute activities.

☑ PLAN

Substitution follows a basic three-step procedure. The first step is to assess the needs and desires being satisfied by the drug lifestyle. This can be accomplished by reviewing the results of the "What Will Be Missed from the Drug Lifestyle" exercise described earlier (see Appendix 28). The second step in the substitution process is to assist clients in identifying substitute activities that fulfill the needs and desires previously satisfied by the drug lifestyle. The degree to which these alternative activities are productive is a general estimate of their ability to promote long-term change and steer the individual away from future drug use opportunities. The third step in the substitution process is implementing these alternative strategies, even if they appear to make the client uncomfortable at first. What the client needs to realize is that change rarely feels comfortable and because drug lifestyle activities have become habitual, breaking the habit is no small task. It has been estimated that it takes several months of repeated performance of an unfamiliar behavior before the behavior starts feeling "comfortable" (Marlatt & George, 1984). Accordingly, if the client should slip and return to old drug use patterns within several months, he or she may need to return to Step 1 and repeat the entire sequence. This does not mean that the individual will be problem-free after several months, just that the new behavior will feel more comfortable or natural after several months of repeated performance.

In embracing activities that are constructive, harmless, or less harmful than drug abuse, the person is demonstrating a learned process. Through observation and repeated performance of these behaviors the client may eventually find the substitute activities sufficiently reinforcing to continue engaging in them. Unfortunately, there are few non-drug lifestyle behaviors as immediately gratifying as drug use. By the same token, there are few non-drug lifestyle activities as distally destructive or damaging as those that follow the use of drugs. It would seem imperative, then, that the individual learn to balance short- and long-term expectancies (as described in Chapter 5) as a way of achieving an optimal level of personal fulfillment. The trade-off in abandoning the drug lifestyle is reduced immediate gratification in exchange for greater long-term satisfaction and fewer long-range negative consequences. Cognitive reframing can also be incorporated into the substitution process by emphasizing to clients that they are not so much losing an "old friend" (drug lifestyle) as gaining a "new ally" (path less traveled) capable of supplying them with greater long-term satisfaction, fulfillment, and success. Involvements must shift from drug-related preoccupations to the regular performance of activities incompatible with the drug lifestyle if the individual is to have any chance of abandoning the lifestyle. However, commitment must also change.

COMMITMENT

A robust relationship is believed to exist between involvement and commitment. Accelerated involvement may encourage increased commitment, and a rise in commitment may spur increased involvement. The bidirectional relationship that exists between these two elements of socialization can be used to promote effective follow-up and aftercare. In appreciating the value of this relationship it is important to keep in mind that performance of an action, even without initial commitment, may result in behavioral change through creation of a cognitively dissonant mental set. As such, the client should be advised to enact alternative behaviors even if these behaviors feel uncomfortable at first, with the understanding that this feeling will eventually be replaced by the reassurance that comes with repetition and familiarity. Once the behavior is comfortable, familiar, and regular, the natural tendency is to reinterpret one's commitment to that behavior in an effort to achieve greater cognitive-behavioral consonance. This could eventually foster a growing commitment to the behavior, which, in turn, might serve to encourage further involvement in the activity and stimulate the natural process of social reinforcement that occurs with repeated performance of a particular response. The crossover between involvement and commitment may, in fact, explain the appearance of a self-perpetuating system of rewards that accrue as the person becomes less involved with drugs and more involved with activities incompatible with the drug lifestyle.

The attachment, belief, and commitment that comprise Hirschi's (1969) social control theory of delinquency and drug abuse, all relate, as does identity, to the commitment process hypothesized to subserve socialization into a lifestyle. It is hypothesized that an emotional bond must form between the individual and relevant agents of social influence, even if this is nothing more than a mutual dislike for conventional society, for socialization to take root. As such, attachment is a necessary precondition for commitment to a particular life path. Belief in the validity of the socialization agents' position or ideas is also instrumental in the formation of an abiding commitment to a lifestyle, conventional or otherwise. Hirschi's notion of commitment—namely, working toward goals and objectives defined by the socializing agent—is a third element that contributes to a growing commitment to a drug or other lifestyle. Finally, a person's identity plays a key role in the development of commitment. It is assumed that people only accept, and ultimately commit to, information congruent with their self-view. If an experience is incongruent with a person's self-view then the individual will either distort the experience to make it more compatible with his or her self-view or modify the self-view to make it more compatible with the experience. These four factors eventually merge to form a sense of commitment to the rules, roles, relationships, and rituals proposed by the socializing agent.

☑ SKILL   Forming Commitments Incompatible with the Drug Lifestyle

Forming commitments to people and activities incompatible with the drug lifestyle is essential for continued desistance from old drug use patterns. Reinforcement of non-drug behavior and constructive social support networks are consequently critical for drug-free living. Social support is one of the more effective avenues of abstinence promotion and relapse prevention, according to the results of studies conducted on people who have exited an alcohol- (Booth et al., 1992), cocaine- (Higgins, Budney, Bickel, & Badger, 1994), or tobacco- (Gruder et al., 1993) based lifestyle. Of male veterans released from an inpatient treatment program, those who demonstrated commitment to aftercare by attending weekly follow-up sessions were three times more likely to be abstinent nine months later than patients who dropped out of aftercare (Walker, Donovan, Kivlahan, & O'Leary, 1983). Likewise, the degree to which a group of clients perceived support from their AA sponsors was found to correspond with completion of aftercare substance abuse programming (Huselid, Self, & Gutierres, 1991). Although these findings are correlational in nature and subject to multiple interpretations, they nonetheless suggest that social support may aid in the formation and maintenance of a commitment to non-drug living.

☑ ASSESSMENT   Schedule of Family and Community Support

Appendix 29: Schedule of Family and Community Support is designed to identify areas of social support available to clients. In addition to the social support clients might reasonably anticipate from family, extended family, and friends, clients also must list local sources of community support, ranging from alcohol and drug counseling to welfare assistance. The therapist should ensure that clients complete all sections of this survey, even though some respondents may tend to perceive certain areas as irrelevant to their current or projected life circumstances. It is essential that the therapist understand the primary purpose of this schedule; namely, to stimulate the client's thinking on personal sources of family and community support and, if such support is lacking, motivate the client to explore and identify alternative networks of social subsistence available in the community. Information provided could be critical in the planning of effective aftercare programming and follow-up services.

☑ PLAN

The first step in forming a commitment to a non-drug life pattern is to identify potential areas of social support, perhaps with the aid of the Schedule of Family and Community Support. From here the therapist can implement the community reinforcement approach (CRA) proposed by Sisson and Azrin (1989) in which natural sources of reward for non-drug living are identified, expanded, and reinforced. CRA interventions, which are conducted either individually or in small groups, address four basic issues. First, clients are taught to negotiate with others for positive change in sessions attended by one or more family members or close friends. Second, clients learn to identify, avoid, and manage high-risk situations (people, places, and things associated with past drug use) with and without the help of their support network. Third, employment and vocational training are furnished to unemployed clients. Fourth, clients are encouraged to develop hobbies, recreational interests, and social relationships incompatible with the drug lifestyle. According to lifestyle theory, before the CRA or any other program can instill commitment to a non-drug life pattern, clients must acquire self-respect, whereby they come to believe that they deserve more out of life than the drug lifestyle and that they are reasonably capable of attaining this new life.

Contingency management is another therapeutic technique relevant to the formation of commitment to a non-drug lifestyle. Bigelow, Stitzer, Griffiths, and Liebson (1981) have established certain guidelines in this regard by describing how a therapist and client might collaborate in constructing a relapse prevention contract. In a cooperative effort to devise a plan of action, the therapist and client outline the steps to be taken if a slip or lapse occurs (e.g., punishment). However, punishment is not the sole consequence covered by the contract. Reinforcement of positive behaviors and corrective steps to be taken in the event of a lapse or relapse are both discussed in the body of the contingency management contract. Hence, the client may agree to participate in or do something he or she may not believe in or want to do, such as buy lunch for someone he or she dislikes (punishment) or attend additional therapy sessions (correction) should he or she lapse or relapse, and reward him or herself with a vacation should he or she remain drug-free for 6 months. The consequences should be graded from short- to long-term so that the client can work for both proximal and distal rewards, while learning to avoid the short-and long-term negative consequences of drug use. Budney et al. (1991) successfully implemented contingency management procedures as part of an outpatient follow-up conducted with a group of cocaine abusers subsequent to their release from an inpatient substance abuse treatment program.

Commitment is an internalized process that clearly responds to external influences. One such influence is the behavior of the therapist. Woody and his colleagues at the Veterans Administration Medical Center in Philadelphia determined that therapists achieved varying degrees of success with methadone-maintained opiate abusers, based on the quality of the therapist–client relationship (Woody, McLellan, Luborsky, & O'Brien, 1990). However, the therapist effect was stronger for supportive-expressive counseling than for a cognitive-behavioral technique. Although the small sample size precludes drawing definitive conclusions on the relationship between outcome and process, it may be that the quality of the therapeutic relationship has a more direct bearing on the results obtained with unstructured, as opposed to structured, interventions. The fact that more structured procedures, such as the cognitive-behavioral approach, may be less influenced by the nature of the therapeutic relationship should in no way be interpreted as meaning that the therapeutic relationship is unimportant in cognitive-behavioral therapy or that direct confrontation is the optimal approach to use in intervening with clients. Miller, Benefield, and Tonigan (1993), in fact, report that confrontation may be counterproductive when intervening with alcohol-abusing clients. This implies that in creating an atmosphere conducive to change the therapist should eschew head-on disputes, incredulity, direct challenges, and sarcasm. A good rule of thumb in working with such clients may be to confront lifestyle thinking and behavior, but avoid attacking the client directly; keeping in mind that initially the client will tend to identify with the thinking and behavior of the drug lifestyle.

IDENTIFICATION

Rather than adopting a personified view of identity, as have Gordon Allport (1961), Carl Jung (1961), and Carl Rogers (1959), lifestyle theory considers the self a perceptual process capable of organizing behavior and governing one's interpretation of internal events and environmental situations. Lifestyle theory speculates that a sense of self or identity derives from an interactive relationship that forms between the individual and his or her surroundings. As such, identity is prominently influenced by social roles and relationships (Mead, 1934), which, in turn, are swayed by the person's evolving sense of self. For this reason, involvement in drug use and commitment to drug-related goals may be both a cause and effect of a drug-based self-view. Because a negative identity (e.g., drug addict, criminal) is preferable to no identity at all, some people choose to enact involvements and commitments that fulfill a deviant self-image. Involvement, commitment, and identification may be instrumental in the evolution of the drug lifestyle precisely because they are effective in managing existential fear. Involvement reduces existential fear by assisting the individual in structuring his or her time, commitment eases the fear by furnishing goals to pursue, and identification attenuates the fear by giving the individual a sense of self. A brief discussion of the primary components and functions of the self-system should help clarify the role of identity in the formation of the drug lifestyle.

The elements of identity reveal the structure of the self. Schemas, the cognitive representations of reality that are coded into memory and that mediate a person's interpretation of future events, are the building blocks of the self-system. Borrowing from the work of Kelly (1955), lifestyle theory asserts that schemas are organized into bipolar categories (e.g., good–bad, weak–strong, intelligent–unintelligent). This breakdown into bipolar categories would appear to be in harmony with the nature of human cognition, because research shows that children normally learn by forming basic-level categories that are then assimilated into superordinate groupings of increasing complexity (Roberts & Cuff, 1989). It is speculated that there may even be something universal about bipolar categories in the sense that the fundamental unit of the central nervous system, the neuron, operates on a simple bipolar principle (fire–don't fire) to produce complex behavior. As with neural networks, schematic networks become increasingly more intricate over time. The differentiation of a simple bipolar concept (strong–weak) is portrayed in Figure 7-1. As this diagram illustrates, the concept of strong–weak may be differentiated into physical versus emotional strength as the child matures. At even higher levels of cognitive complexity the individual may subdivide physical strength into brawn versus stamina and emotional strength into self-control versus endurance. By integrating and synthesizing

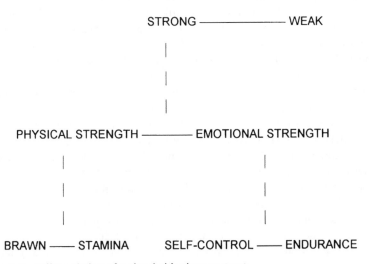

Figure 7-1 Differentiation of a simple bipolar construct.

these constructs the person is in a position to better comprehend the world, manage the environment, and predict future problems and events, all of which serve to support survival.

Perhaps the most important and interesting schemas are those that represent the self. Beyond self-description, self-schemas furnish the individual with rules and procedures for development of the self-system (Pratkanis & Greenwald, 1985). One of these rules is that self-schemas are heavily influenced by a person's interactions with others (Horowitz, 1989). Therefore, social relations, roles, and interpersonal expectations influence the formation of self-schema and account for individual and group differences in the content of these self-representations. The self-image and role identity life tasks described in Chapter 2 undoubtedly contribute to the development of the self-system, as do expectancies, values, attributions, and specific behaviors. A multitude of possible selves also work their way into a person's self-system. These possible selves—the ideal self, powerful self, glorified self, undesired self, and not-me self, to name just a few—serve as incentives for future behavior and the formation of specific life goals (Markus & Nurius, 1986). Possible selves not only motivate the individual to pursue certain goals, but also help the self-system process information. Hewitt and Genest (1990) report that an ideal self can function as a schema for coding and retrieving verbal information, whereas Deutsch, Kroll, Weible, Letourneau, and Goss (1988) note that ideal traits may play as important a role in the operation of the self-system as self-descriptive traits. The results of these two studies insinuate that possible selves may have as much impact on behavior as do self-appraisals formed from current experience.

According to lifestyle theory, identity serves four basic functions: self-monitoring, self-organization, self-reference, and self-verification. The self-monitoring function reflects a person's willingness to examine information that is incongruent with his or her current self-view. This function gives rise to a working self-concept in which the self is found to be in dynamic interaction with the surrounding environment and subject to continually shifting emphases and priorities (Markus & Wurf, 1987). The second major function of identity, self-organization, facilitates growth of the self-system by enhancing the cognitive complexity and integration of self-schema. In a literature review of the third identity factor, self-reference, Higgins and Bargh (1987) ascertained that processing information in relation to the self may lead to deeper symbolization, patterning, and storage of information than if the self is not referenced, because the self-system is more elaborately defined and data within it more precisely encoded than non-self mental representations. The search for information consistent with one's world-view, also known as self-verification, contributes to selective attention and biased interpretations of new information. Research suggests that people pay more attention to, and are more accepting of, feedback that is compatible with their self-conceptions and general world-view (Swann & Read, 1981) and that people with negative self-views are more apt to seek unfavorable evaluations

(Swann, Hixon, Stein-Seroussi, & Gilbert, 1990) and interact with partners who provide them with negative feedback (Swann, Pelham, & Krull, 1989) than are persons who hold positive self-views.

☑ SKILL Identity Transformation

The self-labeling displayed by persons involved in the drug lifestyle must be challenged and rectified if these individuals are to feel sufficiently empowered to abandon the drug lifestyle. Labeling oneself an "alcoholic," "addict," or "dope fiend" only reinforces the negative self-view and low self-efficacy that fuel chronic substance misuse. Encouraging clients to explore their identities with an eye toward helping them form a more positive self-view would seem a viable way of buttressing their ability to avoid future drug use opportunities. According to lifestyle theory, the identity transformation process is twofold: First, clients must challenge the restrictions they have placed on their behavior in identifying with the drug lifestyle. Second, clients must expand their base of operations by incorporating new experiences and activities into their self-view. This denotes that the identity transformation process requires both the rejection of old drug-centered patterns and the development of a new, more inclusive self-definition. However, abandonment of the drug lifestyle can be anxiety provoking, in part because the individual is left without a clear sense of identity. The therapist must consequently assist the client in identifying attributes, experiences, and behaviors that can be incorporated into a self-view that is incompatible with the misuse of substances. Much like the mutual interaction that develops between involvement and commitment, identity is a function of a person's involvements and commitments but also influences the behaviors the person enacts and the goals he or she pursues.

☑ ASSESSMENT Bipolar Identity Survey

By way of review, lifestyle theory postulates that schemas and self-schemas have their foundation in simple bipolar categories. This implies that people learn to construe the world by contrasting bipolar opposites. However, as the cognitive system matures these bipolar categories become increasingly more complex, integrated, and mutually dependent. In Appendix 30: Bipolar Identity Survey, the client is asked to list positive and negative behaviors, parental messages, stories, movies, accomplishments, traits, physical characteristics, and nicknames from the past. The contrast supplied by these positive and negative attributes is designed to clarify the structural parameters of the client's self-system. Given the wide range of responses one is likely to encounter on this instrument, only general interpretive guidelines can be offered. The therapist should concentrate on (a) cataloging the behaviors and characteristics clients associate with themselves, (b) assisting clients in forming an understanding of their general self-view, (c) determining the level of complexity displayed by the individual components of the self-system, and (d) evaluating the degree of schematic fractionalization versus integration present in the system. Because of the personal nature of some of the questions, it is probably best if the results of the Bipolar Identity Survey are discussed in individual sessions or small groups of clients who are reasonably familiar with one another.

☑ PLAN

Identity transformation is a major goal of lifestyle intervention. The therapist might initiate this process by encouraging the client to adopt new behaviors, values, and expectancies that contribute to the construction of new self-schema. However, integration of these self-schema may require additional work. For this reason, cognitive complexity is given high priority in therapeutic interventions. Research indicates that cognitive complexity may shield people from experiencing the debilitating effects of stress (Linville, 1987), depression (Dance & Kuiper, 1987), and frustration (Dixon & Baumeister, 1991). A developmental phenomenon, cognitive complexity evolves with age (Bigner, 1974). Nevertheless, it is possible to promote cognitive complexity by engaging clients in a Socratic dialogue (Frankl, 1984) or strengthening their cognitive restructuring skills (Ellis, 1970). Interjecting information incongruent with a client's current self-view in an effort to create cognitive dissonance has also been found effective in modifying attitudes and values (Rokeach, 1983), and may achieve its effect by enhancing cognitive complexity. Once a client's conceptual abilities have been expanded, the natural inclination to self-verify (Swann, 1983) reinforces and solidifies these patterns. It should be noted that there is nothing inherently good or bad about self-verification. If the person is verifying a negative identity, then self-verification will be negative; if, on the other hand, the individual is verifying a positive identity, then self-verification tends to be positive.

Fragmentation of the self-system occurs when the situational specificity of the self-monitoring function predominates over the integrative functions of self-organization, self-referencing, and self-verification. Sensitivity to information incompatible with one's current self-view is mandatory for good mental health, but so is an organized, congruent self-system. Otherwise, a seriously fragmented identity, whereby the individual holds incompatible and conflicting views of him- or herself, will occur; a situation ripe for the development of discontinuity (Jekyll and Hyde syndrome). The integration and synthesis of disparate self-schema into an organized self-system is a long and arduous task, yet one that is essential for the psychological adjustment of the human organism. Skafte (1987) noted that "experiencing oneself as part of the social matrix returns the self, in a sense, to its original birthplace, and bestows a feeling of being larger and more complete" (p. 399). Skafte advocates the use of videotape replays of prior group interactions to propel the group into becoming an object unto itself, thereby accelerating the process of unification for both the group and individual group members. This technique has notable limitations, but if incorporated into a larger program of self-exploration it may be of some value in promoting the conditions necessary for effective integration of a fragmented sense of personal identity.

The vehicles that might be used to effect one's escape from the drug lifestyle via the identity transformation process vary widely, but group and family approaches are two of the more powerful interventions. Eradication of socialization patterns that support the drug lifestyle demands acquisition of new skills and relationships, both of which can be accessed through group and family therapy. A recent investigation into self-concept change provides additional support for this hypothesis. In this study, Tice (1992) surmises that behaviors performed publicly exert a more profound effect on self-concept than the same behaviors performed privately, despite the fact that subjects in the public situation had no contact with their audience. This insinuates that the internalization process believed to precede a change in identity may be strengthened by the belief that one is making a public commitment to change. It is noteworthy that in this study high self-monitoring subjects and persons who anticipated future interaction with their audience were better able to internalize a public behavior than low self-monitoring subjects and persons who believed that they would have no further contact with their audience. In group therapy clients are asked to make a commitment in front of peers, some of whom they may have dealings with outside of therapy. In family therapy the client is contemplating changes that will be witnessed by other family members. In either case, the public nature of the client's actions and assertions holds greater promise of internalization and potential change than commitments made alone or in front of a therapist with whom the client may have only limited future contact.

CONCLUSION

A great deal has been written about drug abuse as a variant of obsessive–compulsive disorder. That habitual drug use exhibits characteristics of an obsessive–compulsive nature is fairly obvious from even causal observation. However, this does not necessarily place habitual drug use on the so-called obsessive–compulsive spectrum. Selective serotonin reuptake inhibitors (SSRIs) such as fluoxetine (Prozac), fluvoxamine (Luvox), and clomipramine (Anafranil)[1] have been found effective in the treatment of obsessive–compulsive disorder, presumably because of the role serotonin, a neurotransmitter substance, plays in the genesis of this disorder (Hollander, 1991). However, a double-blind investigation on fluoxetine in the treatment of cocaine abuse failed to reveal any fluoxetine-placebo outcome differences (Grabowski et al., 1995). Lifestyle theory speculates that the obsessive–compulsive nature of the drug lifestyle may be attributable to the

---

[1]Clomipramine (Anafranil) is chemically classified as a tricyclic antidepressant but is frequently grouped with the SSRIs because of its powerful serotonin reuptake inhibiting properties.

interaction of involvement, commitment, and identification in a lifestyle that is organized around short-term expectancies and goals. As people become more preoccupied with drugs through increased involvement, begin to arrange their goals and priorities around drug-related activities, and achieve a sense of identity from their use of substances, it is anticipated that they will display an obsessive–compulsive-like drive to engage in this behavior, particularly if this behavior provides them with short-term gratification that dissipates rapidly. Hence, substance abuse may acquire its obsessive–compulsive-like properties, not from its position on the obsessive–compulsive spectrum, but from its ability to stimulate patterns of involvement, commitment, and identity that take on an obsessive–compulsive quality.

Before concluding this chapter, it seems appropriate to consider the interactive nexus that apparently links involvement, commitment, and identity in the socialization of the drug lifestyle. These three elements of socialization are also highly interdependent when it comes to constructing a reinforcing non-drug lifestyle. As non-drug involvements, commitments, and identifications intensify, clients will be in a better position to avoid future substance abuse opportunities. Another noteworthy consideration is that each element benefits from a strengthening of the other two elements. Hence, if identity is a major stumbling block for a particular client, but commitment and involvement are more readily accessible, then the therapist would be well advised to emphasize commitment and involvement early on. This will oftentimes lead to initial changes in identity that can then be used to foster subsequent expansion of both the involvement and commitment bases of a new life pattern. By the same token, if the individual has trouble with one element in the triad, this will tend to adversely affect the other two elements. This implies that the interdependence of involvement, commitment, and identification may be either an asset or liability in intervening with persons with prior allegiance to the drug lifestyle. It is recommended, then, that therapists take what clients offer in terms of involvement, commitment, and identity and work to expand the scope of the behaviors these individuals use to define themselves by taking note of the interdependence and crossover that exists between these three major elements of socialization.

Chapter 8

Practice, Application, and Usage

In most, if not all, areas of scientific inquiry, knowledge is useful only to the extent that it can be applied. It seems fitting, then, that application serves as the centerpiece of discussion in this, the final chapter of a book on substance abuse treatment. Commencing with a review of factors that should probably be considered in structuring one's interactions with clients, this chapter is designed to assist clinicians with the difficult task of applying knowledge obtained through a theoretical analysis of the drug lifestyle. The first section presents ways to enhance the comprehensiveness, specificity, efficiency, flexibility, relevance, stimulatory power, and instructional value of the intervention. This is followed by a dialogue on how the information contained in this book can be efficaciously shared with clients. The perceived advantages and disadvantages of the individual, group, and programmatic methods of conducting substance abuse interventions are thoroughly examined. In the third section, case study material is introduced in an effort to demonstrate specifically how the assessments and interventions described in this book apply to individual clients. Several issues requiring further attention, study, and reflection with respect to the continued development of the lifestyle paradigm are scrutinized in the final section of this chapter.

GUIDES TO APPLICATION

In making the transition from theory to application, clinicians might want to consider the comprehensiveness, specificity, efficiency, flexibility, relevance, stimulatory power, and instructional value of their planned intervention.

Comprehensiveness

Comprehensiveness refers to the fact that all pertinent issues, areas, and topics are covered by the proposed intervention. Although no single intervention is capable of covering all bases, lifestyle theory seeks to furnish the therapist with a general overview of the areas he or she might want to explore with clients. Comprehensiveness should not be confused with efforts to construct a "blueprint" for change. This is because lifestyle theory holds firmly to the belief that change is a personalized experience in which relationship issues and trust are as important as specific intervention techniques and objectives. The comprehensiveness of a change plan can perhaps be best understood in a review of the three primary goals of intervention: arresting the lifestyle; instructing the client in skills designed to manage lifestyle-supporting conditions, choices, and cognitions; and providing effective aftercare through resocialization. Comprehensiveness, therefore, is designed to instill a sense of confidence in the breadth and scope of one's evaluation and subsequent intervention.

Specificity

As the previous section denotes, comprehensiveness entails assessing all major areas of potential concern. However, this does not mean that each of these areas will work their way into the client's change plan. Lifestyle theory asserts that therapeutic interventions must be tailored to the personal needs, attributes, and experiences of the identified client. The dilemma facing programs that conceptualize desistance from the drug lifestyle as a uniform process is the reality that no single approach is effective in all situations, with all types of clients. Lifestyle theory recommends that clinicians map out the client's individual strengths and weaknesses as a means to constructing a change plan that is at once comprehensive and specific. Comprehensiveness and specificity are therefore complementary, rather than antagonistic, processes. In combination, they may augment the efficiency or cost-effectiveness of one's therapeutic interventions. Hence, a comprehensive evaluation pinpoints specific areas for intervention, thereby preventing duplication of services. Once areas of deficit or low efficacy and strength or high efficacy have been identified, the therapist can begin to assemble an individualized change plan that identifies major areas of both strength and weakness and integrates these with goals for the development of new competencies and personal skills designed to aid the client in identifying the path less traveled.

Efficiency

Comprehensiveness and specificity are reconcilable processes potentially capable of enhancing the effectiveness of one's interventions with clients. In this age of managed care and broad-based budget cuts, however, there is a conspicuous lack of guidance as to how cost effectiveness might be achieved. The lifestyle approach seeks to redress the lack of attention to the actual mechanics of cost effectiveness by encouraging empirical documentation of the cost-to-benefit ratio of one's interventions. Program evaluation and applied research are two avenues through which the efficiency of an intervention might be assessed, evaluated, and enhanced. It is the efficiency criterion, in point of fact, that is responsible for lifestyle theory's strong emphasis on applied research. Even though the lifestyle paradigm is largely congruent with current research developments in the substance abuse field and follows from the author's ongoing clinical research with clients, more rigorous examination of the model's underlying assumptions and tenets is required. This is particularly true of the assessment devices and procedures outlined in the appendixes of this book.

Flexibility

Flexibility is the fourth criterion that should be considered in offering effective drug programming services to clients with a substance abuse problem. An organized plan of action is clearly advantageous in identifying specific goals for each session. However, unanticipated issues may surface from time to time, and the therapist must choose between addressing these issues or ignoring them and proceeding with the planned intervention. The position adopted by lifestyle theory is that a therapist must be sufficiently flexible to abandon a planned intervention if a more pertinent or timely issue surfaces over the course of a session. After all, flexibility is one of the attributes lifestyle therapists are attempting to instill in clients. To demonstrate rigidity in one's interactions with clients is to miss an opportunity to influence clients through the modeling of flexible behavior. Lack of flexibility on the part of the therapist may be viewed by some clients as a sign of weakness—an interpretation that might then be used to justify the client's own inflexible behavior and fear of making a commitment to change.

Relevance

The majority of issues and skills described in this book appear to be sufficiently ecumenical to permit extension beyond their original drug context, without significant loss of explanatory power. However, if clients fail to perceive an intervention as relevant to themselves or their situations, they may refuse to invest the time and energy necessary to achieve a consummate level of commitment to the change process. For this reason, it is critical that a client's problems with drugs be highlighted during the early stages of intervention, but that the focus gradually shift to other issues as programming progresses. The purpose this serves is two-fold. First, the initial emphasis on drugs imbues an intervention with face validity by helping clients see the relevance of the program to their own personal situations. Clients are therefore more willing to devote the necessary time and effort to the task of establishing initial changes in behavior. Second, the gradual shift from drugs as the primary focus of treatment serves to challenge the client's belief that drug abuse is his or her sole or core problem, and mobilizes and expands the client's self-awareness by reframing drug abuse as a personal problem in which socialization into a lifestyle of short-term gain is the overriding concern.

Stimulating Power

Therapy need not be boring to be effective. Lifestyle theory, in fact, maintains that efficacy is enhanced by the stimulatory power of the intervention. Games, role plays, and practical exercises hold the potential of stimulating change by igniting a client's interest in new ideas, skills, and activities. Cinematic productions and television specials that address relevant substance abuse issues may also advance the treatment enterprise. As the reader may recall, the drug lifestyle is conceptualized as an extreme role that is unattainable in real life, but one with which some people identify strongly. What films such as *Clean and Sober, The Doors,* and *Drugstore Cowboy* demonstrate, is that the drug lifestyle can perhaps best be understood in movies, where the prototypic features of the lifestyle can be extracted and merged into a single character. In constructing an idealized portrait of a fictionalized character, which in some cases may be based on a real-life person or situation, Hollywood occasionally captures the caricature of the drug lifestyle. By using these movies to educate clients about the lifestyle, the therapist is providing clients with the opportunity to reorient their drug-related attitudes and beliefs.

Instructional Value

Instructional value is the seventh and final factor therapists may want to consider in devising a change plan for clients. The lifestyle approach to change is designed to teach clients basic social, coping, life, thinking, and information processing skills. Lifestyle theory rejects the notion that substance abuse is a disease or addiction, but instead conceives of such behavior as a lifestyle characterized by interlocking conditions, choices, cognitions, and skill deficits. Accordingly, a key goal of intervention with substance abusers is skills training. An intervention that educates and instructs is viewed as having potentially more impact than an intervention that ignores these issues. To boost client interest in learning, it may be helpful to challenge clients to seek out new learning experiences. The therapist can model this knowledge-seeking attitude by sharing with clients how he or she endeavors to acquire new information each time he or she conducts a therapeutic intervention. If internalized, this knowledge-seeking attitude can assist clients in managing the problems of everyday living.

METHODS OF APPLICATION

Lifestyle intervention normally occurs through one of three therapeutic venues: individual counseling, group and family therapy, or as part of a comprehensive program. There are advantages and disadvantages to each method. Cost containment, convenience, and privacy are the chief advantages of the individual approach to intervention. The individual and group methods are less expensive than the programmatic approach because only one staff person is normally required for implementation of these two methods. This can be a drawback as well, however, in that a single therapist cannot be all things to all clients. The individual method of intervening with substance-abusing clients is appreciably more convenient than the group and programmatic models because only one client is treated at a time; this, in turn, helps clinicians avoid the system-wide confounds of group, family, or programmatic interventions. The downside to the convenience of the individual method is its inability to provide direct feedback on interpersonal transactions (except for those that transpire between the therapist and client). The individual model also affords clients more privacy than either the group or program methods, a great advantage when addressing sensitive issues. The disadvantage of such privacy is that research has shown that performing a behavior publicly, as in a group or family session, facilitates internalization and increases the probability that the behavior will be executed outside of therapy (Tice, 1992).

Group and family interventions permit social interaction and behavioral rehearsal of interpersonal skills, which, in turn, expedite the development and pursuit of pertinent interpersonal objectives and goals. The group method also affords clients the opportunity to learn from peers, parents, and siblings, either through imitation or counter-imitation (see Harburg, DiFranceisco, Webster, Gleiberman, & Schork, 1990). Family therapy enjoys the added benefit of encouraging modification of ongoing interactive patterns within an existing system that can then be used to inspire positive change in that system. The principal advantage of the group method, however, is that it permits alteration of socialization patterns. A drawback to the group approach is that clients may imitate the negative behaviors of peers or family members. One way this can be handled is through a "mixed group" format, in which clients displaying varying levels of commitment to change, as measured by the Prochaska and DiClemente (1988) model (i.e., precontemplation, contemplation, action, maintenance), are included in the same group. Obviously, the mixed group format cannot be used with preexisting groups, such as families. Although the group method may not be as flexible or as private as the individual model, or as comprehensive as the programmatic model, it plays a pivotal role in helping substance-abusing clients change.

The principal advantage of the programmatic method is that it furnishes clinicians a comprehensive evaluation of potential targets for intervention and is capable of addressing a wider range of issues than either the individual or group methods. As such, the therapist need not be all things to all people, but can concentrate on the domain with which he or she is most familiar and proficient. However, there is one inevitable disadvantage and two potential disadvantages to the programmatic approach. The inescapable drawback is its cost. A comprehensive program demands more staff, resources, and coordination than individual or group interventions administered by a single therapist. *Splitting* and dogmatism are limitations of the programmatic approach for which potential solutions are available. Substance abusers, like persons committed to a criminal, gambling, sexual, or eating disorder lifestyle, are adept at splitting program staff by forming alliances and pitting one staff member against another. The presence of multiple staff invites this particular form of client manipulation. Opportunities for splitting can be reduced, however, by training staff in the use of effective communication. Dogmatism occurs when program staff come to believe that there is only one way to treat substance abuse and only one path out of the drug lifestyle. Although placing client choice and skill development high on its list of program priorities, the lifestyle approach acknowledges that not all clients respond favorably to the same intervention. Consequently, variety and flexibility are potential solutions for the problem of program dogmatism.

The lesson to be learned from this review of the individual, group, and programmatic methods of assisted change is that although all three strategies are potentially useful with substance-abusing clients, no single method will prove effective in all situations. These three methods must therefore be creatively integrated with the client's unique life situation to achieve maximum clinical effectiveness. Interventions that capitalize on the unique advantages of the individual, group, and program methods will achieve the greatest measure of success. To secure an optimal level of integration and productivity the clinician must strive to counterbalance the assorted limitations of these three methods, capitalize on the individual strengths of each method, and maximize the comprehensiveness, specificity, efficiency, flexibility, relevance, stimulatory power, and instructional value of specific interventions. Quite obviously, available funding and staff experience/training must also be considered in designing a therapeutic system capable of promoting change in persons previously preoccupied with drugs and committed to the caricature of the drug lifestyle. In the following case, the information presented throughout this book will be discussed and applied to the situation of a 40-year-old man.

A CASE HISTORY: WINSTON

Background

Winston is a 40-year-old man with a 24-year substance abuse history. Currently serving a 60-month sentence for bank robbery, Winston has had numerous dealings with the criminal justice system, including three prior incarcerations. He insists that the only times he has ever ceased or significantly reduced his use of drugs since age 18 has been while confined in jail or prison. As the oldest of four children, Winston was put in the position of looking after three younger siblings. The abuse he received at the hands of an alcohol-abusing stepfather and the shock of seeing his sister killed by a drunk driver certainly contributed to his future involvement with drugs. However, his desire to be part of an "older crowd," a group he viewed as having earned the respect and fear of others in the neighborhood, is what Winston identifies as the driving force behind his initial use of substances. Winston's inaugural exposure to drugs came in the form of intravenous heroin use at age 16, and during his lifetime he has abused alcohol, barbiturates, methamphetamine, psilocybin, and phencyclidine, but his preference is for heroin and cocaine. Winston entered the Lifestyle Change program, a prison-based intervention program administered by the author, in an effort to understand himself better and identify alternatives to his former preoccupation with drugs.

Initial Assessment

Results from Winston's completion of the Drug Lifestyle Screening Interview (DLSI) (Appendix 2), outlined in Table 8-1, suggest a pattern of behavior consistent with the drug lifestyle. Scores of 10 or higher on this measure normally suggest significant preoccupation, commitment, and identification with the drug lifestyle. A total score of 17, therefore, connotes a high degree of prior involvement in drug lifestyle activities. Winston achieved maximum scores on the Irresponsibility/Pseudoresponsibility, Interpersonal Triviality, and Social Rule Breaking/Bending subscales and a moderate score on the Stress-Coping Imbalance subscale. This would seem to imply that stress has played a less significant role in Winston's misuse of substances than has poor responsibility, drug-based rituals and relationships (interpersonal triviality), and self-image (social rule breaking/bending). As Winston himself relates, his pursuit of drug lifestyle objectives was based largely on his desire to be one of the "bad boys in

Table 8-1   DLSI Scores for Winston

Scale	Score
Irresponsibility/pseudoresponsibility	5
Stress-coping imbalance	2
Interpersonal triviality	5
Social rule breaking/bending	5
Total DLSI Score	17

the neighborhood." He also found drugs to be effective in structuring his time and achieving certain short-term goals with minimal effort.

Intervention

The first step in the intervention process is to arrest the lifestyle by defining and highlighting crises stemming from one's preoccupation with drugs. The crisis for Winston began with his arrest for bank robbery, his confinement in the city jail, and his medically unassisted withdrawal from heroin. It was at this point that Winston began to realize that if he wished to avoid future incarceration and follow a constructive life path, he would have to abandon the drug lifestyle. In the Inventory of Negative Consequences (Appendix 4), Winston listed his mother, girlfriend, children, and people in general as those who had been harmed the most by his use of chemicals. Furthermore, he listed school, a possible military career, and various jobs as opportunities and experiences he failed to pursue because of his involvement with drugs; cars, money, and family as possessions and relation-ships he had lost as a consequence of drug use; and stealing his mother's credit card and emptying her account as an experience motivated by drugs that embar-rassed him deeply. With respect to the attribution triad and extension of the arresting phase of treatment, Winston demonstrated strong beliefs in the necessity, the possibility, and his ability to effect change, an encouraging prognostic sign. Although a total score of 77 on the Estimated Self-Efficacy in Avoiding Drugs measure (Appendix 7) could be interpreted as superoptimism, Winston's score on the Superoptimism scale of the Psychological Inventory of Drug-Based Thinking Styles (PIDTS) (Appendix 26A; see Figure 8-1) fails to support this hypothesis. It is speculated, then, that the results of the self-efficacy measure reflect a reasonably strong sense of self-confidence, an attribution that might be capitalized on in devising a program of intervention for Winston.

The three Estimated Self-Efficacy in Avoiding Drugs (Appendix 7) items receiving less than maximum scores from Winston were drug-related cues (remi-niscing about past drug experiences), availability (coming across a stash of hidden drugs), and social influence (receiving pressure from former drug associates to accompany them to a place where drugs are used). Consequently, these three current–contextual conditions were targeted for intervention. A cue-exposure pro-cedure was used to reduce the craving elicited by drug-related cues. Winston was exposed to a brief videotape depiction of people injecting heroin; after the fourth session he was switched to a coping version of the cue-exposure model. Winston's responses on the Drug-Related Cues Checklist (Appendix 12) (see Table 8-2) indicate a general trend toward extinction over the course of 18 sessions. The fact that withdrawal-like symptoms (cold chills, increased heart rate, nervousness) predominated over drug-like symptoms (decreased heart rate, general sense of bodily relaxation) in Winston's reactions to videotape portrayals of opiate use, lends support to Siegel's (1988) opponent process interpretation of drug-related

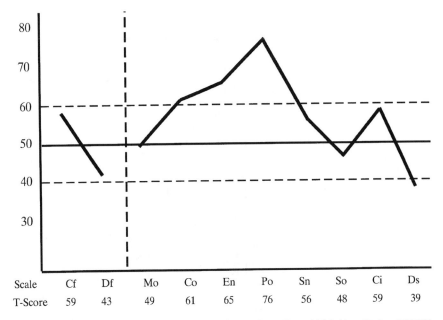

Scale	Cf	Df	Mo	Co	En	Po	Sn	So	Ci	Ds
T-Score	59	43	49	61	65	76	56	48	59	39

Figure 8-1 Winston's Psychological Inventory of Drug-Based Thinking Styles (PIDTS) profile.

cues (see Walters, 1994c, for a complete explanation of Siegel's model). Furthermore, there was a shift in the types of symptoms reported over the course of treatment, with worry and anger becoming more prominent during the final seven sessions. Availability was addressed by reviewing how Winston might reduce his access to future drug-use opportunities by avoiding certain people, places, and things. In addition to demonstrating less than maximum confidence in his ability to resist interpersonal pressure on the Estimated Self-Efficacy in Avoiding Drugs (Appendix 7) measure, Winston also scored in the borderline range on the Interpersonal Influence Scale (Appendix 14) (total score = 17). Interpersonal influence was addressed in a series of role-play exercises through which Winston was instructed in strategies designed to assist him in more effectively resisting pressure from others to use drugs.

Winston generated 24 alternatives to the 8 situations listed on the Multiple Options Analysis procedure (Appendix 16), which yields an average of 3 alternative solutions per situation. Having registered a borderline score on this measure, Winston was enrolled in a short course designed to improve his lateral thinking skills. Just prior to enrolling in the Lifestyle Change program, Winston earned his General Equivalency Diploma (GED). He also participated in two vocational training workshops. Both training programs served to expand Winston's options for future employment. Although no major problems were noted with respect to

Table 8-2 Drug-Related Cues Checklist Results Over 18 Sessions of Training

Symptoms	\multicolumn{18}{c}{Session number}																	
	1	2	3	4	5	6	7	8	9	10	11	12	13	14	15	16	17	18
2. Lightheaded							2			2	1							
4. Tension in face, neck, or jaw							2											
5. "Lump" in throat			1	1	1	2	1	1	2	3		1	1	1		2		
6. Increased heart rate	2		5	5		1	1	5	2	1	1	2	1	1				
7. Decreased heart rate		1																
9. Upset or quivering stomach		1			2				3	3	1							
11. Uncontrollable shaking											1	1			1			
12. Tension in arms/chest/hands			3	1	1	1	1	1	1	1								
13. "Nervous" movement of arms/legs						2			1	2				1				
14. Cold chills	2	3	5	6		4	4	2	4		4	4	2	1	2	1		1

122

Symptom																		
15. General sense of bodily relaxation	1							1										
16. Feeling anxious or "on edge"	1		1															
18. Worry												2	1	1	1			
19. Anger												3	1	1	1	1	1	2
20. Disgust												2	1	2	1		2	1
22. Confusion	1				1		1				1							
28. Excitement	1	1			1													
29. A general state of well-being				3														
30. A feeling of being "high"		1			1													
TOTAL NUMBER OF SYMPTOMS REPORTED	9	8	15	17	8	10	12	9	13	12	9	12	8	5	7	5	5	4

Note: The numerals in the boxes represent the frequency of that symptom during a single session (six trials per session). The Total Number of Symptoms Reported box, located at the bottom of the form, is a tally of the total number of symptoms reported during that session. It should be noted that this number may exceed the sum of the individual items because low-frequency items are not reported.

Winston's life skills, his responses on the Social-Communication Skills Checklist (Appendix 17) suggested that he may experience difficulty showing affection and requesting favors, advice, and direction from others. These social skill deficits were addressed as part of a structured group therapy experience in which participants received preliminary instruction, engaged in various role plays, and received feedback on their performance from the therapist and other group members. With time, Winston became more proficient in the performance of the targeted social skills. Winston's responses to the Values Inventory (Appendix 22) demonstrated that his priorities in the social and work value areas had been low in the past and that he wished to increase his future investment in these values. A program of values clarification, as well as training in certain value skills (relatedness, responsibility, and industriousness), was therefore initiated. Winston's ratings on the Expectancies Grid (Appendix 23) highlighted the positive short-term effects of drug use and deemphasized their negative long-term impacts. To help Winston achieve a better balance between long- and short-term consequences, he received instruction in goal-setting.

Winston was asked to record common constructional errors using the Self-Monitoring of Constructional Errors form (Appendix 24). After 7 days of self-monitoring it became apparent that overgeneralization was a major problem for Winston. This constructional error was addressed in individual sessions in which overgeneralization was discussed and Winston was given suggestions on how he might avoid this constructional error in the future (e.g., by keeping problems and issues in their proper perspective; by focusing on the larger picture, rather than being sidetracked by smaller details). The results of Winston's PIDTS profile, reproduced in Figure 8-1, indicate that Winston defends his thinking and lifestyle principally through power orientation, cutoff, and entitlement. An above-average-score on the Confusion (Cf) scale, in light of other information, appears to reveal a help-seeking attitude that may have increased the overall elevation of the thinking style scales, but is not believed to have significantly altered the overall pattern of scale relationships. Winston's power orientation and propensity to cutoff in response to frustration were addressed through exercises and self-instructional training designed to enhance his capacity for self-control. The entitlement issue was pursued through a program of cognitive restructuring, with emphasis on teaching Winston to discriminate between his wants and needs. It is noteworthy that although these interventions were carried out using both group and individual formats, Winston responded better to the group method. Results from the Fear Checklist (Appendix 27) imply that Winston's fears and concerns center predominantly on issues of intimacy, rejection, and social relations. These issues were addressed in both group (role playing and feedback) and individual (directed discussion) therapy.

Involvement, commitment, and identification with behaviors incompatible with the drug lifestyle were emphasized during the last several months of Winston's enrollment in the Lifestyle Change program. Several drug-related activities and feelings Winston indicated he would miss once he was no longer involved in the drug lifestyle included hustling, staying out all night, and interacting with wild women. These features of involvement in the drug lifestyle were managed through substitution (working as a substitute for hustling, intimacy as a substitute for wild women), values reorientation (valuing relatedness and responsibility over immediate pleasure), and cognitive restructuring. Commitment was assessed through the Schedule of Family and Community Support (Appendix 29) and engineered through the development of a series of behavioral contracts, several of which were negotiated with treatment staff and one of which was made with significant others in Winston's life. Identity was initially assessed through a review of Winston's responses on the Bipolar Identity Survey (Appendix 30; see Figure 8-2), the results of which indicated that Winston seeks attention and

BIPOLAR IDENTITY SURVEY

1a. List 3 positive messages you recall receiving from your parents/caregivers

Keep up the good work in school; we knew you could do it if you tried.

1b. List 3 negative messages you recall receiving from your parents/caregivers

You are dumb for following other people; you'll wind up in jail just like your uncle.

2a. List two behaviors for which you were consistently rewarded as a child

Doing good in school; taking charge of younger brother while mother worked.

2b. List two behaviors for which you were consistently punished as a child

Hooking school; stealing and lying.

4a. Favorite TV show during childhood

"Gunsmoke."

4b. TV show you disliked as a child

"Lassie."

5a. A favorite movie

"The Mack."

5b. A movie you did not like

Any Elvis movie.

6a. Two things you have done in your life that you are proud of

Getting my GED; Living to be 40.

6b. Two things you have done in your life that you are ashamed of

Stole from mother; breaking the law.

7a. Two personal traits you see as positive

Making people laugh; trying to help young kids do right.

7b. Two personal traits you see as negative.

Keeping a job; keeping a relationship going.

9a. Single word that is likely to be used to describe your personality

Funny.

9b. Single word that is unlikely to be used to describe your personality

Weak.

10a. Two characteristics you have observed in others that attract you to them

Strength; Sense of humor.

10b. Two characteristics you have observed in others that repulse you

Weakness; Laziness.

12a. What you want people to remember you by

He meant well; damn, he sure got his life together.

12b. What you don't want people to remember you by

Nothing.

Figure 8-2   Several of Winston's responses on the Bipolar Identity Survey.

approval, but avoids intimacy, perhaps because he fears rejection. Hence, by playing the "clown" he is able to attract attention and approval, without having to risk the prospect of rejection that normally accompanies intimacy. In therapy he learned that he could be funny without using drugs and worthwhile without being the center of attention. After 9 months in the Lifestyle Change program, Winston began to develop a new identity, one that no longer centered around drugs. However, identity transformation is a slow, gradual process that Winston will need to continue reinforcing through increased involvement and commitment to non-drug activities before it can become as comfortable and natural as the drug-centered identity that has directed his behavior for the last 24 years.

Outcome

Winston attended Lifestyle Change program activities for 9 months before being transferred to another federal facility to participate in a 500-hour comprehensive drug program. While involved in programming, Winston remained disciplinary report–free and demonstrated good responsibility and work performance. However, the ultimate test will be when Winston is released from prison. On several occasions Winston has stated that this will be the first time he has ever left prison with the intent of remaining drug free. It cannot be determined at this time whether he has formed sufficient involvement, commitment, and identification with activities incompatible with the drug lifestyle to make good on these initial intentions.

CONCLUSION

Because social roles are believed to be the forerunners of lifestyles, it is speculated that lifestyles should be subject to the same effects and influences as social roles. One such influence is the cultural and historical context of a lifestyle. Although lifestyles are designed to minimize the amount of change people experience, they may tend to self-modify in response to certain cultural and historical influences. The reader is referred to Walters (1994c) for a discussion on the role of culture in the formation of the drug lifestyle. Zimmer-Hofler and Dobler-Mikola (1992), on the other hand, offer insight into the effect history can have on drug use patterns and lifestyles. Passage of the Harrison Act in 1914, for instance, made heroin consumption illegal and drastically altered the roles, demographics, and ingestion patterns of those who used it. For example, the number of women who used opiates in the United States dropped dramatically after it was made illegal. These findings suggest that the drug lifestyle may self-modify in response to cultural, historical, and other contextual influences. It is therefore imperative that theorists avoid conceptualizing substance misuse as a stationary phenomenon and that therapists consider the possibility that they may need to alter their approach in response to feedback that the intervention is ineffective, inappropriate, or no longer pertinent to the drug lifestyle as it currently exists. It is also suggested that the assessments, procedures, and techniques described in this book may need to be revised, modified, or even discarded in response to the continually changing lifestyle picture brought about by permutations of cultural and historical influence. That is to say, flexibility is not only a criterion that must be considered in framing specific interventions, it is also something that should be considered in applying the lifestyle model to real-life situations.

The reality of self-modifying social roles and lifestyles intimates that the drug lifestyle will never be fully discerned because it is continually in motion, although at a significantly slower speed than that registered by an organism functioning in an adaptive mode. Those who would use the principles of the lifestyle paradigm must realize that no single approach, procedure, or technique is universally effective in intervention for substance abuse. Therapists must therefore seek to understand the way a client constructs reality and use this to match the client to a particular form or method of intervention. In this book, the lifestyle approach is offered as an alternative to the more contemporarily popular disease and social work models. To effectively implement this approach, clinicians must appreciate the situational sensitivity of the lifestyle concept. This is why weighing comprehensiveness, specificity, efficiency, flexibility, relevance, stimulatory power, and instructional value is vital to the successful application of the information and procedures contained in this book. Beyond educating therapists on the features and limitations of the present model, the future of the lifestyle paradigm rests with its ability to stimulate research that adequately documents the strengths and weaknesses of the approach utilized. Only through a program of formal research endeavor will scientists and clinicians be in a position to address the value, feasibility, and generalizability of the concepts described in this book. Successful application of the lifestyle model consequently requires that therapists be educated about the advantages and potential disadvantages of the model and that investigators probe the validity of the conceptual paradigm that supports the lifestyle treatment approach. Therapists must remain open to the ideas contained in the lifestyle approach and be flexible in adapting them for each situation. A variety of approaches can be used, each with the same goal—to build the self-reliance and self-esteem of clients. Initiating this approach, among others, can help therapists provide effective treatments to the clients they have today, and those they will meet tomorrow.

References

Alcoholics Anonymous World Services. (1980). *Alcoholics Anonymous.* New York: Author.

Allport, G. W. (1961). *Pattern and growth in personality.* New York: Holt, Rinehart, & Winston.

Ayers, D. J., Duguid, S., Montague, C., & Wolowidnyk, S. (1980). *Effects of the University of Victoria Program: A post-release study.* Report prepared for the Ministry of the Solicitor General of Canada, Ottawa.

Bagdy, E. (1984). Levels of symbolization within the circles of experiences of learning autogenic training. *Magyar Pszichologiai Szemle, 41,* 201–213.

Bandura, A. (1982). Self-efficacy mechanism in human agency. *American Psychologist, 37,* 122–147.

Beck, A. T. (1976). *Cognitive therapy and mental disorders.* New York: International Universities Press.

Beck, A. T., Rush, A. J., Shaw, B. F., & Emery, G. (1979). *Cognitive therapy of depression.* New York: Guilford.

Beck, J. L. (1981). Employment, community treatment center placement, and recidivism: A study of released federal offenders. *Federal Probation, 45,* 3–8.

Becker, G. S. (1968). Crime and punishment: An economic approach. *Journal of Political Economy, 76,* 169–217.

Bennett, T. (1986). A decision-making approach to opioid addiction. In D. B. Cornish & R. V. Clarke (Eds.), *The reasoning criminal: Rational choice perspectives on offending* (pp. 83–103). New York: Springer-Verlag.

Berg, G., Laberg, J. C., Skutle, A., & Ohman, A. (1981). Instructed versus pharmacological effects of alcohol in alcoholics and social drinkers. *Behavior, Research, and Therapy, 19,* 55–66.

Biernacki, P. (1990). Recovering from opiate addiction without treatment: A summary. *NIDA Research Monograph Series, 98,* 113–119.

Bigelow, G. E., Stitzer, M. L., Griffiths, R. R., & Liebson, I. A. (1981). Contingency management approaches to drug self-administration and drug abuse: Efficacy and limitations. *Addictive Behaviors, 6,* 241–252.

Bigner, J. J. (1974). A Wernerian developmental analysis of children's descriptions of siblings. *Child Development, 45,* 317–323.

Binkoff, J. A., Monti, P. M., Zwick, W., Abrams, D. B., Pedraza, M., & Monroe, S. (1986). *Relationship between problem drinkers' performance in alcohol-specific role plays and post-treatment drinking.* Poster presented at the 7th Annual Meeting of the Society of Behavioral Medicine, San Francisco, CA.

Birke, S. A., Edelmann, R. J., & Davis, P. E. (1990). An analysis of the abstinence violation effect in a sample of illicit drug users. *British Journal of Addiction, 85,* 1299–1307.

Booth, B. M., Russell, D. W., Soucek, S., & Laughlin, P. R. (1992). Social support and outcome of alcoholism treatment: An exploratory analysis. *American Journal of Drug and Alcohol Abuse, 18,* 87–101.

Bradley, B. P., Phillips, G., Green, L., & Gossop, M. (1989). Circumstances surrounding the initial lapse to opiate use following detoxification. *British Journal of Psychiatry, 154,* 354–359.

Brandon, T. H., Tiffany, S. T., & Baker, T. B. (1986). The process of smoking relapse. *NIDA Research Monograph Series, 72,* 104–117.

Brennan, P. L., & Moos, R. H. (1990). Life stressors, social resources, and later life problem drinking. *Psychology and Aging, 5,* 491–501.

Briddle, D. W., Rimm, D. C., Caddy, G. R., Krawitz, G., Sholis, D., & Wunderlin, R. J. (1978). The effects of alcohol and cognitive set on sexual arousal to deviant stimuli. *Journal of Abnormal Psychology, 87,* 418–430.

Brown, H. P., & Peterson, J. H. (1990). Rationale and procedural suggestions for defining and actualizing spiritual values in the treatment of dependency. *Alcoholism Treatment Quarterly, 7,* 17–46.

Brown, S. A., Vik, P. W., McQuaid, J. R., Patterson, T. L., Irwin, M. R., & Grant, I. (1990). Severity of psychosocial stress and outcome of alcoholism treatment. *Journal of Abnormal Psychology, 99,* 344–348.

Buchanan, W. L. (1992). Eating disorders: Obesity. In L. L'Abate, J. E. Farrar, & D. A. Serritella (Eds.), *Handbook of differential treatments for addictions* (pp. 189–210). Boston: Allyn & Bacon.

Budney, A. J., Higgins, S. T., Delaney, D. D., Kent, L., & Bickel, W. K. (1991). Contingent reinforcement of abstinence with individuals abusing cocaine and marijuana. *Journal of Applied Behavior Analysis, 24,* 657–665.

Cautela, J. R. (1967). Covert sensitization. *Psychological Reports, 20,* 459–468.

Chaney, E. F., O'Leary, M. R., & Marlatt, G. A. (1978). Skill training with alcoholics. *Journal of Consulting and Clinical Psychology, 46,* 1092–1104.

Chick, J., Ritson, B., Connaughton, J., Stewart, A., & Chick, D. A. (1988). Advice versus extended treatment for alcoholism: A controlled study. *British Journal of Addiction, 83,* 159–170.

Childress, A. R., McLellan, A. T., Ehrman, R., & O'Brien, C. P. (1987). Extinction of conditioned responses in abstinent cocaine or opioid users. *NIDA Research Monograph Series, 76,* 189–195.

Childress, A. R., McLellan, A. T., Ehrman, R., & O'Brien, C. P. (1988). Classically conditioned responses in opioid and cocaine dependence: A role in relapse? *NIDA Research Monograph Series, 84,* 25–43.

Childress, A. R., McLellan, A. T., & O'Brien, C. P. (1986). Conditioned responses in a methadone population: A comparison of laboratory, clinical, and natural setting. *Journal of Substance Abuse Treatment, 3,* 173–179.

Collins, R. L., & Lapp, W. M. (1991). Restraint and attributions: Evidence of the abstinence violation effect in alcohol consumption. *Cognitive Therapy and Research, 15,* 69–84.

Condiotte, M. M., & Lichtenstein, E. (1981). Self-efficacy and relapse in smoking cessation programs. *Journal of Consulting and Clinical Psychology, 49,* 648–658.

Cooney, N. L., Baker, L., & Pomerleau, O. F. (1983). Cue exposure for relapse prevention in alcohol treatment. In R. J. McMahon & K. D. Craig (Eds.), *Advances in clinical therapy* (pp. 174–210). New York: Brunner/Mazel.

Cooper, M. L. (1994). Motivations for alcohol use among adolescents: Development and validation of a four-factor model. *Psychological Assessment, 6,* 117–128.

Corbin, R. M. (1980). Decisions that might not get made. In T. S. Wallsten (Ed.), *Cognitive processes in choice and decision behavior.* Hillsdale, NJ: Erlbaum.

Cox, W. M., & Klinger, E. (1988). A motivational model of alcohol use. *Journal of Abnormal Psychology, 97,* 168–180.

Critchlow, B. (1986). The powers of John Barleycorn: Beliefs about the effects of alcohol on social behavior. *American Psychologist, 41,* 751–764.

Crowley, T. J. (1988). Learning and unlearning drug abuse in the real world: Clinical treatment and public policy. *NIDA Research Monograph Series, 84,* 100–121.

Curry, S., Marlatt, G. A., & Gordon, J. R. (1987). Abstinence violation effect: Validation of an attributional construct with smoking cessation. *Journal of Consulting and Clinical Psychology, 55,* 145–149.

Cushman, P. (1974). Detoxification of rehabilitated methadone patients: Frequency and predictors of long term success. *American Journal of Drug and Alcohol Abuse, 1,* 393–408.

Dance, K. A., & Kuiper, N. A. (1987). Self-schemata, social roles, and a self-worth contingency model of depression. *Motivation and Emotion, 11,* 251–268.

Darkes, J., & Goldman, M. S. (1993). Expectancy challenge and drinking reduction: Experimental evidence for a mediational process. *Journal of Consulting and Clinical Psychology, 61,* 344–353.

Davison, G. C., Tsujimoto, R., & Glaros, A. (1973). Attribution and the maintenance of behavior change in falling asleep. *Journal of Abnormal Psychology, 82,* 124–135.

de Bono, E. (1977). *Lateral thinking: A textbook of creativity.* Markham, England: Penguin Books.

de Bono, E. (1981). *CoRT thinking program*. Toronto: Pergamon.

de Bono, E. (1983). The direct teaching of thinking as a skill. *Phi Delta Kappan, 64,* 703–716.

Denney, M. R., Baugh, J. L., & Hardt, H. D. (1991). Sobriety outcome after alcoholism treatment with biofeedback participation: A pilot inpatient study. *International Journal of the Addictions, 26,* 335–341.

Denoff, M. S. (1988). An integrated analysis of the contributions made by irrational beliefs and parental interaction to adolescent drug abuse. *International Journal of the Addictions, 23,* 655–669.

Deutsch, F. M., Kroll, J. F., Weible, A. L., Letourneau, L. A., & Goss, R. L. (1988). Spontaneous trait generation: A new method for identifying self-schemas. *Journal of Personality, 56,* 327–354.

DiLeo, F. B. (1982). The activation and experiential integration of in-depth psychic introjects in psychedelic-activated psychotherapy. *International Journal of Eclectic Psychotherapy, 1,* 33–35.

Dixon, T. M., & Baumeister, R. F. (1991). Escaping the self: The moderating effect of self-complexity. *Personality and Social Psychology Bulletin, 17,* 363–368.

Dusenbury, L., & Botvin, G. J. (1992). Substance abuse prevention: Competence enhancement and the development of positive life options. *Journal of Addictive Diseases, 11,* 29–45.

D'Zurilla, T. J., & Goldfried, M. R. (1971). Problem-solving and behavior modification. *Journal of Abnormal Psychology, 78,* 107–126.

Eastman, C., & Norris, H. (1982). Alcohol dependence, relapse, and self-identity. *Journal of Studies on Alcohol, 43,* 1214–1231.

Einhorn, H. J., & Hogarth, R. M. (1978). Confidence in judgment: Persistence in the illusion of validity. *Psychological Review, 85,* 395–416.

Ellis, A. (1970). *The essence of rational psychotherapy: A comprehensive approach to treatment.* New York: Institute of Rational Living.

Emmelkamp, P. M. G. (1986). Behavior therapy with adults. In S. L. Garfield & A. E. Bergin (Eds.), *Handbook of psychotherapy and behavior change* (3rd ed., pp. 385–442). New York: Wiley.

Eppley, K. R., Abrams, A. I., & Shear, J. (1989). Differential effects of relaxation techniques on trait anxiety: A meta analysis. *Journal of Clinical Psychology, 45,* 957–974.

Eriksen, L., Bjornstad, S., & Gertestam, K. G. (1986). Social skills training in groups for alcoholics: One-year treatment outcome for groups and individuals. *Addictive Behaviors, 11,* 309–329.

Eysenck, H. J. (1964). *Crime and personality.* Boston: Houghton-Mifflin.

Fanning, P. (1994). *Visualization for change* (2nd ed.). Oakland, CA: New Harbinger.

Fattah, E. H. (1982). A critique of deterrence research with particular reference to the economic approach. *Canadian Journal of Criminology, 24,* 79–90.

Faupel, C. E., & Klockars, C. B. (1987). Drugs-crime connections: Elaborations from the life histories of hard-core heroin addicts. *Social Problems, 34,* 54–68.

Field, G. (1985). The cornerstone program: A client outcome study. *Federal Probation, 49,* 50–55.

Frankl, V. E. (1984). *Man's search for meaning: An introduction to Logotherapy* (3rd ed.). New York: Simon & Schuster.

Fromme, K., & Dunn, M. E. (1992). Alcohol expectancies, social and environmental cues as determinants of drinking and perceived reinforcement. *Addictive Behaviors, 17,* 167–177.

Gelderloos, P., Walton, K. G., Orem-Johnson, D. W., & Alexander, C. N. (1991). Effectiveness of the transcendental meditation program in preventing and treating substance misuse: A review. *International Journal of the Addictions, 26,* 293–325.

Gilberstadt, H., & Duker, J. (1965). *A handbook for clinical and actuarial MMPI interpretation.* Philadelphia: Saunders.

Goldberg, J., Zwibel, A., Safir, M. P., & Merbaum, M. (1983). Mediating factors in the modification of smoking behavior. *Journal of Behavior Therapy and Experimental Psychiatry, 14,* 325–330.

Grabowski, J., Rhoades, H., Elk, R., Schmitz, J., Davis, C., Creson, D., & Kirby, K. (1995). Fluoxetine is ineffective for treatment of cocaine dependence or concurrent opiate and cocaine dependence: Two placebo controlled double-blind trials. *Journal of Clinical Psychopharmacology, 15,* 163–174.

Greenfield, T. K., Guydish, J., & Temple, M. T. (1989). Reasons students give for limiting drinking: A factor analysis with implications for research and practice. *Journal of Studies on Alcohol, 50,* 108–115.

Gruder, C. L., Mermelstein, R. J., Kirekendol, S., Hedeker, D., Wong, S. C., Schreckengost, J., Warnecke, R. B., Burzette, R., & Miller, T. Q. (1993). Effects of social support and relapse prevention training as adjuncts to a televised smoking-cessation intervention. *Journal of Consulting and Clinical Psychology, 61,* 113–120.

Gueron, J. (1980). The supported-work experiment. In E. Ginzberg (Ed.), *Employing the unemployed* (pp. 73–93). New York: Basic Books.

Hall, S. M., Havassy, B. E., & Wasserman, D. A. (1990). Commitment to abstinence and acute stress in relapse to alcohol, opiates, and nicotine. *Journal of Consulting and Clinical Psychology, 58,* 175–181.

Harburg, E., DiFranceisco, W., Webster, D. W., Gleiberman, L., & Schork, A. (1990). Familial transmission of alcohol use: II. Imitation of and aversion to parent drinking (1960) by adult offspring (1977)—Tecumseh, Michigan. *Journal of Studies on Alcohol, 51,* 245–256.

Hathaway, S. R., & McKinley, J. C. (1940). A multiphasic personality schedule (Minnesota): I. Construction of the schedule. *Journal of Psychology, 10,* 249–254.

Hawkins, J. D., Catalano, R. F., Gillmore, M. R., & Wells, E. A. (1989). Skills training for drug abusers: Generalization, maintenance, and effects on drug use. *Journal of Consulting and Clinical Psychology, 57,* 559–563.

Hester, R. K., & Miller, W. R. (1988). Empirical guidelines for optimal client-treatment matching. *NIDA Research Monograph Series, 77,* 27–38.

Hewitt, P. L., & Genest, M. (1990). The ideal self: Schematic processing of perfectionistic content in dysphoric university students. *Journal of Personality and Social Psychology, 59,* 802–808.

Higgins, E. T., & Bargh, J. A. (1987). Social cognition and social perception. *Annual Review of Psychology, 38,* 369–425.

Higgins, S. T., Budney, A. J., Bickel, W. K., & Badger, G. J. (1994). Participation of significant others in outpatient behavioral treatment predicts greater cocaine abstinence. *American Journal of Drug and Alcohol Abuse, 20,* 47–56.

Hirschi, T. (1969). *Causes of delinquency*. Berkeley: University of California Press.

Hollander, E. (1991). Serotenergic drugs and the treatment of disorders related to obsessive-compulsive disorder. In M. Pato & J. Zohar (Eds.), *Current treatments of obsessive-compulsive disorder* (pp. 173–192). Washington, DC: American Psychiatric Association.

Horowitz, M. J. (1989). Relationship schema formulation: Role-relationship models and intrapsychic conflict. *Psychiatry, 52*, 260–274.

Hover, S., & Gaffney, L. R. (1991). The relationship between social skills and adolescent drinking. *Alcohol and Alcoholism, 26*, 207–214.

Hunt, W. A., Barnett, L. W., & Branch, L. G. (1971). Relapse rates in addiction programs. *Journal of Clinical Psychology, 27*, 455–456.

Huselid, R. F., Self, E. A., & Gutierres, S. E. (1991). Predictors of successful completion of a halfway-house program for chemically-dependent women. *American Journal of Drug and Alcohol Abuse, 17*, 89–101.

Ingram, J. A., & Salzberg, H. C. (1990). Effects of in vivo behavioral rehearsal on the learning of assertive behaviors with a substance abusing population. *Addictive Behaviors, 15*, 189–194.

Jeffrey, R., & Woopert, S. (1974). Work furlough as an alternative to incarceration: An assessment of its effects on recidivism and social cost. *Journal of Criminal Law and Criminology, 65*, 404–415.

Johnston, L. D., O'Malley, P. M., & Bachman, J. G. (1991). *Drug use among American high school seniors, college students and young adults 1975–1990*. Washington, DC: U.S. Government Printing Office.

Jung, C. G. (1961). The theory of psychoanalysis. In H. Read, M. Fordham, & G. Adler (Eds.), *Collected works* (Vol. 4). Princeton, NJ: Princeton University Press.

Kazdin, A. E. (1975). *Behavior modification in applied settings*. Homewood, IL: Dorsey.

Kelly, G. A. (1955). *The psychology of personal constructs*. New York: Norton.

Kipper, D. A. (1977). The Kahn Test of Symbol Arrangement and criminality. *Journal of Clinical Psychology, 33*, 777–781.

Lang, A. R., Goeckner, D. J., Adesso, V. J., & Marlatt, G. A. (1975). The effects of alcohol and aggression in male social drinkers. *Journal of Abnormal Psychology, 84*, 505–518.

Leigh, B. C., & Stacy, A. W. (1994). Self-generated alcohol outcome expectancies in four samples of drinkers. *Addiction Research, 1*, 335–348.

Linehan, M. M. (1993). *Cognitive-behavioral treatment of borderline personality disorder*. New York: Guilford.

Linkenbach, J. (1990). Adlerian techniques for substance abuse prevention and intervention. *Individual Psychology: Journal of Adlerian Theory, Research, and Practice, 46*, 203–207.

Linquist, C. M., Lindsay, T. S., & White, G. D. (1979). Assessment of assertiveness in drug abusers. *Journal of Clinical Psychology, 35*, 676–679.

Linville, P. W. (1987). Self-complexity as a cognitive buffer against stress-related illness and depression. *Journal of Personality and Social Psychology, 52*, 663–676.

Liskow, B. I., & Goodwin, D. W. (1987). Pharmacological treatment of alcohol intoxication, withdrawal and dependence: A critical review. *Journal of Studies on Alcohol, 48*, 356–370.

Litman, G. K., Stapleton, J., Oppenheim, A. N., Peleg, M., & Jackson, P. (1983). Situations related to alcoholism relapse. *British Journal of Addiction, 78,* 381–389.

Lochman, J. E., Burch, P. R., Curry, J. F., & Lampron, L. B. (1984). Treatment of generalization effects of cognitive-behavioral and goal-setting interventions with aggressive boys. *Journal of Consulting and Clinical Psychology, 52,* 915–916.

Ludwig, A. M. (1985). Cognitive processes associated with "spontaneous" recovery from alcoholism. *Journal of Studies on Alcohol, 46,* 53–58.

Marks, P. A., Seeman, W., & Haller, D. L. (1974). *The actuarial description of personality: An atlas for use with the MMPI.* Baltimore: Williams & Wilkins.

Markus, H., & Nurius, P. (1986). Possible selves. *American Psychologist, 41,* 954–969.

Markus, H., & Wurf, E. (1987). The dynamic self-concept: A social psychological perspective. *Annual Review of Psychology, 38,* 299–337.

Marlatt, G. A. (1978). Craving for alcohol, loss of control, and relapse: A cognitive behavioral analysis. In P. E. Nathan, G. A. Marlatt, & T. Løberg (Eds.), *Alcoholism: New directions in behavioral research and treatment.* New York: Plenum.

Marlatt, G. A., & George, W. H. (1984). Relapse prevention: Introduction and overview of the model. *British Journal of Addiction, 79,* 261–273.

Marlatt, G. A., & Gordon, J. R. (1980). Determinants of relapse: Implications for the maintenance of behavior change. In P. O. Davidson & S. M. Davidson (Eds.), *Behavioral medicine: Changing health lifestyles* (pp. 410–472). New York: Brunner/Mazel.

Marlatt, G. A., & Gordon, J. R. (Eds.). (1985). *Relapse prevention: Maintenance strategies in the treatment of addictive behaviors.* New York: Guilford.

Marlatt, G. A., Kosturn, C. F., & Lang, A. R. (1975). Provocation to anger and opportunity for retaliation as determinants of alcohol consumption in social drinkers. *Journal of Abnormal Psychology, 84,* 652–659.

Marlatt, G. A., & Marques, J. K. (1977). Meditation, self-control and alcohol abuse. In R. B. Stuart (Ed.), *Behavioral self-management: Strategies, techniques and outcomes* (pp. 117–153). New York: Brunner/Mazel.

Marlatt, G. A., & Rohsenow, D. R. (1980). Cognitive processes in alcohol use: Expectancy and the balanced placebo design. In N. K. Mello (Ed.), *Advances in substance abuse* (pp. 155–199). Greenwich, CT: JAI Press.

Maultsby, M. C. (1975). *Help yourself to happiness through rational self-counseling.* New York: Institute for Rational Living.

McClelland, D. C., Davis, W. N., Kalin, R., & Wanner, E. (1972). *The drinking man.* New York: Free Press.

McCusker, C. G., & Brown, K. (1990). Alcohol-predictive cues enhance tolerance to and precipitate "craving" for alcohol in social drinkers. *Journal of Studies on Alcohol, 51,* 494–499.

Mead, G. H. (1934). *Mind, self, and society.* Chicago: University of Chicago Press.

Meichenbaum, D. H. (1974). *Cognitive behavior modification.* Morristown, NJ: General Learning Press.

Meyer, R. E., & Mirin, S. M. (1979). *The heroin stimulus: Implications for a theory of addiction.* New York: Plenum.

Miller, W. R. (1992). The effectiveness of treatment for substance abuse: Reasons for optimism. *Journal of Substance Abuse Treatment, 9,* 93–102.

Miller, W. R., Benefield, R. G., & Tonigan, J. S. (1993). Enhancing motivation for change in problem drinking: A controlled comparison of two therapist styles. *Journal of Consulting and Clinical Psychology, 61,* 455–461.

Miller, W. R., & Dougher, M. J. (1989). Covert sensitization: Alternative treatment procedures for alcoholism. *Behavioural Psychotherapy, 17,* 203–220.

Mischel, W. (1974). Processes in delay of gratification. *Advances in Experimental Psychology, 7,* 249–292.

Monti, P. M., Abrams, D. B., Binkoff, J. A., Zwick, W. R., Liepman, M. R., Nirenberg, T. D., & Rohsenow, D. J. (1990). Communication skills training, communication skills training with family and cognitive behavioral mood management training for alcoholics. *Journal of Studies on Alcohol, 51,* 263–270.

Moore, M. (Guest), with Wilson, J. Q. (Moderator). (1984). *National Institute of Justice Crime File: Drinking and crime* [Film]. Washington, DC: National Institute of Justice.

Moore, R. W. (1983). Art therapy with substance abusers: A review of the literature. *Arts in Psychotherapy, 10,* 251–260.

Mulford, H. A. (1970). Education and drinking behavior. In G. L. Maddox (Ed.), *The domesticated drug: Drinking among collegians* (pp. 81–97). New Haven, CT: College & University Press.

Murphy, T. J., Pagano, R. R., & Marlatt, G. A. (1986). Lifestyle modification with heavy alcohol drinkers: Effects of aerobic exercise and meditation. *Addictive Behaviors, 11,* 175–186.

Novaco, R. (1975). *Anger control: The development and evaluation of an experimental treatment.* Lexington, MA: DC Heath.

Oei, T. P. S., & Jackson, P. (1980). Long-term effects of group and individual social skills training with alcoholics. *Addictive Behaviors, 5,* 129–136.

Oei, T. P. S., & Jackson, P. R. (1982). Social skills and cognitive behavioral approaches to the treatment of problem drinking. *Journal of Studies on Alcohol, 43,* 532–547.

O'Farrell, T. J., Cutter, H. S. G., & Floyd, F. J. (1985). Evaluating behavioral marital therapy for male alcoholics: Effects on marital adjustment and communication from before to after treatment. *Behavior Therapy, 16,* 147–167.

Penk, W. W., Robinowitz, R., & Fudge, J. W. (1978). Differences in interpersonal orientation of heroin, amphetamine, and barbiturate users. *British Journal of Addiction, 73,* 82–88.

Pernanen, K. (1976). Alcohol and crimes of violence. In B. Kissen & H. Begletier (Eds.), *The biology of alcoholism* (Vol. 4). New York: Plenum.

Piaget, J. (1963). The attainment of invariants and reversible operations in the development of thinking. *Social Research, 30,* 283–299.

Platt, J. J., Perry, G. M., & Metzger, D. S. (1980). The evolution of a heroin addiction treatment program within a correctional environment. In R. R. Ross & P. Gendreau (Eds.), *Effective correctional treatment.* Toronto: Butterworth.

Posner, I., Leitner, L. A., & Lester, D. (1994). Diet, cigarette smoking, stressful life events and subjective feelings of stress. *Psychological Reports, 74,* 841–842.

Pratkanis, A. R., & Greenwald, A. G. (1985). How shall the self be conceived? *Journal of the Theory of Social Behaviour, 15,* 311–329.

Preston, K. L., Bigelow, G. E., Bickel, W., & Liebson, I. A. (1987). Three-choice drug discrimination in opioid-dependent humans: Hydromorphone, naloxone and saline. *Journal of Pharmacology and Experimental Therapeutics, 243,* 1002–1009.

Prochaska, J. O., & DiClemente, C. C. (1988). Toward a comprehensive model of change. In W. R. Miller & N. Heather (Eds.), *Treating addictive behaviors: Processes of change* (pp. 3–28). New York: Plenum.

Reed, H., & Janis, I. L. (1974). Effect of induced awareness of rationalizations on smokers' acceptance of fear-arousing warnings about health hazards. *Journal of Consulting and Clinical Psychology, 42,* 748.

Reitman, J. (1974). Without surreptitious rehearsal, information in short-term memory decays. *Journal of Verbal Learning and Verbal Behavior, 13,* 365–377.

Research Triangle Institute. (1976). *Drug use and crime: Report of the panel on drug use and criminal behavior.* Research Triangle Park, NC: Author.

Rist, F., & Watzl, H. (1983). Self assessment of relapse risk and assertiveness in relation to treatment outcome of female alcoholism. *Addictive Behaviors, 8,* 121–127.

Roberts, K., & Cuff, M. D. (1989). Categorization studies of 9- to 15-month-old infants: Evidence for superordinate categorization? *Infant Behavior and Development, 12,* 265–288.

Robins, L. N., Davis, D. H., & Goodwin, D. W. (1974). Drug use by U.S. Army enlisted men in Vietnam: A follow-up on their return home. *American Journal of Epidemiology, 99,* 235–249.

Rogers, C. (1959). A theory of therapy, personality, and interpersonal relationships, as developed in the client-centered framework. In S. Koch (Ed.), *Psychology: A study of a science* (Vol. 13, pp. 184–256). New York: McGraw-Hill.

Rohsenow, D. J., Beach, L. R., & Marlatt, G. A. (1978, July). *A decision-theory model of relapse.* Paper presented at the Summer Conference of the Alcoholism and Drug Abuse Institute, University of Washington, Seattle.

Rohsenow, D. J., Monti, P. M., Binkoff, J. A., Liepman, M. R., Nirenberg, T. D., & Abrams, D. B. (1991). Patient-treatment matching for alcoholic men in communication skill versus cognitive-behavioral mood management training. *Addictive Behaviors, 16,* 63–69.

Rohsensow, D. J., Monti, P. M., Zwick, W. R., Nirenberg, T. D., Liepman, M. R., Binkoff, J. A., & Abrams, D. B. (1989). Irrational beliefs, urges to drink and drinking among alcoholics. *Journal of Studies on Alcohol, 50,* 461–464.

Rokeach, M. (1983). A value approach to the prevention and reduction of drug abuse. *NIDA Research Monograph Series, 47,* 172–194.

Ross, R. R., & Fabiano, E. A. (1985). *Time to think: A cognitive model of delinquency prevention and offender rehabilitation.* Johnson City, TN: Institute of Social Sciences and Art.

Ryan, C., & Butters, N. (1983). Cognitive deficits in alcoholics. In B. Kissen & H. Begleiter (Eds.), *The biology of alcoholism* (Vol. 7, pp. 485–538). New York: Plenum.

Seashore, M., Haberfield, S., Irwin, J., & Baker, K. (1976). *Prisoner education: Project Newgate and other college programs.* New York: Praeger.

Shope, J. T., Dielman, T. E., Butchart, A. T., Campanelli, P. C., & Kloska, D. D. (1992). An elementary school-based alcohol misuse prevention program: A follow-up evaluation. *Journal of Studies on Alcohol, 53,* 106–121.

Shorkey, C., & Sutton-Smith, K. (1983). Reliability and validity of the Rational Behavior Inventory with a clinical population. *Journal of Clinical Psychology, 39,* 34–38.

Siegel, S. (1988). Drug anticipation and the treatment of dependence. *NIDA Research Monograph Series, 84,* 1–24.

Simpson, D. D., & Marsh, K. L. (1986). Relapse and recovery among opioid addicts 12 years after treatment. *NIDA Research Monograph Series, 72,* 86–103.

Sisson, R. W., & Azrin, N. H. (1986). Family-member involvement to initiate and promote treatment of problem drinkers. *Journal of Behavior Therapy and Experimental Psychiatry, 17,* 15–21.

Sisson, R. W., & Azrin, N. (1989). The community reinforcement approach. In R. K. Hester & W. R. Miller (Eds.), *Handbook of alcoholism treatment approaches: Effective alternatives* (pp. 242–257). New York: Pergamon.

Sjoberg, L., & Johnson, T. (1978). Trying to give up smoking: A study of volitional break-downs. *Addictive Behaviors, 3,* 149–164.

Sjoberg, L., Samsonowitz, V., & Olsson, G. (1978). Volitional problems in alcohol abuse. *Gotteberg Psychological Reports, 8,* No. 5.

Skafte, D. (1987). Video in groups: Implications for a social theory of the self. *International Journal of Group Psychotherapy, 37,* 389–402.

Skutle, A., & Berg, G. (1987). Training in controlled drinking for early-stage problem drinkers. *British Journal of Addiction, 82,* 493–501.

Stall, R., & Biernacki, P. (1986). Spontaneous remission from the problematic use of substances: An inductive model derived from a comparative analysis of the alcohol, opiate, tobacco, and food/obesity literatures. *International Journal of the Addictions, 21,* 1–23.

Swann, W. B., Jr. (1983). Self-verification: Bringing social reality into harmony with the self. In J. Suls & A. G. Greenwald (Eds.), *Psychological perspectives on the self* (Vol. 2, pp. 33–66). Hillsdale, NJ: Erlbaum.

Swann, W. B., Jr., Hixon, J. G., Stein-Seroussi, A., & Gilbert, D. T. (1990). The fleeting gleam of praise: Behavioral reactions to self-relevant feedback. *Journal of Personality and Social Psychology, 43,* 59–66.

Swann, W. B., Jr., Pelham, B. W., & Krull, D. S. (1989). Agreeable fancy or disagreeable truth? How people reconcile their self-enhancement and self-verification needs. *Journal of Personality and Social Psychology, 57,* 782–791.

Swann, W. B., Jr., & Read, S. J. (1981). Acquiring self-knowledge: The search for feedback that fits. *Journal of Personality and Social Psychology, 41,* 1119–1128.

Thorn, D. (1987). Problem solving for innovation in industry. *Journal of Creative Behavior, 21,* 93–107.

Tice, D. M. (1992). Self-concept change and self-presentation: The looking glass is also a magnifying glass. *Journal of Personality and Social Psychology, 63,* 435–451.

Tuchfeld, B. S. (1981). Spontaneous remission in alcoholics: Empirical observations and theoretical implications. *Journal of Studies on Alcohol, 42,* 626–641.

Vaillant, G. E., & Milofsky, E. S. (1982). Natural history of male alcoholism: IV. Paths to recovery. *Archives of General Psychiatry, 39,* 127–133.

Walker, R. D., Donovan, D. M., Kivlahan, D. R., & O'Leary, M. R. (1983). Length of stay, neuropsychological performance, and aftercare: Influences on alcohol treatment outcome. *Journal of Consulting and Clinical Psychology, 51,* 900–911.

Walters, G. D. (1990). *The criminal lifestyle: Patterns of serious criminal conduct.* Newbury Park, CA: Sage.

Walters, G. D. (1992). Drug-seeking behavior: Disease or lifestyle? *Professional Psychology: Research and Practice, 23,* 139–145.

Walters, G. D. (1994a). Discriminating between high and low volume substance abusers by means of the Drug Lifestyle Screening Interview. *American Journal of Drug and Alcohol Abuse, 20,* 19–33.

Walters, G. D. (1994b). *Drugs and crime in lifestyle perspective.* Thousand Oaks, CA: Sage.

Walters, G. D. (1994c). *Escaping the journey to nowhere: The psychology of alcohol and other drug abuse.* Washington, DC: Taylor & Francis.

Walters, G. D. (1995a). Predictive validity of the Drug Lifestyle Screening Interview: A two-year follow-up. *American Journal of Drug and Alcohol Abuse, 21,* 187–194.

Walters, G. D. (1995b). The natural history of substance misuse in an incarcerated criminal population. Manuscript submitted for publication.

Walters, G. D., & Willoughby, F. W. (1995). *The Psychological Inventory of Drug-Based Thinking Styles (PIDTS): Preliminary data.* Unpublished manuscript.

Weiner, B. (Ed.). (1974). *Achievement motivation and attribution theory.* Morristown, NJ: General Learning Press.

Wexler, M. (1975). Personality characteristics of marijuana users and nonusers in a suburban high school. *Cornell Journal of Social Relations, 10,* 267–288.

Wilson, J. Q., & Herrnstein, R. J. (1985). *Crime and human nature.* New York: Simon & Schuster.

Wilson, W. J. (1987). *The truly disadvantaged.* Chicago: University of Chicago Press.

Wolpe, J. (1969). *The practice of behavior therapy.* New York: Pergamon.

Woody, G. E., McLellan, A. T., Luborsky, F. L., & O'Brien, C. P. (1990). Psychotherapy and counseling for methadone-maintained opiate addicts: Results of research studies. *NIDA Research Monograph Series, 104,* 9–23.

Yamaguchi, K., & Kandel, D. B. (1984). Patterns of drug use from adolescence to young adulthood: II. Sequences of progression. *American Journal of Public Health, 74,* 668–672.

Yochelson, S., & Samenow, S. E. (1976). *The criminal personality: Vol. I. A profile for change.* New York: Jason Aronson.

Zimmer-Hofler, D., & Dobler-Mikola, A. (1992). Swiss heroin-addicted females: Career and social adjustment. *Journal of Substance Abuse Treatment, 9,* 159–170.

Zucker, R. A., & Gomberg, E. S. L. (1986). Etiology of alcoholism treatment reconsidered: The case of a biopsychosocial approach. *American Psychologist, 41,* 783–793.

Appendix 1:
Participant Handbook

The approach described in this handbook acknowledges that people begin using drugs for different reasons. Some use drugs to feel good, others because they are curious, and still others because they desire peer acceptance. The lifestyle model of drug-seeking behavior is less concerned with why people start using drugs than with why they continue using them after it becomes apparent that drugs are causing them serious life problems. One possible explanation is that with repetition drug-seeking behavior takes on the appearance of a lifestyle. The drug lifestyle is a set of decisions, behaviors, and thinking patterns that blinds the individual to the reality of his or her situation and allows the individual to continue using substances despite the associated long-term negative consequences. If your friends and family insist that you have an alcohol or drug problem, but you don't see it; if you are constantly looking for excuses to drink alcohol or use other drugs; if you find yourself spending more and more time with drug users; then the drug

This handbook is meant to serve as an aid in a professionally conducted program of treatment intervention and should not be used without appropriate supervision. Copyright © 1995 by Glenn D. Walters.

lifestyle may be something with which you are already familiar. This manual is designed to assist you in your efforts to abandon the drug lifestyle, under the watchful eye of a trained professional.

Before learning about the behavioral, cognitive, developmental, and change aspects of a drug lifestyle, you must first understand that the lifestyle approach to drug-seeking behavior is built on a foundation known as the three Cs. The three Cs (conditions, choice, and cognition) are believed to be instrumental in the formation of the drug lifestyle. **Conditions** are internal (heredity, intelligence) and external (family relationships, peer pressure) variables that either increase or decrease a person's chances of becoming a user or abuser of substances. Although conditions may limit or expand a person's options in life, they do not determine behavior. Instead, people choose how they will respond to the conditions of their lives. **Choice,** therefore, is the second of the three Cs. The third C, **cognition,** is how a person supports, justifies, and rationalizes his or her decisions by distorting his or her thinking. No one wants to think of themselves as a bad person; so when we make bad decisions or our choices wind up hurting others, we adjust our thinking in order to avoid feeling bad.

BEHAVIORAL PATTERNS

The drug lifestyle is a caricature (an exaggerated picture of reality, like the caricatures drawn of politicians and celebrities) that many people approach, but few people achieve in a complete or final form. One of the primary goals of this program, then, is to decide, with the aid of a trained therapist, how closely you, the client, resemble this caricature or ideal. This can be accomplished by comparing yourself against the four behavioral characteristics of a drug lifestyle: irresponsibility/pseudoresponsibility, stress-coping imbalance, interpersonal triviality, and social rule breaking/bending. Your therapist may ask you certain questions designed to help him or her estimate your proximity to the drug lifestyle caricature, so it is important that you answer these questions as honestly and completely as possible.

Irresponsibility/Pseudoresponsibility   Irresponsibility means not fulfilling your obligations to others—your family, friends, or employer—or being unaccountable for your actions by missing appointments, being delinquent in paying your bills, or failing to consider the consequences of your actions. Pseudoresponsibility, on the other hand, is a fake or superficial pattern of responsibility in which you give the appearance of being responsible (providing financial support for yourself and your family, maintaining employment, staying out of serious trouble with the police), but fail to meet personal obligations to family members (missing important family functions because of a growing preoccupation with drugs).

Stress-Coping Imbalance   Drug use may start out as a desire to feel good and indulge oneself. However, by the time drug abuse becomes a lifestyle, self-indulgence has been replaced by stress-coping imbalance. The drug lifestyle is characterized by an ever-increasing level of stress that is managed through drug use or some other form of psychological escape. The reason this is termed stress-coping imbalance is that the person's habitual manner of handling stress (escaping through drug use) creates more long-term stress problems and contributes to an escalating pattern of drug usage (in an effort to manage the rising level of stress caused by the drugs). In addition, because drugs are effective in reducing stress in the short-run, the person has little motivation to learn more effective long-term coping strategies.

Interpersonal Triviality　As you get more involved with drugs you may notice that you are spending less time with your family and more time with other drug users. As the drug lifestyle progresses, deep and meaningful relationships tend to shrink in importance, whereas superficial, often exploitive, relationships tend to prosper and grow. This is what is referred to as interpersonal triviality. Interpersonal triviality also occurs when you use drugs as a substitute for meaningful human interaction. For this reason, rituals (repetitive patterns of behavior that center on the purchase, preparation, or use of a drug) become increasingly more important as you move into the more advanced stages of the drug lifestyle. These rituals can become so powerful that when interrupted in the performance of a ritual you may become angry at being cheated from experiencing the full drug effect.

Social Rule Breaking/Bending　If you are committed to the drug lifestyle then you are probably not adverse to breaking the rules of society as a way of achieving access to drugs. However, rule-breaking behavior often comes with a high price. For this reason, people committed to the drug lifestyle generally prefer to bend the rules—lying, conning, deceiving—rather than break them. Social rule bending is less likely to lead to arrest, and if you are "caught in the act," the consequences are ordinarily less severe than if you are caught stealing, robbing, or committing other social rule–breaking acts. People involved in the drug lifestyle will engage in social rule–breaking behavior if they believe their opportunities for social rule bending are limited. However, if given the choice between the two, most drug users will select the social rule–bending option because it is much less likely to separate them from the drugs they crave.

COGNITION

Cognition, or thinking, is the way you justify and rationalize your drug-seeking behavior. The lifestyle model identifies eight thinking patterns critical in maintaining a drug lifestyle. Each will be discussed briefly in this section.

Mollification　People who abuse drugs like to avoid responsibility for their actions by proving to themselves and others that they had no choice but to use drugs. By blaming your parents, peers, or society, however, you are failing to take responsibility for your actions. Lifestyle theory refers to this as mollification. In not assuming responsibility for your decisions and behavior, you are eliminating potential avenues of change and intervention, which in the end only serves to protect the drug lifestyle.

Cutoff   Commitment to the drug lifestyle requires that you be able to eliminate common roadblocks to drug use. The phrase "fuck it" is the most common cutoff observed in clinical populations of drug users. It is also possible that drugs may serve as a cutoff for future drug use. For example, you may stop off at a bar on your way home from work for a couple of beers and wind up consuming an entire case of beer along with a fifth of whisky, because the first two beers served as a cutoff by interfering with your judgment and eliminating your original intent to limit yourself to a couple of drinks.

Entitlement   Before indulging in the use of drugs you must first grant yourself permission to use the substance in question. Drug-involved people often tell themselves that they are entitled to use drugs because they have had a hard life, a rough week, or a bad day. Some drug users can, in fact, be rather creative in the way they grant themselves permission to use drugs, sometimes going so far as to manipulate a conflict with a spouse or employer in order to justify going out and getting drunk or using drugs. The idea that you are "addicted" or "out of control" and that this somehow negates your ability to make rational decisions is another example of entitlement in the service of continued drug use.

Power Orientation   The thinking that governs the drug lifestyle is not only motivated by immediate gratification, but by the desire for interpersonal control, as well. The drug user may attempt to counteract weak personal control by finding ways to manipulate and control others. Power orientation is also expressed in a person's use of drugs to achieve a sense of control and predictability over his or her own behavior. In other words, drugs normally have a fairly predictable effect; you can, therefore, gain a temporary sense of predictability over a seemingly unmanageable life by using these substances and experiencing the anticipated effect, even if this effect is no longer enjoyable.

Sentimentality   We all have a need to view ourselves in a positive, constructive light; drug-involved individuals are no exception. They tend to distort their thinking in order to deny behavior that is destructive to both themselves and others. Rather than making excuses because of perceived injustices, as is the pattern with mollification, sentimentality involves justifying your actions by noting all the positive things you have accomplished over a certain period of time. Religion, love of your family, and the welfare of strangers are ways one might reduce guilt through sentimentality. The major difference between sentimentality and true caring and concern is that whereas true caring and concern is focused on another person, sentimentality is a selfish attempt to shine a positive light on yourself by performing one or more good deeds.

Superoptimism   Because the human body is able to withstand a great deal before it eventually breaks down, people often use drugs for months, perhaps even years, before experiencing the negative side effects of the drug lifestyle. This contributes to the formation of an attitude of invulnerability in the minds of people who are able to initially escape the devastating physical and social consequences of habitual drug use, even though they may have observed many of the same consequences in others. This is because you convince yourself that you will somehow be able to escape the negative repercussions of the drug lifestyle "for the time being." However, this only makes your eventual fall that much more dramatic.

Cognitive Indolence   People who abuse drugs are as lazy in thought as they are in action. Like water running down hill, people involved in the drug lifestyle take the path of least resistance, although this path is fraught with pitfalls and booby traps at every turn. If you are committed to the drug lifestyle then you have probably taken many shortcuts, knowing full well that these shortcuts may eventually end in disaster. However, those committed to the drug lifestyle are much more interested in pursuing the short-term pleasure of drug use than worrying about long-term effects. The lazy thinking that is cognitive indolence also causes many drug abusers to take an uncritical view of their plans and ideas.

Discontinuity   People engaged in the drug lifestyle often have trouble following through on commitments and good intentions. When you are engaged in discontinuity you may also have trouble remaining focused on goals because you are readily sidetracked and distracted by things going on around you. This lack of consistency in thought and behavior is called discontinuity and is what often frustrates a person's attempts at long-term change. It also gives rise to a Jekyll and Hyde pattern in which the person wears two different masks, one when using drugs and the other during periods of relative sobriety.

DEVELOPMENTAL STAGES

The drug lifestyle is said to progress through four distinct developmental stages.

Pre-Drug Lifestyle Stage   During this stage drug use is motivated chiefly by curiosity, excitement, and the desire for peer acceptance. Although the individual may experiment with a wide variety of substances and may even encounter drug-related difficulties, he or she has not yet made a commitment to the drug lifestyle. Well over half the people (mostly juveniles) who enter this stage do not proceed to the next stage of drug lifestyle development. As a result, this stage contributes a higher rate of voluntary attrition (drop out) than any of the three stages that follow it.

Early Drug Stage   This stage is marked by increasing commitment to the drug lifestyle in defining your goals and interests in life. It is also during this stage that a growing preoccupation with drug-related activities and a dawning identification with the drug lifestyle becomes apparent. With an escalation in the frequency of use comes a reduction in the number of different substances consumed, or at least preferred. There is a low to moderate degree of attrition from this stage, not as much as during the pre-drug lifestyle stage, but significantly more than is observed during the advanced stage.

Advanced Drug Stage   Commitment, preoccupation, and identification are at their height during this stage. In fact, commitment to drug lifestyle goals and activities is so strong that persons functioning at this stage are more dangerous to themselves (from overdose, suicide) and others (inadvertently through drunk driving or crime) than at any other point in the drug lifestyle sequence. Very few people voluntarily drop out of the lifestyle during the advanced stage because of the high level of commitment to the drug ideal.

Burnout/Maturity   Due to the combined influence of age and the wear and tear of the drug lifestyle, people eventually enter a state of burnout or maturity. A decline in physical energy and reduced sensitivity to drug effects is referred to as burnout, whereas psychological changes in values and priorities come under the heading of maturity. Burnout is inevitable, maturity is not. Treatment is designed to stimulate maturity so that it accompanies the natural burnout process. Burnout in the absence of maturity results in continued drug use, often at a lower level, and puts the individual at risk for future relapse.

It is important for you to understand that a person can regress to an earlier stage in the lifestyle development sequence at any time, even after spending years in the burnout/maturity stage. This could occur if you used a slip as a pretense to return to the lifestyle, or if you were to identify a new primary drug of abuse. As a case in point, you may burn out on cocaine without achieving maturity and return to the early stage with a new primary drug of abuse (alcohol, for example). These factors need to be considered in planning and constructing an effective program of behavior change and relapse prevention.

LIFESTYLE MODEL OF BEHAVIORAL CHANGE

The lifestyle model of behavioral change follows three phases: foundation, vehicles for change, and a reinforcing non-drug lifestyle.

Foundation   The foundation is a sense of disgust with your past use of drugs and current drug-related thinking. This might take the form of generating images of the people who have been hurt, including yourself, by your involvement in the drug lifestyle. Later phases of treatment will fail to take root if you have not constructed a solid foundation. Furthermore, the foundation needs to be continually reinforced once it has been laid, or you run the risk of relapse.

Vehicles for Change   A vehicle is a tool used by clients to challenge drug-related thinking and behavior and develop social, coping, and general life skills. Vehicles that have been found effective in assisting people interested in abandoning the drug lifestyle include group counseling, drug education, vocational guidance, stress management, social skills training, and self-inspection. However, these vehicles cannot stand on their own; they require the continued support of a solid foundation and the realization of a reinforcing non-drug lifestyle.

Reinforcing Non-Drug Lifestyle   By the time you have entered the final phase of the change process, you have already made a number of changes in the way you think, feel, and act. This final step in the process is to identify reinforcers in the community you can use to avoid old drug lifestyle patterns. Making commitments to yourself by considering the effect your behavior has had on your family and friends, changing your priorities, identifying a non-drug career, and finding non-drug hobbies and entertainment are ways to encourage development of a reinforcing non-drug lifestyle.

COMMON VEHICLES FOR THE EIGHT THINKING PATTERNS

Thinking pattern	Vehicle for change
Mollification	Learn to accept responsibility for the decisions you have made in life and stop offering excuses for your past drug usage.
Cutoff	Explore alternative coping strategies designed to teach you how to manage stress and frustration more effectively.
Entitlement	Challenge thoughts of ownership and privilege and your tendency to misidentify wants as needs. Stop using your drug addiction to justify continued drug usage.
Power orientation	Shift your attention away from the external environment, issues of control, and mood manipulation, and seek to develop internal controls and self-discipline.
Sentimentality	You must own up to the pain that has been caused by your use of drugs and accept the fact that performing a few good deeds does not erase the harm created by your involvement in the drug lifestyle.

Thinking pattern	Vehicle for change
Superoptimism	Become more realistic in your self-appraisal and learn to develop reality-based creative thinking skills.
Cognitive indolence	Avoid taking shortcuts and become more critical of your thoughts, ideas, and plans.
Discontinuity	Formulate goals and learn to identify cues associated with "getting off track." In addition, know how to get yourself back on track by accepting responsibility for your actions and continually reevaluating your goals and progress.

PROGRAM CONTINUATION

This is only the first part of the handbook you will be using to effect your escape from the drug lifestyle. Your therapist will provide additional information, homework assignments, exercises, and other materials designed to assist you further. It is important to understand that this information is designed to help you challenge old lifestyle patterns and construct a new, non-drug lifestyle. You may, therefore, want to store this handbook and related materials in a large file folder so that you have ready access to the information.

Appendix 2: Drug Lifestyle Screening Interview (DLSI)

I. Personal Data

Name _____ Reg. No. _____ Sex _____

Age _____ Race ____ Education _____ Marital _____

II. Irresponsibility/Pseudoresponsibility

a. Did you drop out of high school before completing the 12th grade? _____

b. Have you ever been fired from a job or quit a job without warning? _____

c. Have you ever gotten into trouble for not paying your bills? _____

d. Have you ever been cited for failure to pay child support? _____

e. Did you regularly neglect the psychological needs of loved ones? _____

Note: Responding Yes receives a score of 1 and responding No a score of 0.

Irresponsibility/Pseudoresponsibility Score _____

III. Stress-Coping Imbalance

a. On a scale from 1 to 3, 1 representing a low level of stress and 3 a high
    degree of stress, rate your level of stress:
    1. Right before you began using drugs _____
    2. After you had been using drugs for 6 months _____
b. How did you handle stress during the period you were using drugs?

    _____

Note: Score 2 points if subject responds by using drugs, 1 point if they report
some other form of escapism, and 0 points if they appeared to use more effective
coping strategies.
Stress-Coping Imbalance Score _____

IV. Interpersonal Triviality

a. Did you spend more time with drug users or non-drug users?
    1. Before you started using drugs yourself   Yes/No
    2. During the early stages of your drug usage   Yes/No
    3. During the advanced stages of drug involvement   Yes/No
b. A ritual is a routinized pattern of behavior which accompanies use of a
    particular drug. Indicate the degree to which rituals were part of your use of
    drugs (check one of the options listed below):
    Not at all _____ (0)
    To a moderate degree _____ (1)
    To a high degree _____ (2)
c. List the specific rituals individual engaged in while using drugs.

    _____
    _____
    _____
    _____

d. Did you find yourself engaging in empty and meaningless conversations
    ("bullshit") with other drug users once you became involved in regular drug
    usage?
    _____ Yes (1)   _____ No (0)
Interpersonal Triviality Score _____

V. Social Rule Breaking (SRBr)/Bending (SRBe)

a. Have you ever engaged in the following behaviors (one point each):
    1. panhandling _____ (SRBe)
    2. burglary _____ (SRBr)

    3. lying to family members in order to get money for drugs _____ (SRBe)

    4. selling drugs _____ (SRBr)

    5. suspension from school for misbehavior _____ (SRBr)

    6. acting as a go-between in a drug deal _____ (SRBe)

    7. writing bad checks you intended to cover at a later date _____ (SRBe)

    8. stealing money from mother's purse/father's wallet < age 14 _____
      (SRBr)

b. Age of onset: Rule Breaking _____   Rule Bending _____

Social Rule Breaking/Bending Score _____

TOTAL DLSI SCORE _____

Appendix 3: Administration and Scoring Key for DLSI

ADMINISTRATION

I. Personal Data

Fill in personal data information.

II. Irresponsibility/Pseudoresponsibility

Inquire about the five areas under this heading and score a "1" if respondent answers "yes" and a "0" if respondent answers "no." For question *b* ("Have you ever been fired from a job or quit a job without warning?"), score a "1" if individual reports having never held a legitimate job. Being laid off for economic reasons does not qualify as being fired for the purposes of this item.

III. Stress-Coping Imbalance

Ask respondent, "On a scale from 1 to 3, 1 representing a low level of stress, 2 a medium or moderate level of stress, and 3 a high level of stress, how would you rate your level of stress right before you began using drugs?" Then ask, "How would you rate your level of stress after you had been using drugs for 6 months?"

Next, ask how the respondent handled stress during the periods in which he or she was using drugs. Ask for specific examples if the respondent provides a general or unscorable response (e.g., "I would just go ahead and deal with it anyway" or "There's nothing I can't handle").

IV. Interpersonal Triviality

Ask respondent if he or she spent more time with drug users or non-drug users (a) before initiating own drug use, (b) during the initial stages of drug involvement (i.e., first several months), and (c) during the advanced stages of the drug lifestyle (i.e., when most highly involved with drugs).

Define for respondent what a ritual is and provide examples if he or she seems to have problems understanding the concept. Then ask the participant to rate the degree to which rituals were involved in his or her own use of chemicals (i.e., a high degree, a moderate degree, or not at all). Ask for a description of the specific rituals in order to check respondent's understanding.

Ask respondent if he or she has engaged in frivolous communications by inquiring about whether he or she has experienced empty and meaningless conversations with other drugs users since becoming involved in a regular pattern of drug use.

V. Social Rule Breaking/Bending

Ask respondent the eight questions in subsection *a* and place a "1" where the answer is "yes" and a "0" where the answer is "no."

Briefly define the difference between social rule breaking (violating the rules of the home, school, and society; to include breaking the law) and social rule bending (bending the rules or going around them as represented by deception, lying, and manipulation). Ask respondent which (social rule breaking or social rule bending) he or she displayed *on a regular basis first,* and record this age. Then inquire about the age at which the other behavior began. If the individual states that he or she never engaged in social rule breaking or social rule bending behavior, place an NA in the space provided for age.

SCORING

I. Personal Data

No scoring required.

II. Irresponsibility/Pseudoresponsibility

Sum the five items. Maximum score on this subscale is 5.

III. Stress-Coping Imbalance

Score 1 point if stress level before initial drug use was 2 or 3. Score 1 point if stress level after 6 months of drug use was 3. Score 1 point if stress level went up from the pre-drug level after using drugs (i.e., 1 to 2, 1 to 3, 2 to 3). Score 2 points if individual reports having handled stress during periods of drug involvement by "using drugs," "drinking," or "getting high." Score 1 point if individual fails to report the use of drugs to combat stress, but mentions some other form of escapism or ineffective coping (e.g., running away, withdrawing, violence, crime). If respondent reports both drug use and other forms of escapism, count only the drug use. Maximum score on this subsection is 5.

IV. Interpersonal Triviality

Score 1 point if individual spent more time with drug users than non-drug users during either the early or advanced stages of his or her drug involvement. Score 1 additional point if individual reports having spent more time with non-drug users before he or she began using drugs and more time with drug users during both the early and advanced stages of drug involvement. Score 2 points for a high degree of ritualism, 1 point for a moderate degree of ritualism, and 0 for no ritualism. Score 1 point if respondent replies yes to part d ("Did you find yourself engaging in empty and meaningless conversations ['bullshit'] with other drug users once you became involved in regular drug usage?") of this subsection. Maximum score on this subsection is 5.

V. Social Rule Breaking/Bending

Score 1 point for each "yes" response to items followed by SRBr (Social Rule Breaking) and 1 point for each "yes" answer to items followed by SRBe (Social Rule Bending). If a regular pattern of social rule breaking began before age 16 score 1 point (Social Rule Breaking) and if a regular pattern of social rule bending began before age 16 score 1 point (Social Rule Bending). Maximum scores on this subsection are 5 for Social Rule Breaking and 5 for Social Rule Bending. Sum the subtotals for the Social Rule Breaking and Social Rule Bending categories and then divide by 2. If the result is a decimal, round up. The maximum score on this subsection is 5.

VI. Total DLSI Score

Add the Irresponsibility/Pseudoresponsibility, Stress-Coping Imbalance, Interpersonal Triviality, and Social Rule Breaking/Bending subtotals to derive the total DLSI score. The maximum score the total DLSI can achieve is 20.

Appendix 4: Inventory of Negative Consequences

Instructions: Describe the negative consequences of your drug-oriented lifestyle by completing the following lists.

1. List the people who have been hurt by your involvement with drugs.

    1.

    2.

    3.

    4.

2. List the opportunities and experiences you missed or failed to pursue because of your involvement with drugs.

1.

2.

3.

4.

3. List the possessions and relationships you have lost as a result of your involvement with drugs.

1.

2.

3.

4.

4. List situations in which you felt embarrassed by what you did or did not do because of your involvement with drugs.

1.

2.

3.

4.

Appendix 5: LOCUS Test

Instructions: On a scale from 1 to 5, rate the degree to which you currently perceive the following five events to be the result of outside forces (e.g., other people, society, environmental circumstances, chance) or your own decision making: 1 represents exclusive external responsibility, 2 represents moderate external responsibility, 3 represents equal amounts of external and internal (own decision making) responsibility, 4 represent moderate personal or internal responsibility, and 5 represents exclusive personal or internal responsibility. Calculate your total score by summing your ratings for the five events.

	Outside forces			Own decision making
1. Your initial use of drugs	1	2	3	4	5
2. Your current or most recent use of drugs	1	2	3	4	5
3. Your most recent conflict with another person	1	2	3	4	5
4. Your enrollment in this program	1	2	3	4	5
5. Your current emotional state	1	2	3	4	5

TOTAL SCORE _____

Appendix 6:
Change Thermometer

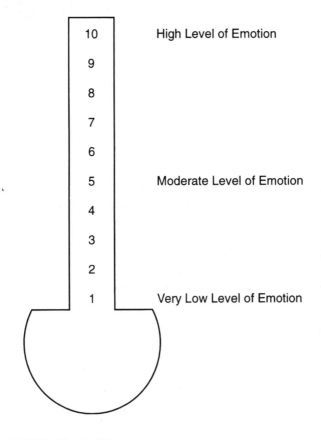

10   High Level of Emotion

9

8

7

6

5   Moderate Level of Emotion

4

3

2

1   Very Low Level of Emotion

Appendix 7:
Estimated Self-Efficacy
in Avoiding Drugs

Instructions: Imagine you are on the streets and you encounter the following situations. Using the 5-point scale provided below, rate the degree to which you believe you would be able to resist the urge to use drugs.

 0 = no confidence (would avoid drugs less than 50% of the time)
 1 = mildly confident (would avoid drugs approx. 50 to 74% of the time)
 2 = moderately confident (would avoid drugs approx. 75 to 89% of the time)
 3 = highly confident (would avoid drugs approx. 90 to 99% of the time)
 4 = extremely confident (would avoid drugs 100% of the time)

PART A

1. You get fired from your job 4   3   2   1   0
2. You feel depressed or sad 4   3   2   1   0
3. You are "hassled" by a counselor at the center
   where you go for drug treatment follow-up 4   3   2   1   0

4. You feel overwhelmed by responsibilities 4   3   2   1   0
5. You are bored 4   3   2   1   0

PART B

6. You feel good about "staying clean" for 6 months . . 4   3   2   1   0
7. You must speak in front of a group of ex-drug
    abusers about your recent success in remaining
    drug-free 4   3   2   1   0
8. Someone whose opinion you respect tells you
    that it may be possible to "dabble" in drugs without
    becoming addicted or getting "caught up" 4   3   2   1   0

PART C

9. You watch a movie where people are using
    drugs in a way reminiscent of how you
    once used drugs 4   3   2   1   0
10. You walk by a corner where you used to
    "cop" drugs 4   3   2   1   0
11. You feel a restlessness inside that reminds you of
    how you used to feel when you went without
    drugs for several days 4   3   2   1   0
12. You are in a conversation with someone you used
    drugs with in the past and they start reminiscing
    about a particular drug experience you both went
    through several years ago 4   3   2   1   0

PART D

13. You come across a large stash of drugs you had
    hidden so well you had forgotten about it
    for several years 4   3   2   1   0
14. You are told by a colleague at work that he or she
    knows where you can get some "really
    good" drugs 4   3   2   1   0

PART E

15. You receive pressure from a group of old friends to go
    with them to a bar or disco where you know there
    will be a lot of drugs and drinking 4   3   2   1   0
16. You feel lonely 4   3   2   1   0
17. You have trouble making new friends 4   3   2   1   0
18. You are approached by a former drug associate who
    states that he has been using drugs for years without
    any problems and that if you go out with him he will
    teach you the secret to his success 4   3   2   1   0
19. You are surrounded by a group of old drug associates
    who respond to your desire to remain drug-free as a
    sign that you are "selling out" to the system and so
    should no longer be trusted or be allowed to be part
    of their group 4   3   2   1   0
20. You pick up on subtle messages from the people you
    care about most that they believe it is just a matter of
    time before you start using drugs again 4   3   2   1   0

After completing the 20 items, total the scores by section (A, B, C, D, and E) and then total the sections. Next, divide each section score by the number of items within it (e.g., 5 in Section A, 3 in Section B, and so on) to obtain the average estimate per item and record this figure on the line to the right of the = sign.

Score for Section A _____ ÷ 5 = _____

Score for Section B _____ ÷ 3 = _____

Score for Section C _____ ÷ 4 = _____

Score for Section D _____ ÷ 2 = _____

Score for Section E _____ ÷ 6 = _____

TOTAL SCORE _____ ÷ 20 = _____

Appendix 8: Imagery Exercise Questionnaire

Instructions: Close your eyes and draw a simple two-dimensional box with four equal sides in your mind. (10-second pause) Now add a third dimension to this image. Make the box three-dimensional by adding depth. (10-second pause) Were you able to successfully convert the square into a cube? If not take another 10 seconds to get a good image of a cube in your mind. (10-second pause) Now run your hand over the cube. Is the surface rough or smooth to the touch? (10-second pause) Does it feel warm, hot, cold? Or maybe you can identify a specific temperature. (10-second pause) What color or combination of colors is your cube? (10-second pause) Is it solid or transparent? (20-second pause) Put you nose up to the cube. What does it smell like? (10-second pause) Put the cube in your mouth. What does it taste like? (20-second pause) Imagine what the cube would sound like if you dropped it on the floor. (20-second pause) Now complete the Imagery Exercise Questionnaire.

QUESTIONNAIRE

1. Were you able to visualize the two-dimensional box?   ☐ Yes   ☐ No

2. Were you able to visualize the three-dimensional cube?   ☐ Yes   ☐ No

3. Were you able to touch the cube?   ☐ Yes   ☐ No
3a. If so, what did the surface feel like?

_____

_____

   Did it have a temperature? If so, what was it?

_____

_____

4. Did your cube have color?   ☐ Yes   ☐ No
4a. If so, what was the color?

_____

_____

5. Were you able to determine whether the cube
      was solid or transparent?   ☐ Yes   ☐ No
5a. If so, which was it?

_____

_____

6. Were you able to smell the cube?   ☐ Yes   ☐ No
6a. If so, what did it smell like?

_____

_____

7. Were you able to taste the cube?   ☐ Yes   ☐ No
7a. If so, what did it taste like?

_____

_____

8. Were you able to hear the sound of the cube
hitting the floor?   ☐ Yes   ☐ No
8a. If so, what kind of sound did it make?

_____

_____

Appendix 9:
Self-Monitoring
of Drug-Related
Thoughts and Behaviors

Instructions: Make a mark in the proper column each time you engage in the behaviors and thoughts listed below.

	Day 1	Day 2	Day 3	Day 4	Day 5	Day 6	Day 7	TOTAL
Behaviors								
1. Buy drugs								
2. Use drugs								
3. Associate with known drug users								
4. Refuse drugs offered to you								
Thoughts								
1. Think about buying drugs								
2. Think about using drugs								
3. Think about an enjoyable drug experience								
4. Think about a negative drug experience								

Appendix 10: Sample Behavioral Contract

INITIAL CHANGE CONTRACT

The drug program at this facility is based on the lifestyle model of intervention, which conceives of drug abuse as a lifestyle. Consistent with the lifestyle approach to intervention, this program is broken down into three phases. The first phase is designed to encourage termination of drug use and drug-related activities so that clients can benefit from future phases of intervention. This phase normally lasts 1 to 3 weeks and blends into the second phase. The second phase of intervention involves the assessment of skills and training in social, coping, life, and thinking skills identified as deficient during the assessment. This phase normally lasts 6 to 12 weeks. The final phase of intervention entails follow-up and resocialization. This will necessitate coordinating aftercare services with a community-based outpatient program or mental health professional to maintain and solidify the changes made during the first two phases of intervention. The major portion of this phase takes place after release and may last anywhere from 6 to 48 months.

The Client Agrees:

1. To refrain from drug use, drug dealing, and other forms of disruptive behavior while enrolled in this program.
2. To submit to regular urinalysis or breathalyzer evaluations designed to detect the presence of prohibited substances.
3. To actively participate in all program sessions, complete all "in session" and "homework" assignments, and dedicate oneself to the change process.
4. To keep all information revealed by others during group sessions confidential.
5. To allow certain exercises and sessions to be videotaped for therapeutic and program purposes. Videotaping for reasons other than programming will require that the taping agent secure the informed consent of clients.
6. To understand and abide by the rules and guidelines established by program staff and realize that any violations of these rules and guidelines may result in expulsion from the program.

Therapy Staff Agree:

1. To provide a high quality professional program of drug abuse programming.
2. To encourage client change through support, training, and feedback.
3. To keep all personal information disclosed by clients confidential except where limited by law. This means that release of information outside of the program will require that the client sign a Release of Information form.
4. To coordinate release with an aftercare agency or professional in order to maintain and solidify the changes made in the formal program.
5. To allow clients to withdraw from the program upon signing a Withdrawal from Programming form.

Support Group Members Agree:

1. To attend support group meeting made available through the program.
2. To learn to differentiate between positive support and behaviors that reinforce a drug lifestyle.
3. To make an effort to provide clients with positive support and avoid engaging in behaviors that reinforce or encourage the client's drug use.

This contract is agreed to by the following parties:

_____

    Client's Printed Name

_____   _____

    Client's Signature   Date

_____   _____

Therapy Team Member's Signature   Date

_____   _____

Support Group Member's Signature   Date

_____   _____

Support Group Member's Signature   Date

_____   _____

Support Group Member's Signature   Date

_____   _____

Support Group Member's Signature   Date

Appendix 11:
Lifestyle Stress Test

Instructions: Rate each of the following 20 situations and issues in terms of how often you experienced each in the month in which you were most heavily involved with drugs (first column) and in the past 30 days (second column), using the following scale:

   0 = never experienced the situation
   1 = at least one time, but no more than once a week
   2 = several times a week, but not daily
   3 = at least once a day

	Month used drugs the most	Past 30 days
1. Money or financial concerns		
2. Feeling irritated with other people		
3. Setting goals or standards that you could not realistically achieve		
4. Arguing with others about relatively trivial matters		
5. Feeling that you have lost control over your life		
6. Problems communicating with spouse, family, friends, or boss		
7. Being saddled with too much responsibility		
8. Feeling pressured at work to meet unrealistic deadlines or achieve beyond your capabilities		
9. Worrying about things over which you have little control		
10. Having trouble accepting compliments		
11. Not having sufficient time for hobbies, leisure, or recreation		
12. Feeling "crowded" by others		
13. Spending too much time sitting and not enough time exercising		
14. Having trouble saying no to unrealistic requests from others		
15. Trying to do too many things at one time		
16. Getting into physical fights with others		
17. Wanting to change your life but not knowing how		
18. Sense of being overwhelmed by the noise created by others		
19. Feeling bored		
20. Being "put down" by others		
TOTAL SCORE		
PERSONAL SCORE (odd-numbered items)		
INTERPERSONAL SCORE (even-numbered items)		

Appendix 12: Drug-Related Cues Checklist

Instructions: Check any of the symptoms listed below that you experience in response to the stimulus that is presented to you. Mark your answers under column 1. Then rate the degree to which the stimulus is something you can relate to (if the stimulus is a videotape) or something that seems genuine to you (if the stimulus is a drug replica).

	Physical symptoms	1	2	3	4	5	6
1.	Headache						
2.	Lightheaded						
3.	Flushing of face or neck						
4.	Tension in face, neck, or jaw						
5.	"Lump" in throat						
6.	Increased heart rate						
7.	Decreased heart rate						

Physical symptoms		1	2	3	4	5	6
8.	Heartburn						
9.	Upset or quivering stomach						
10.	Sweaty palms						
11.	Uncontrollable shaking						
12.	Tension in arms/chest/hands						
13.	"Nervous" movement of arms/legs						
14.	Cold chills						
15.	General sense of bodily relaxation						
	Psychological symptoms						
16.	Feeling anxious or "on edge"						
17.	Feeling uptight						
18.	Worry						
19.	Anger						
20.	Disgust						
21.	Fear						
22.	Confusion						
23.	Sadness or depression						
24.	Urge to use drugs						
25.	Joy or happiness						
26.	Feeling of power						
27.	Increased energy						
28.	Excitement						
29.	A general state of well-being						
30.	A feeling of being "high"						

Indicate the degree to which you are able to relate to this film portrayal of drug use or view the drug replica as realistic by circling one of the five numbers listed below:

    1 = Cannot relate to videotape/drug replica unrealistic.

    2 = Can vaguely relate to videotape/drug replica vaguely realistic.

    3 = Can relate somewhat to videotape/drug replica somewhat realistic.

    4 = Can relate reasonably well to videotape/drug replica reasonably realistic.

    5 = Can relate very well to film portrayal/drug replica highly realistic.

Appendix 13:
Access to Drug Use

1. List the specific *people* and types of *people* that encouraged you to use drugs in the past.

a. _____

b. _____

c. _____

d. _____

e. _____

f. _____

2. List the specific *places* and kinds of *places* in which you used drugs in the past.

a. _____

b. _____

c. _____

d. _____

e. _____

f. _____

3. List the specific *things* and categories of *things* that appear to have supported your use of drugs in the past.

a. _____

b. _____

c. _____

d. _____

e. _____

f. _____

Appendix 14: Interpersonal Influence Scale

Instructions: Select the option that best reflects your attitudes, behaviors, and beliefs.

1. My drug use
    a. has nearly always occurred alone.
    b. has sometimes occurred in the company of others.
    c. has nearly always occurred in the company of others.
2. The worst thing I could ever imagine is
    a. being rejected by people I respect.
    b. being alone.
    c. having no self-respect.
3. If someone were to tell me something I knew nothing about
    a. I would check out the situation myself.
    b. I would wonder if what they were telling me was true.
    c. I would accept what they said without question.

4. If someone were to approach me with a plan to get drugs they swore carried no risk of getting caught I would
   a. jump at the opportunity.
   b. think about the opportunity for awhile and if it seemed to make sense probably go along with it.
   c. reject the idea without considering it further.
5. In situations where people make fun of me or try to put me down my usual response is to
   a. ignore them.
   b. feel hurt or angry but not express these feelings.
   c. tell them off.
6. When in a group
   a. I tend to go along with the group.
   b. I generally go along with the group unless I strongly disagree with something that is being said or done.
   c. I am often the first one to speak out against what the group thinks or does.
7. My main goal in life is to
   a. achieve personal satisfaction.
   b. do something other people will notice.
   c. have other people like me.
8. My first use of drugs was
   a. something I felt forced to do because of peer pressure.
   b. something I chose to do but mostly because of the fact my peers were involved with drugs.
   c. something I did alone and which had nothing to do with peer influence.
9. If I were to come into contact with an old drug-using associate I would
   a. act as if I did not know him or her.
   b. speak to him or her but keep the conversation short and curt.
   c. drop what I am doing in order to spend some time with an "old friend."
10. Pressure from people I respect that is designed to get me to use drugs is likely to lead me to
   a. use the drugs.
   b. agree to use the drugs with the intent of finding an excuse for why I must leave before the drugs are actually used.
   c. lose respect for these individuals and avoid any further contact with them.

Appendix 15: Suggested Role Plays for Social Perspective Taking

1. You must talk a close friend into seeking treatment for a serious cocaine problem.

2. Your car has just been hit by a drunk driver.

3. You must bail your brother out of jail after his arrest for possession of heroin.

4. You are a bartender who must tell an obviously inebriated patron that you can no longer serve him or her drinks.

5. You must counsel an employee who is having trouble at work because of his or her use of amphetamines.

6. Your spouse comes home intoxicated on an unprescribed tranquilizer after missing your 4-year-old's birthday party.

7. You find marijuana and rolling papers in your 14-year-old's backpack.

8. You receive an unwelcome advance from someone who is apparently high on drugs.

9. You learn that your spouse or lover has contracted the HIV virus from using intravenous drugs.

10. You are discussing an issue with a friend who tells you that you are wrong and he or she is right because this person is on LSD, which he or she asserts is the only path to truth and understanding.

Appendix 16: Multiple Options Analysis

Instructions: You will be asked to generate as many options as you can (up to a maximum of nine) for each of the following eight situations. You will be given 1 minute to respond to each item, one item at a time. It is important to keep in mind that the object of this exercise is to generate as many alternative solutions and options as possible for each item.

1. You want to determine whether a bookcase will fit into a space between your sofa and desk but have no tape measure or ruler handy. List as many alternative options for making this determination as you can.
1.
2.
3.
4.
5.
6.
7.
8.
9.

2. You go out to your car in the morning and notice that it won't start. You have to be at work, which is 10 miles away, for a very important meeting that starts in 30 minutes. List as many alternative options for dealing with this situation as you can.

1.
2.
3.
4.
5.
6.
7.
8.
9.

3. You are in town and someone you know approaches you for a "few dollars" so that she can buy food for her children. However, you know this individual has a serious drug problem and you suspect that she will use the money for drugs. List as many alternative options as come to mind in administering to this old acquaintance.

1.
2.
3.
4.
5.
6.
7.
8.
9.

4. You and another individual must move a 1,000-pound safe from a truck in the street to the third floor of an office building with no elevator. List as many alternative options as you can so that you might accomplish this task.

1.
2.
3.
4.
5.
6.
7.
8.
9.

5. Entertaining a group of friends at an expensive restaurant, you notice that you are $35 short of covering the bill (not including the tip). Furthermore, the restaurant does not take personal checks, will only accept American Express (which you do not have), and has no automatic teller machine. List as many alternative options as you can for correcting your oversight.

1.

2.

3.

4.

5.

6.

7.

8.

9.

6. Somebody has broken the windows in the front of your house twice in the past month. You suspect a neighborhood teenager but have no solid evidence that he is the culprit. List as many alternative options as cross your mind for correcting this situation.

1.

2.

3.

4.

5.

6.

7.

8.

9.

7. Your boss, who happens to be physically attracted to you but for whom you have no feelings in return, informs you that unless you engage in sexual relations with him or her you will be fired. List as many alternative options as you can for managing these unwelcome proposals.

1.

2.

3.

4.

5.

6.

7.

8.

9.

8. You are divorced and your ex-wife (or ex-husband) has custody of the children. However, your ex-wife/ex-husband has a serious alcohol problem and you are concerned about the welfare of your two young children. List as many alternative options as come to mind for how you might handle this situation.

1.
2.
3.
4.
5.
6.
7.
8.
9.

Appendix 17:
Social-Communication
Skills Checklist

Instructions: Check off the skills you perform infrequently and/or have difficulty performing.

_____ accepting criticism without getting defensive
_____ acknowledging confusion or admitting you are wrong
_____ apologizing for something you have done
_____ asking for assistance
_____ asking for directions
_____ compromising
_____ criticizing someone
_____ ending a conversation
_____ expressing an opinion
_____ giving orders
_____ greeting another person
_____ initiating a conversation with a stranger

_____ maintaining a conversation
_____ requesting a favor
_____ resisting the impulse to yell at someone
_____ saying "no"
_____ saying "yes"
_____ sharing an idea with someone
_____ showing affection
_____ starting a conversation
_____ taking orders
_____ telling a joke
_____ turning down an unreasonable request

Appendix 18: Role Play
Rating Scale

Person being rated _____

Person conducting the rating _____

Nonverbal behavior	S	NI
Body relaxation		
Eye contact		
Facial expression		
Gestures		
Posture		
Voice		

(continued)

Verbal behavior	S	NI
Clarity of expression		
Completeness		
Continuity		
Precision/specificity		
Responsiveness		

S = Satisfactory, NI = Needs Improvement

Appendix 19: Suggested Social-Communication Role Plays

1. Asking directions after getting lost in a city with which you are unfamiliar.
2. Sending a meal back at a restaurant because it is not cooked to your satisfaction.
3. Dealing with a rude customer at your place of employment.
4. Apologizing for something you know you should not have said or done.
5. Holding a conversation with someone you do not know.
6. Requesting that a fellow employee switch days off with you.
7. Interacting with someone who has just jumped in front of you in line.
8. Asking someone out on a date.
9. Showing affection toward a baby.
10. Dealing with an unreasonable request.

Appendix 20: Index of Life Skills

Instructions: Check the skills you feel confident and competent performing.

Area I: Personal Hygiene
_____ hair care
_____ skin and nail care
_____ dental care
Area II: Clothing Maintenance
_____ shopping for clothes
_____ mending clothes
_____ polishing shoes
_____ using washer/dryer
_____ ironing

Area III: Food Skills
_____ shopping for food
_____ preparing meals
_____ setting/clearing table
_____ doing dishes
Area IV: Housing
_____ finding an apartment/house
_____ keeping up with rent/mortgage
_____ furnishing an apartment/house
_____ minor maintenance
         on house/apartment

Area V: Job Skills

_____ preparing a résumé of your
       experiences and training
_____ filling out a job
       application
_____ interviewing for a job
_____ acting responsibly at work
_____ handling disagreements with
       a boss or supervisor

Area VI: Transportation

_____ purchasing a car
_____ automobile maintenance
_____ identifying alternative modes
       of transportation

Area VII: Money Management

_____ opening a bank account
_____ budgeting
_____ balancing a checkbook
_____ seeking/securing a loan

Area VIII: Leisure-Time Activities

_____ identifying hobbies and
       outside interests
_____ structuring time outside of
       your work environment
_____ finding non-drug-using friends
       and associates
_____ identifying interests you
       share with others

Area IX: Telephoning Skills

_____ opening and closing
       conversations
_____ identifying cues in phone
       conversations
_____ getting your point across

Area X: Dating Skills

_____ asking someone whom you
       find attractive out on a date
_____ planning a date
_____ preparing for a date
_____ ending a date

Appendix 21: Review of Academic and Occupational Skills

Name _____

Date _____

Part I: Experience

Years of formal education _____

If less than 12 years, did subject achieve GED? _____

Has subject ever enrolled in college? _____

If so, list colleges, credits, dates, and majors _____

_____

_____

Vocational training (along with year completed)

_____

_____

Jobs held (list job title, avg. hrs/week, dates of employment)

_____

_____

_____

On-the-job training (type of training, date completed)

_____

_____

Part II: Interests

Educational goals _____

_____

_____

Occupational goals _____

_____

_____

Appendix 22:
Values Inventory

Instructions: Rate the value (0 = none, 1 = low, 2 = moderate, 3 = high) you (a) have placed, (b) currently place, and (c) would like to place on the following priorities and situations.

		(a) In the past when most involved in drug abuse	(b) At the present time	(c) Future ideal
1.	Family			
2.	Job			
3.	Sex			
4.	Knowledge			
5.	Sharing			

	(a) In the past when most involved in drug abuse	(b) At the present time	(c) Future ideal
6. Mastery			
7. Pleasure			
8. Education			
9. Friends			
10. Productivity			
11. Excitement			
12. Truth			
13. Love			
14. Competence			
15. Food			
16. Insight			
17. Loyalty			
18. Achievement			
19. Power			
20. Wisdom			
Items 1+5+9+13+17			
Items 2+6+10+14+18			
Items 3+7+11+15+19			
Items 4+8+12+16+20			

Appendix 23:
Expectancies Grid

Instructions: Expectancies are the beliefs people have about what they think will happen should they engage in a specific behavior such as drug use. Fill in each box of the grid below with the positive and negative short- and long-term consequences of drug use. Then, using a scale from 1 to 10 (1 = highly unlikely, 5 = somewhat likely, 10 = very likely), rate the probability of each consequence. The first rating should represent the expectancies you had of each consequence when you were most heavily involved with drugs; the second rating, which should be written in a different color pen or pencil, should indicate your current evaluation of the probability of each consequence's occurrence.

1. Positive short-term	2. Negative short-term
3. Positive long-term	4. Negative long-term

Appendix 24:
Self-Monitoring of
Constructional Errors

Instructions: Make a mark in the proper column each time you engage in the constructional errors listed below.

	Day 1	Day 2	Day 3	Day 4	Day 5	Day 6	Day 7	TOTAL
Selective abstraction								
Arbitrary inference								
Dichotomous thinking								
Magnification/ minimization								
Overgeneralization								
Personalization								

Definitions. Selective abstraction: Focusing on a small detail to the exclusion of other, more important, features of the situation. Arbitrary inference: Coming to a conclusion without supporting evidence or in the face of contradictory evidence. Dichotomous thinking: Breaking experiences into mutually exclusive categories (win-lose, good-bad); also known as black-and-white thinking. Magnification: Overestimation of the significance of a particular event. Minimization: Underestimation of the significance of a particular event. Overgeneralization: Drawing a conclusion from an isolated event and then applying this conclusion to related and unrelated situations. Personalization: Inappropriately relating events to oneself; taking impersonal messages personally.

Copyright © 1995 by Glenn D. Walters.

Appendix 25:
Lapse Versus Relapse

Instructions: It is important to understand that there are no correct answers to this questionnaire, just personal opinions. Indicate whether you agree or disagree with the following 12 statements by circling "A" for agree or "D" for disagree. For the purposes of this questionnaire, a *slip* or *lapse* is defined as an isolated instance of drug use, whereas a *relapse* is specified as one's return to a lifestyle pattern of drug use.

1. A slip usually has a catastrophic effect on a person's future chances of recovery. . . . . A   D
2. Successes as well as failures should be taken into account in avoiding future relapse. . . . . A   D
3. It is unwise to generalize from a single occurrence. . . . . A   D
4. The only way relapse can be prevented is by avoiding all drug-related thoughts and opportunities. . . . . A   D

5. Relapse is not a black-and-white issue, but contains a
   number of gray areas as well. . . . . A   D

6. If one slips and uses a drug once, then there is a sharp increase
   in one's chances of progressing to more serious forms of drug
   involvement. . . . . A   D

7. People often relapse because of a lack of willpower. . . . . A   D

8. Rather than becoming preoccupied with lapses and slips, one
   should view such occurrences as learning experiences
   potentially capable of assisting one in avoiding future relapse. . . . A   D

9. Situational factors are at least as important as personal factors
   in promoting relapse. . . . . A   D

10. The craving produced by drugs is so great that to inadvertently
    become involved, even if one's involvement is unintentional,
    is normally sufficient to bring about relapse. . . . . A   D

11. To think about drugs is to use drugs. . . . . A   D

12. The mind can convince the body of just about anything. . . . . . . A   D

Scoring: Score 1 point for "Agree" answers to Items 1, 4, 6, 7, 10, and 11 and 1 point for "Disagree" answers to Items 2, 3, 5, 8, 9, and 12.

TOTAL SCORE _____

Appendix 26A:
Psychological Inventory of Drug-Based Thinking Styles (PIDTS)

Name _____ Facility _____

Age _____ Sex _____ Race _____ Education _____

Marital _____

Instructions: The following items, if answered honestly, are designed to help you better understand your thinking and behavior. For the purposes of this inventory, *drug* refers to both alcohol and various illegal substances used to achieve an altered state of consciousness. Please take the time to complete each of the 80 items on this inventory using the 4-point scale defined below:

    4 = strongly agree
    3 = agree
    2 = uncertain
    1 = disagree

1. I will allow nothing to get in the way of me getting
   what I want 4   3   2   1

2. I find myself blaming society and external circumstances
   for the problems I have had in life 4   3   2   1

3. My mind is free of any serious psychological problems
   or difficulties 4   3   2   1

4. Even though I may start out with the best of intentions I
   have trouble remaining focused and staying "on track" 4   3   2   1

5. There is nothing I can't do if I try hard enough 4   3   2   1

6. When pressured by life's problems I have said "the hell
   with it" and followed this up by using drugs 4   3   2   1

7. I see no reason to change my behavior at this point in my life . . 4   3   2   1

8. I have found myself blaming other people who have been
   hurt by my drug use by saying things like "they deserved
   what they got" or "they should have known better" 4   3   2   1

9. I use drugs in order to change the way I feel or manipulate
   my mood state 4   3   2   1

10. I occasionally think of things too horrible to talk about 4   3   2   1

11. I am afraid of losing my mind 4   3   2   1

12. The way I look at it, I've paid my dues and am therefore
    justified in taking what I want 4   3   2   1

13. The more I got away with drug use the more I thought
    there was no way my parents, spouse, or the authorities
    would ever catch up with me 4   3   2   1

14. I believe that using drugs is no big deal as long as you
    don't hurt other people in the process 4   3   2   1

15. I have helped friends and family with money I have
    acquired dishonestly 4   3   2   1

16. I am uncritical of my thoughts and ideas to the point that
    I ignore the problems and difficulties associated with
    these plans until it is too late 4   3   2   1

17. It is unfair that I have been hassled for my use of drugs
    when bank presidents, lawyers, and politicians get away
    with all sorts of illegal and unethical behaviors every day . . 4   3   2   1

18. I find myself arguing with others over relatively
    trivial matters 4   3   2   1

19. I can honestly say that I took into account the feelings of
    other people even when I was using drugs heavily 4   3   2   1

20. When frustrated I find myself saying "fuck it" and then engaging in some irresponsible or irrational act 4 3 2 1

21. I have many fewer problems than other people 4 3 2 1

22. Even when I got into trouble for using drugs I would convince myself that I didn't require any assistance because I could stop anytime I wanted 4 3 2 1

23. I find myself taking shortcuts, even if I know these shortcuts will interfere with my ability to achieve certain long-term goals 4 3 2 1

24. When not in control of a situation I feel weak and helpless and experience a desire to exert power over others 4 3 2 1

25. Despite the drug lifestyle I have led, deep down I am basically a good person 4 3 2 1

26. I will frequently start an activity, project, or job but then never finish it 4 3 2 1

27. I regularly hear voices and see visions that others do not hear or see 4 3 2 1

28. When it's all said and done, society owes me 4 3 2 1

29. I have said to myself more than once that if it wasn't for someone else's nosiness I would have never gotten into trouble for my drug use 4 3 2 1

30. I tend to let things go which should probably be attended to, based on my belief that they will work themselves out . . . 4 3 2 1

31. There have been times when I intended to limit myself to a few drinks or a small amount of drug only to end up drunk or stoned 4 3 2 1

32. I have made mistakes in life 4 3 2 1

33. Before entering treatment I would give myself permission to use drugs by telling myself that I needed the drugs to function 4 3 2 1

34. I like to be on center stage in my relationships and conversations with others, controlling things as much as possible 4 3 2 1

35. When questioned about my motives for engaging in drug use, I have justified my behavior by pointing out how hard my life has been 4 3 2 1

36. I have trouble following through on good initial intentions . 4 3 2 1

37. I find myself expressing tender feelings toward animals or little children in order to make myself feel better about my use of drugs 4 3 2 1

38. There have been times in my life when I felt I was above the law 4 3 2 1

39. It seems that I have trouble concentrating on the simplest of tasks 4 3 2 1

40. I tend to act impulsively under stress 4 3 2 1

41. Why should I be made to appear worthless in front of friends and family when it is so easy to take from others 4 3 2 1

42. I have never had any regrets about my drug lifestyle 4 3 2 1

43. I tend to put off until tomorrow what should have been done today 4 3 2 1

44. Although I have always realized that I might get into trouble for using drugs I would convince myself that there was no way I would get into trouble *this time.* 4 3 2 1

45. I have justified my involvement in crime and other irresponsible acts by telling myself that I had no choice in that I was addicted to drugs 4 3 2 1

46. I make it a point to read the financial section of the newspaper before turning to the sports page or entertainment section 4 3 2 1

47. People have difficulty understanding me because I tend to jump around from subject to subject when talking 4 3 2 1

48. I get at least 4 to 5 hours of sleep most nights 4 3 2 1

49. Nobody tells me what to do and if they try I will respond with intimidation, threats, or I might even get physically aggressive . 4 3 2 1

50. When I use drugs or act irresponsibly I will perform a "good deed" or do something nice for someone as a way of making up for the harm I have caused 4 3 2 1

51. I have difficulty critically evaluating my thoughts, ideas, and plans 4 3 2 1

52. Nobody before or after can do it better than me because I am stronger, smarter, or slicker than most people 4 3 2 1

53. I have rationalized my use of drugs with statements such as "everybody else is doing it so why shouldn't I" 4 3 2 1

54. If challenged I will sometimes go along by saying "yeah, you're right," even when I know the other person is wrong, because it's easier than arguing with them about it 4 3 2 1

55. I am not seriously mentally ill 4 3 2 1

56. The way I look at it I'm not really a bad person because I never intended to hurt anyone 4 3 2 1

57. I still find myself saying "the hell with working a regular job, I'll get high or drunk instead" 4 3 2 1

58. I sometimes wish I could take back certain things I have said or done 4 3 2 1

59. Looking back over my life I can see now that I lacked direction and consistency of purpose 4 3 2 1

60. Strange odors, for which there is no explanation, come to me for no apparent reason 4 3 2 1

61. When on the streets I believed I could use drugs and avoid the negative consequences (addiction, compulsive use) that I observed in others 4 3 2 1

62. I tend to be rather easily sidetracked so that I rarely finish what I start 4 3 2 1

63. If there is a shortcut or easy way around something I will find it 4 3 2 1

64. I have trouble controlling my angry feelings 4 3 2 1

65. I believe that I am a special person and that my situation deserves special consideration 4 3 2 1

66. There is nothing worse than being seen as weak or helpless . . 4 3 2 1

67. I view the positive things I have done for others as making up for the negative things 4 3 2 1

68. Even when I set goals I frequently do not obtain them because I am distracted by events going on around me . . . 4 3 2 1

69. I have never "blacked out" except perhaps when I was drunk or using drugs 4 3 2 1

70. When frustrated I will throw rational thought to the wind with such statements as "fuck it" or "the hell with it" 4 3 2 1

71. I have told myself that I would never have had to use drugs if I didn't have such a stressful life 4 3 2 1

72. I can see that my life would be more satisfying if I could learn to make better decisions 4 3 2 1

73. There have been times when I felt entitled to use drugs because of the way my life was going 4 3 2 1

74. I rarely considered the consequences of my actions when I was in the community 4 3 2 1

75. A significant portion of my life on the streets was spent trying to control people and situations 4 3 2 1

76. When I first began using drugs I was very cautious, but as time went by and I didn't get into serious trouble I became

overconfident and convinced myself that I could get away
with just about anything 4   3   2   1

77. As I look back on it now, I was a pretty good person even
though I used drugs .4   3   2   1

78. There have been times when I have made plans to do
something with my family and then canceled these plans so
that I could hang out with my friends or use drugs 4   3   2   1

79. I tend to push problems to the side rather than deal with
them 4   3   2   1

80. I have used good behavior (abstaining from drug use for a
period of time) or various situations (fight with a spouse)
to give myself permission to use drugs and engage in other
irresponsible acts 4   3   2   1

Appendix 26B:
PIDTS Scoring Key

1.	En	+	28.	En	+	55.	Cf	−
2.	Mo	+	29.	So	+	56.	Sn	+
3.	Cf	−	30.	Ci	+	57.	Co	+
4.	Ds	+	31.	Co	+	58.	Df	−
5.	So	+	32.	Df	−	59.	Ds	+
6.	Co	+	33.	En	+	60.	Cf	+
7.	Df	+	34.	Po	+	61.	So	+
8.	Mo	+	35.	Mo	+	62.	Ds	+
9.	Po	+	36.	Ds	+	63.	Ci	+
10.	Df	−	37.	Sn	+	64.	Co	+
11.	Cf	+	38.	En	+	65.	En	+
12.	En	+	39.	Cf	+	66.	Po	+
13.	So	+	40.	Co	+	67.	Sn	+
14.	Mo	+	41.	Po	+	68.	Ds	+
15.	Sn	+	42.	Df	+	69.	Cf	−
16.	Ci	+	43.	Ci	+	70.	Co	+
17.	Mo	+	44.	So	+	71.	Mo	+
18.	Po	+	45.	Mo	+	72.	Df	−
19.	Sn	+	46.	Df	+	73.	En	+
20.	Co	+	47.	Ds	+	74.	Ci	+
21.	Df	+	48.	Cf	−	75.	Po	+
22.	So	+	49.	Po	+	76.	So	+
23.	Ci	+	50.	Sn	+	77.	Sn	+
24.	Po	+	51.	Ci	+	78.	Ds	+
25.	Sn	+	52.	So	+	79.	Co	+
26.	Ds	+	53.	Mo	+	80.	En	+
27.	Cf	+	54.	Ci	+			

Note: + scoring direction: strongly agree = 4, agree = 3, uncertain = 2, disagree = 1; − scoring direction: strongly agree = 1, agree = 2, uncertain = 3, disagree = 4.

Confusion (Cf)	Items 3(−), 11(+), 27(+), 39(+), 48(−), 55(−), 60(+), 69(−)
Defensiveness (Df)	Items 7(+), 10(−), 21(+), 32(−), 42(+), 46(+), 58(−), 72(−)
Mollification (Mo)	Items 2(+), 8(+), 14(+), 17(+), 35(+), 45(+), 53(+), 71(+)
Cutoff (Co)	Items 6(+), 20(+), 31(+), 40(+), 57(+), 64(+), 70(+), 79(+)
Entitlement (En)	Items 1(+), 12(+), 28(+), 33(+), 38(+), 65(+), 73(+), 80(+)
Power orientation (Po)	Items 9(+), 18(+), 24(+), 34(+), 41(+), 49(+), 66(+), 75(+)
Sentimentality (Sn)	Items 15(+), 19(+), 25(+), 37(+), 50(+), 56(+), 67(+), 77(+)
Superoptimism (So)	Items 5(+), 13(+), 22(+), 29(+), 44(+), 52(+), 61(+), 76(+)
Cognitive indolence (Ci)	Items 16(+), 23(+), 30(+), 43(+), 51(+), 54(+), 63(+), 74(+)
Discontinuity (Ds)	Items 4(+), 26(+), 36(+), 47(+), 59(+), 62(+), 68(+), 78(+)

Appendix 26C: PIDTS *T*-Score Conversions

Raw Score					PIDTS Scales						Raw Score
	Cf	**Df**	**Mo**	**Co**	**En**	**Po**	**Sn**	**So**	**Ci**	**Ds**	
8	29	35	37	30	31	32	21	32	29	30	8
9	31	38	39	31	34	35	24	34	31	31	9
10	33	40	41	33	36	37	27	36	33	33	10
11	35	43	43	35	38	39	29	38	35	35	11
12	37	45	45	37	40	41	32	40	37	37	12
13	39	48	47	39	43	43	35	42	39	39	13
14	41	50	49	40	45	45	37	44	41	41	14
15	43	53	52	42	47	47	40	46	43	43	15
16	45	55	54	44	49	49	43	48	45	45	16

(continued)

PIDTS Scales

Raw Score	Cf	Df	Mo	Co	En	Po	Sn	So	Ci	Ds	Raw Score
17	47	57	56	46	52	51	45	50	47	46	17
18	49	60	58	48	54	53	48	52	49	48	18
19	51	63	60	50	56	55	51	55	51	50	19
20	53	65	62	52	59	57	53	57	53	52	20
21	55	68	64	53	61	59	56	59	55	54	21
22	57	70	66	55	63	61	59	61	57	56	22
23	59	73	68	57	65	63	61	63	59	58	23
24	61	75	71	59	68	66	64	65	61	59	24
25	63	78	73	61	70	68	67	67	63	61	25
26	65	80	75	63	72	70	70	69	65	63	26
27	67	83	77	64	74	72	72	71	67	65	27
28	69	85	79	66	77	74	75	73	69	67	28
29	71	87	81	68	79	76	78	75	71	69	29
30	74	90	83	70	81	78	80	77	73	71	30
31	76	92	85	72	84	80	83	79	75	72	31
32	78	95	88	74	86	82	86	81	77	74	32

Appendix 27:
Fear Checklist

Instructions: Check off issues and experiences that are or have been personal sources of apprehension and concern for you. Record the number of checks found in the first column (Items 1, 4, 7, 10, 13, and 16) in the box marked "bonding," the number of checks found in the second column (Items 2, 5, 8, 11, 14, and 17) in the box marked "orientation," and the number of checks found in the third column (Items 3, 6, 9, 12, 15, and 18) in the box marked "identity."

1. Intimacy _____	2. Loss of control _____	3. Failure _____
4. Honesty _____	5. Powerlessness _____	6. Disapproval _____
7. Dating _____	8. Inadequacy _____	9. Insignificance _____
10. Social relations _____	11. Rejection _____	12. Other people's opinions _____
13. Closeness _____	14. Weakness _____	15. Success _____
16. Commitment _____	17. Vulnerability _____	18. Anonymity* _____
☐	☐	☐
Bonding	Orientation	Identity

*The state or quality of being unknown or obscure.

Appendix 28:
What Will Be Missed
From a Drug Lifestyle

Instructions: Make a list of the activities and experiences you believe would be missed if you abandon a drug lifestyle starting today.

1. _____
2. _____
3. _____
4. _____
5. _____
6. _____
7. _____
8. _____
9. _____
10. _____

Appendix 29:
Schedule of Family and Community Support

1. Are you married?

☐   Yes, go to Question 1a.

☐   No, go to Question 1b.

  1a. How much support do you believe you can count on from your spouse and why? (Answer and go to Question 2)

_____

_____

  1b. Do you have any intimate relationships to return to? (Answer and go to Question 2)

_____

_____

2. Are there any family members
   you can count on for support?

   ☐   Yes, go to Question 2a.

   ☐   No, go to Question 3.

   2a. List the family members you can count on for financial and/or emotional support and their distance from your planned place of residence.

Name of family member	Distance (in miles)	Type of support (F = financial, E = emotional)

3. Do you have any friends who are
   not involved in crime or drug abuse
   whom you can count on for support?

   ☐   Yes, go to Question 3a.

   ☐   No, go to Question 4.

   3a. List the noncriminal, non-drug-abusing friends you can count on for financial and/or emotional support and their distance from your planned place of residence.

Name of friend	Distance (in miles)	Type of support (F = financial, E = emotional)

4. What support systems are you aware of in your community that might assist
   you with the following problems and issues?

Problem/issue	*Community source or agency*
Alcohol and drugs	_____
Counseling, family	_____
Counseling, personal	_____
Day care/youth services	_____
Employment	_____
	_____
Financial assistance	_____
Food aid	_____
Fuel assistance	_____
Health information/services	_____
	_____
Housing	_____
Legal services	_____
Leisure-time activities	_____
Parenting issues	_____
Parole/probation	_____
Self-help support groups	_____
	_____
Tax information/assistance	_____
Transportation	_____
Veterans services	_____
Volunteer opportunities	_____
Welfare assistance	_____
	_____
_____	_____
_____	_____

Appendix 30: Bipolar Identity Survey

1a. Three positive messages you recall receiving from your parents/caregivers

_____

_____

_____

1b. Three negative messages you recall receiving from your parents/caregivers

_____

_____

_____

2a. Two behaviors for which you were consistently rewarded as a child

_____

_____

2b. Two behaviors for which you were consistently punished as a child

_____

_____

3a. Favorite story as a child

_____

3b. Story you disliked as a child

_____

4a. Favorite TV show during childhood

_____

5a. A favorite movie

_____

6a. Three things you have done in your life that you are proud of

_____

_____

_____

7a. Three personal traits you see as positive

_____

_____

_____

8a. One or two nicknames you like to go by

_____

_____

9a. Single word that is likely to be used to describe your personality

_____

10a. Two characteristics you have observed in others that attract you to them

_____

_____

11a. Three people you admire

_____

_____

_____

12a. What you want people to remember you by

_____

_____

4b. TV show you disliked as a child

_____

5b. A movie you did not like

_____

6b. Three things you have done in your life that you are ashamed of

_____

_____

_____

7b. Three personal traits you see as negative

_____

_____

_____

8b. One or two nicknames you resent

_____

_____

9b. Single word that is unlikely to be used to describe your personality

_____

10b. Two characteristics you have observed in others that repulse you

_____

_____

11b. Three people for whom you have little or no respect

_____

_____

_____

12b. What you don't want people to remember you by

_____

_____

Index